主编 李洪峰

U0611457

第二辑

African Language
and
Culture Studies

非洲语言文化研究

（中英文）

外语教学与研究出版社
FOREIGN LANGUAGE TEACHING AND RESEARCH PRESS
北京 BEIJING

图书在版编目（CIP）数据

非洲语言文化研究. 第三辑 ：汉、英 ／ 李洪峰主编. —— 北京 ：外语教学与研究
出版社，2022.12
ISBN 978-7-5213-4122-5

I. ①非… Ⅱ. ①李… Ⅲ. ①文化语言学－非洲－汉、英 Ⅳ. ①H0-05

中国版本图书馆 CIP 数据核字 (2022) 第 229642 号

出 版 人　王　芳
项目策划　孙凤兰
责任编辑　孙　慧
责任校对　孙凤兰
封面设计　郭　莹
出版发行　外语教学与研究出版社
社　　址　北京市西三环北路 19 号（100089）
网　　址　https://www.fltrp.com
印　　刷　北京捷迅佳彩印刷有限公司
开　　本　710×1000　1/16
印　　张　11.5
版　　次　2022 年 12 月第 1 版 2022 年 12 月第 1 次印刷
书　　号　ISBN 978-7-5213-4122-5
定　　价　50.00 元

如有图书采购需求，图书内容或印刷装订等问题，侵权、盗版书籍等线索，请拨打以下电话或关注官方服务号：
客服电话：400 898 7008
官方服务号：微信搜索并关注公众号"外研社官方服务号"
外研社购书网址：https://fltrp.tmall.com

物料号：341220001

编辑团队

主　　编：李洪峰

编辑部主任：马秀杰

编辑部成员：李春光　魏媛媛　赵　磊　王　婷　苏晓楠　张经纬

编 辑 单 位：北京外国语大学非洲学院

　　　　　　《非洲语言文化研究》编辑部

编辑部电话：010–88816484

编辑部邮箱：jalcs@bfsu.edu.cn

版权声明

　　对于本书所收录文章，作者承担其知识产权等保证责任。作者保证其享有该文章著作权及其他合法权益，保证无"抄袭""剽窃""一稿两投或多投"等学术不端行为，保证其文章中不含有任何违反我国法律法规的内容，保证不侵害其他任何方的任何合法权益。

　　作者同意将其作品整体以及附属于作品的图、表、摘要或其他可以从作品中提取部分的全部复制传播的权利，包括但不限于复制权、发行权、信息网络传播权、表演权、翻译权、汇编权等，许可外语教学与研究出版社有限责任公司使用。未经作者和本出版单位事先书面授权，任何机构和个人不得以任何形式予以转载、摘录、使用或实施其他任何侵害作者和本出版单位合法权益的行为，否则作者和本出版单位将依法予以追究。

目　　录

非洲语言与文学

非洲社会与文化

书评

征稿启事

Contents

African Language and Literature

African Society and Culture

Book Review

Call for Papers

"新非洲流散":奇玛曼达·阿迪契小说中的身份叙事 ①

袁俊卿

上海师范大学人文学院

摘　要:尼日利亚作家奇玛曼达·阿迪契在长篇小说《紫木槿》《半轮黄日》和《美国佬》中,有意无意地勾勒出非洲流散者身份认同的嬗变过程:从本土流散者的不知道"我是谁"或"我应该是谁",到为了追寻自我的民族身份认同而试图构建由单一民族构成的"比亚夫拉共和国",再到重新认同"尼日利亚"这个多民族国家。一国之内,某个民族常以其他民族为参照,而在全球化的语境中,由于冲破了时空阻隔,个体或群体面临的不再是本国内的其他民族,而是全球化权力格局中的其他国家,尤其是英美等西方大国。况且,个体、民族和国家的身份构建不仅需要自我认同,还需要"他者"的认可。身份问题关乎民族、国家的兴亡,同时,它也是发达国家给发展中国家设置的一个"陷阱",即发展中国家的个体要想得到发达国家的"承认",就必须尽量摆脱母国的"痕迹",逐渐"他者化",而"他者化"的过程就是自身主体性被他者塑造的过程。

关键词:"新非洲流散";主体性;奇玛曼达·阿迪契

New African Diaspora: Identity Narratives in Chimamanda Adichie's Novels

Yuan Junqing

School of Humanities, Shanghai Normal University

Abstract: Nigerian writer Chimamanda Adichie has intentionally or unintentionally

① 本文系上海市哲学社会科学规划课题"东非英语文学中的主体性重构"(项目编号:2022ZWY011)和国家社科基金重大项目"非洲英语文学史"(项目编号:19ZDA296)的阶段性研究成果。

收稿日期:2022-04-21

作者信息:袁俊卿,上海师范大学比较文学与世界文学国家重点学科讲师,研究方向为非洲英语文学和流散文学,电子邮箱:lyyuanjunqing@126.com。

sketched the evolution of the identity of African diasporas in the novels *Purple Hibiscus, Half of a Yellow Sun* and *Americanah*: from the native diasporas' not knowing "who I am" or "who I am supposed to be" to trying to build a "Republic of Biafra" consisting of a single nationality for the purpose of pursuing self-identity, and then to re-identifying "Nigeria". Within a country, a certain nationality often uses other nationalities as a reference. However, in the context of globalization, instead of facing other nationalities in their own countries, because of broken barriers of time and space, individuals and groups are facing other countries in the context of globalized power, especially western countries such as Britain and the United States. Moreover, the construction of the identity of individuals, nationalities and nations requires not only self-identification, but also the recognition by "others". The issue of identity is related to the rise and fall of nationalities and nations. At the same time, it is also a "trap" that the developed countries have set for the developing countries. That is, if they want to be "recognized" by the developed countries, they must try to get rid of the "traits" of their home country and gradually become "others". And the process of becoming "others" is the process by which one's subjectivity is shaped by others.

Keywords: New African Diaspora; subjectivity; Chimamanda Adichie

2021 年，坦桑尼亚裔作家阿卜杜勒拉扎克·古尔纳（Abdulrazak Gurnah）被授予诺贝尔文学奖，以表彰他"毫不妥协并充满同理心地深入探索着殖民主义的影响，并关切着那些夹杂在文化和地缘裂隙间难民的命运"的精神（袁俊卿，2021: 56）。"夹杂在文化和地缘裂隙间难民的命运"其实就是非洲流散者的命运。古尔纳的获奖，让非洲流散（African Diaspora）以及与之相关的"流散性"主题再度成为学界关注的焦点。实际上，"'黑人流散'或'非洲流散'直到 20 世纪 50 年代中期或 60 年代才被广泛使用"（Cohen, 2008: 39）。流散研究专家乔治·谢泼森（George Shepperson）和约瑟夫·E·哈里斯（Joseph E. Harris）认为，流散被用来描述非洲人的经历，"是在 1965 年坦桑尼亚达累斯萨拉姆大学举行的非洲历史国际会议上使用的，也可能是在那次会议上创造的"（Patrick, 2009:

3）。可以说，"'非洲流散'一词的现代用法是 20 世纪 50 年代和 60 年代学术和政治运动的产物"（Zeleza & Eyoh, 2003: 6）。此时该术语主要用来描述因奴隶贸易和受殖民主义影响而被迫流离海外的非洲人。对他们来说，家园是一个神秘的、理想化的地方，难以抵达，无法回返。到了 20世纪 80 年代，尼日利亚出现了一种被称为"新非洲流散"（New African Diaspora）的现象，此阶段的流散者大都是相对自愿地移居海外。他们更加自由，与故国保持着密切、稳定的联系，且拥有返回故园的可能性。奇玛曼达·阿迪契（Chimamanda Adichie）、塞菲·阿塔（Sefi Atta）、赫隆·哈比拉（Helon Habila）、克里斯·阿巴尼（Chris Abani）、海伦·奥耶耶米（Helen Oyeyemi）和泰耶·塞拉西（Taiye Selasi）是其中的代表。他们在 21 世纪前 20 年出版了许多代表性作品，形成一股不容小觑的文学力量，这也是尼日利亚英语文学发展的一个阶段性特点。

众所周知，身份问题是流散研究的核心问题，非洲流散也不例外。从整体来看，新非洲流散者的身份问题经过了三重嬗变，这三重嬗变在尼日利亚第三代代表性作家奇玛曼达·阿迪契的创作历程中得到了典型且隐秘地展现。在其长篇小说《紫木槿》（*Purple Hibiscus*, 2003）、《半轮黄日》（*Half of a Yellow Sun*, 2006）和《美国佬》（*Americanah*, 2013）中，阿迪契勾勒出了新非洲流散者身份认同的嬗变过程。（1）对于本土流散者来说，欧洲殖民者的强势入侵和殖民统治瓦解了他们的主体性，令他们的身份迷失了，不知道"我是谁"。这种迷失与异邦流散者的身份迷失具有同构性。（2）在国家独立之初，尤其是在多民族国家中，在其他民族的对照下，本土流散者自身的民族身份得以凸显，并且为了寻求自己的身份，他们甚至试图建构一个由单一民族构成的国家，种族矛盾则加剧了建立单一民族国家的意愿。但是，这种国家之内的个别民族追寻自我身份的行为严重挑战了业已存在的现代国家的主权，极易爆发冲突与战争。（3）异邦流散者由于跨越了国界，来到异国他乡，参照标准不再是自己祖国内的其他民族，而是全球体系中某个具体的目标国家，如美国和英国。在西方国家与非洲这个维度中，异邦流散者不再强调自己的民族身份，而是国家身份，移居国也更倾向于确认流散者的国籍归属。参照标准的变化带来了身份认同的变化，或者说，参照标准的改变促进了身份认同的转变。其实，对于非洲流散者来说，无论是否发生跨越国界的行为，他们都或隐或显地受到西方国家的影响，因为西方国家的殖民侵略和殖民统治已经把他们的语言、教育体制、政治模式、宗教信仰和生活方式深深地嵌入到非洲社会的肌体之中，生于斯长于斯的非洲人不仅受到本土习俗的影响，也受到西方文化的浸染。阿迪契对于身份问题的探讨，就是试图在非洲文化和西方文化的张力下重获自我身份认同，重建完整的主体性的一种尝试，是争取并掌握话语权，发出自己的声音，进而摆脱殖民和后殖民话语的重要步骤。因为"帝国主义的描述从来就不是一种中立的客观表述模式，而是一种高度主观的欧洲中心主义话语，在道义上有利于殖民者"（Rushton, 2014: 184）。只有发出自己的声音，与西方话语进行抵抗、博弈和对话，才能消解业已存在的西方国家对非洲刻板、僵化且单一的负面印象。

1 本土流散者的身份迷失："我是谁？"

欧洲殖民者抵达非洲① 以前，非洲大陆有着自己的传统习俗和族群归属。"迟至 1880 年，非洲大陆约有 80% 是由自己的国王、女王、氏族和家族的首领以大小不等、类型各异的帝国、王国、村社共同体和政治实体的方式进行统治"（博亨，1991: 1）。但是，欧洲的殖民侵略和殖民统治逐渐改变了这种状态。加纳历史学家阿杜·博亨（Adu Boahen）指出，1880 年到 1900 年是欧洲殖民者对非洲的征服阶段，1900 年到 1919 年是殖民占领时期。罗伯茨（Roberts）则认为，到了 1905 年，非洲大部分地区已经被英国、法国、德国、比利时、意大利和葡萄牙等国瓜分，非洲人几乎完全沦为异族统治的对象。从人口规模和土地面积来看，英国无疑是统治非洲的最为重要的帝国力量（罗伯茨，2019）。"到了 1914 年，除了埃塞俄比亚和利比里亚是仅有的例外，整个非洲大陆全都沦为欧洲列强统治下大小不等的殖民地，这些殖民地通常在自然条件上远比原先存在的政治实体大得多，但往往同它们甚少关系或竟毫无关系"（博亨，1991: 1）。殖民列强不顾非洲人民的反对，私自划分势力范围，打破了非洲传统的地理、文化边界。而且，外来宗教、商店、行政机构和教会学校等一系列的殖民机

---

① 这里的非洲主要指撒哈拉沙漠以南的非洲地区。

构对非洲本土传统造成了剧烈的冲击。对非洲来说，殖民侵略和殖民统治"推翻了整个古代的各种信仰和思想，以及古老的生活方式。它使整个民族面临突然的变化。举国上下，毫无准备地发现自己被迫要不就去适应要不就走向灭亡"（博亨，1991: 1）。有着"非洲现代文学之父"之称的尼日利亚作家钦努阿·阿契贝（Chinua Achebe）在《瓦解》（*Things Fall Apart*, 1958）中就描绘了伊博族的传统文化遭到外来文化的冲击和破坏的过程，主人公奥贡卡沃也在本土习俗和外来文化的双重夹击之下上吊而亡。这种状况具有普遍性。"若干世纪以来的生活准则遭到破坏的过程，不仅扩展到曾经沦为殖民地的国家，甚至扩展到曾经保持住国家独立的埃塞俄比亚"（尼基福罗娃，1981: 1-2）。非洲的传统文化遭到瓦解，非洲人的精神世界遭到震荡和颠覆。肯尼亚作家恩古吉·瓦·提安哥（Ngugi Wa Thiong'o）在《大河两岸》（*The River Between*, 1965）中这样写道：

> 白人的到来给人带来一种令人捉摸不定的、难以言喻的东西，这种东西朝着整个山区长驱直入，现在已进入心脏地带，不断地扩大着它的影响。这种影响造成了山里人的分裂，而穆索妮的死就是这种影响的恶果……自从她死以后，时局的发展使人感到担忧，表面上人们保持沉默，但实际上在多数人的心里，虔诚和背叛两种意识却在剧烈地相互斗争。（提安哥，2015: 92）

对于非洲原住民来说，到底是忠于部族传统，做一名传统主义者，还是背弃传统，做一名基督徒？他们拿捏不定，犹疑不决。故而，虔诚和背叛这两种意识在其内心深处剧烈地相互斗争。《大河两岸》的主人公瓦伊亚吉既不是基督徒，也不是传统主义者，而是"中间派"。这种貌似"公允"的立场和态度实则是外来文化和本土文化双重塑造的结果，而这两种文化中的任何一方都没有在瓦伊亚吉的脑海中占据主流。也就是说，在外来文化和宗教的冲击与塑造下，非洲原住民的身份迷失了，不知道"我是谁"或"我应该是谁"，他们处在一种摇摆不定的状态。加纳作家阿玛·阿塔·艾杜（Ama Ata Aidoo）在《幽灵的困境》（*The Dilemma of a Ghost*, 1965）中塑造的阿托·亚乌森亦是如此。他梦到一个幽灵，上上下下徘徊，对他唱着歌:"我应该去海岸角,还是埃尔米纳?我不知道,我不明白,我不知道,我不明白"(艾杜,2017: 41)。这种徘徊、摇摆的状态表明,他们的主体性身份认同还没有建立起来,从而变成了典型的本土流散者。

> 由于殖民者推广殖民语言、传播基督教、侵吞土地、实行种族隔离和分而治之的殖民政策,非洲原住民在自己的国土上被迫进入一种"流散"的文化语境中。他们失去了家园,在自己的土地上流亡;他们被迫接受宗主国的语言,甚至禁止使用本土语言,但是他们又无法完全抛掉部族语言;他们在自我身份认同方面产生了纠结与疑惑,在到底是做一名传统主义者还是基督教徒之间游移不定;他们的灵魂受到西方价值观的统摄,而又难以与传统文化完全剥离,从而在心灵上造成一种既不属于"此"也不属于"彼"的中间状态。(朱振武、袁俊卿,2019: 144)

所谓"本土流散",是因为非洲原住民虽然没有跨国界的生存经历,但显然,本土流散是对非洲人的精神样貌和心理状态的一种概括性描述。在非洲英语文学中,本土流散具有普遍性,如恩古吉·提安哥的小说《孩子,你别哭》(*Weep Not, Child*, 1964)中的恩约罗格、《暗中相会》(*A Meeting in the Dark*, 1974)中的约翰、伊各尼·巴雷特(Igoni Barrett)的小说《黑腚》(*Blackass*, 2015)中的弗洛、库切《夏日》(*Summertime*, 2009)中的马丁与约翰·库切,等等。在《大河两岸》中,恩古吉对非洲原住民在异质文化张力下的精神状态描写得比较直接,主人公的心路历程直接呈现在读者的面前。但在奇玛曼达·阿迪契的第一部小说《紫木槿》中,康比丽的父亲尤金就是一位典型的本土流散者。只不过,尤金的内心冲突和心理波动较为隐秘,需要读者条分缕析,层层剥离,才能窥见其心灵深处的"惊涛骇浪",体悟到他内心的撕裂之苦,领略到那种"于无声处听惊雷"的震颤。

前布克奖评委杰森·考利(Jason Cowley)认为,《紫木槿》是其读过的继阿兰达蒂·洛伊(Arundhati Roy)的《微物之神》(*The God of Small Things*, 1997)之后最好的处女作(Anya, 2005)。这部作品主要描述了康比

丽 "在前往阿巴和恩苏卡的旅途中，通过与祖父努库、姑妈伊菲欧玛及其家人的接触，逐渐改变了性格"（Ojaide, 2012: 34）并逐渐成长的故事。康比丽的父亲尤金是一位虔诚的天主教信徒，妻子、儿女的一切日常生活都必须坚守天主教信条，否则就是犯了大忌，就要受到严厉的惩罚。康比丽和扎扎因为私藏已去世的爷爷的画像，而遭到尤金的暴力相待。尤金认为魔鬼已经来到了家里，而他不允许魔鬼的出现。他用力踢着康比丽，"他越踢越快……他踢啊，踢啊，踢啊……一股咸咸的热乎乎的东西流进我嘴里。我闭上眼睛，滑向了无声之境"（阿迪契，2016: 166-167）。在尤金的暴力踢打下，康比丽内脏出血，断了一根肋骨，差点一命呜呼。但是尤金表面看似冷酷无情、暴力血腥，其内心却异常挣扎。康比丽躺在医院的床上，"爸爸的脸离我很近，我们的鼻尖简直碰在了一起，不过我还是可以看出他目光柔和。他哭着说：'我心爱的女儿。你不会有事的。我心爱的女儿'"（阿迪契，2016: 167）。康比丽从小就在父亲的规训下接受了天主教信仰，没有选择的余地。"我是天主教徒。这是一种身份，虽然我没有太多的选择，但我已经拥有了它"（Adebanwi, 2004）。当西方传教士一手捧着"上帝之书"，一手握着枪支来到非洲的时候，非洲原住民无论是在宗教信仰还是军事实力方面都是无力抵抗的。从这个层面来讲，尤金强迫康比丽等人信奉天主教的过程就是西方殖民者向非洲传播宗教的隐喻。这部小说也可以说是一个政治寓言。尤金的父亲努库是一位传统主义者，有着本部族的传统信仰。在尤金眼中，他的父亲就是异教徒，充满着邪恶和罪恶。"尤金谴责他父亲对木石之神的空虚崇拜，并相信只有他的皈依才能使他从空虚中得到救赎"（Strehle, 2008: 108）。努库自始至终也没有听从尤金的劝说，没有改信天主教。为此，尤金也断绝了与其父亲的来往。努库死后，尤金原本希望按照天主教的仪式举行葬礼，但遭到伊菲欧玛的强烈反对，无奈之下，尤金还是以传统的方式埋葬了父亲。"我给伊菲欧玛送了钱办葬礼，我给了她所需要的一切……为了我们父亲的葬礼"（阿迪契，2016: 156）。尤金的妻子比阿特丽斯也时常遭到暴力，只因为她无法生出更多的儿子。尤金必须恪守天主教对婚姻中一夫一妻制的规定，但是又无法摆脱伊博族中富裕人家应该多妻多子的传统习俗。这种家庭暴力在尼日利亚青年作家欧因坎·布雷思韦特（Oyinkan Braithwaite）的首部长篇小说

《我的妹妹是连环杀手》（*My Sister, the Serial Killer*, 2018）中也有着重体现。阿尤拉未成年时便时常遭受父亲的暴力，长大之后，她对男性表现出一种既需要又恐惧的两难情感。

康比丽、扎扎和比阿特丽斯等人的遭遇表明，"精神的非殖民化只能发生在非殖民化的家庭中——这成为尼日利亚走向独立的必要的第一步"（Strehle, 2008: 107）。如果一个家庭也处在殖民化的境地之中，那么，何谈精神的独立自主？很大程度上，家庭就是国家的象征。"尤金之所以如此，正因为受到西方文化和非洲文化这两种并非势均力敌的异质文化的双重塑造，从而处在一种分裂、纠葛的状态中"（朱振武，2019: 57）。《紫木樨》的叙述者是康比丽，而不是尤金，所以尤金的内心世界是隐而不彰的。如果尤金作为故事的叙述者，那么其内心深处的撕扯、断裂之苦和游移徘徊之状定会表现得十分明显。流散是指"个人或群体选择离开母体文化而在异域文化环境中生存，由此而引起的个体精神世界的文化冲突与抉择、文化身份认同与追寻等一系列问题的文化现象"（张平功，2013: 88）。这也是"全球移民、大流散时代每个种族群体都无法完全回避的"（杨中举，2019: 131）问题。尤金就面临着精神世界的冲突与抉择的问题，他无法彻底做一名天主教信徒，也无法斩断与传统习俗的瓜葛，更不能置家庭伦理于不顾而六亲不认。尤金处在一种深度流散的境况之中，在身份认同的层面，即在到底做一名传统主义者还是天主教信徒之间徘徊不定、纠结游移。[①] 他在精神的暗深处不知道"我"是谁或"我"应该是谁。这就是本土流散者所面临的身份认同困境。但是，本土流散者的身份认同并不是永远迷失的，他们终将迈出探索自我身份认同的步伐。阿迪契的第二部长篇小说《半轮黄日》就鲜明地体现出这一点。

2　建构新的民族国家身份：成为"比亚夫拉人"

在《半轮黄日》中，奥兰纳和奥登尼博对身份问题的讨论，以及伊博族对国民身份的争夺和抗争，就是本土流散者获取自我身份认同和他人对

---

① 对尤金更加细致的分析，详见袁俊卿《异质文化张力下的"流散患者"》，载于《外国文艺》2019 年第 6 期。

自我身份认可的一次努力尝试。"由于对共同历史的认识是任何民族想象中不可缺少的一部分，因此《半轮黄日》是一部历史小说，这是阿迪契的小说构成民族认同文本的最明显方式"（Feldner, 2019: 40）。奥登尼博是恩苏卡大学的一位讲师，时常与一批志同道合的朋友，就某些国内外的重大议题，如去殖民化、泛非主义和民族独立等问题进行探讨。其中，"身份"问题就是重点议题之一。奥登尼博坚持认为非洲人的唯一身份就是部落。

> "我认为非洲人唯一的真实身份是部落……我之所以是尼日利亚人，是因为白人创立了尼日利亚，给了我这个身份。我之所以是黑人，是因为白人把'黑人'建构得尽可能与'白人'不同。但在白人到来之前，我是伊博族人。"（阿迪契，2017: 22）

奥登尼博认为，"尼日利亚人"这个身份是白人给予的。实际上，"尼日利亚"这个现代国家确实是白人建立的。"1914 年，英国总督合并了北部和南部的保护区，他的妻子挑了一个名字，由此诞生了尼日利亚"（阿迪契，2017: 128）。而且，奥登尼博之所以是"黑人"，也是白人建构出来的。白人到来之前，他们并没有意识到自己是"黑人"。自我身份需要"他者"的对照才能凸显出来。在一个全是同样肤色的群体中，群体成员并不会意识到自己的肤色有什么与众不同。在《美国佬》中，伊菲麦露从美国回到尼日利亚，深切的感受即是"我感觉在拉各斯下了飞机后，我不再是黑人了"（阿迪契，2017: 482）。回到祖国，那种在美国才会凸显的种族身份便消失了。奥登尼博认为自己的首要身份便是伊博族人，但是埃泽卡教授与其意见相左。埃泽卡认为，奥登尼博之所以意识到自己是伊博族人，也与白人息息相关。"泛伊博族的理念是面对白人的宰制才产生的。你必须认识到，今天的部落概念也与民族、种族等概念一样，是殖民的产物"（阿迪契，2017: 22）。实际上也确实如此。奥兰纳与奥登尼博持相同立场，他们是"革命恋人"。奥兰纳曾经多次参加伊博族联盟在姆巴埃齐舅舅家举行的集会。在这种政治聚会中，伊博族男人和女人控诉北部地区的学校不接纳伊博族的孩子。所以，他们想筹建伊博族自己的学校。"我的同胞们！我们将盖起我们自己的学校！我们将集资盖我们自己的学校"（阿迪契，

2017：41）！这里的"我们"就是指"伊博族"。其他族群对伊博族的排挤，加深了伊博族的凝聚力和民族身份认同。

奥登尼博和奥兰纳的伊博族身份认同具有代表性，他们并不认可"尼日利亚"这个由殖民者建立起来的现代国家，虽然在尼日利亚建国的时候，伊博族就是其中的一分子。这有着深刻的历史因由。尼日利亚在20世纪初成为英国的殖民地。二战以后，英国的政治、经济和军事实力大为削弱，其殖民地的民族独立运动日益高涨。为了延缓各殖民地的独立进程，维护其在殖民地的一己私利以及反对共产主义在非洲大陆的扩张，英国当局开始对其在非洲的殖民政策进行一系列的调整与改革。在尼日利亚，英国的政策调整以20世纪40—50年代相继出台的《理查兹宪法》《麦克弗逊宪法》和《李特尔顿宪法》为标志。这三部宪法均确定了在尼日利亚实行"分而治之"的原则。"分而治之"的原则把国土面积为336,669平方英里、拥有250多个部族的大国分为三个区域：北区（主要由以豪萨–富拉尼族为主的"北方人民大会党"控制）、西区（主要由以约鲁巴族为主的"尼日利亚行动派"控制）、东区（主要是由伊博族为主的"尼日利亚和喀麦隆国民会议"控制）（刘鸿武，2014：122-126）。这三个区域在民族、宗教、语言以及经济状况等方面差异悬殊，而英国政府正是利用这三个区域的差异企图削弱它们的力量以及减小它们团结抗争的可能性。"地区分治主义作为英国殖民者分而治之政策的结果，事实上已经成为尼日利亚政治的基本特征，它对以后尼日利亚统一国家的稳定构成了潜在的威胁"（刘鸿武，2014：124）。如果说争取尼日利亚的独立这一总体目标可以使得北区、西区与东区的三大政治势力联合起来的话，那么在1960年10月1日尼日利亚取得独立之后，这三大政治势力间的矛盾与冲突便凸显出来了。毕竟，这三大政党只是分别代表不同区域的利益，并不是一个全国性的政党。而且，传统的尼日利亚部族都有自己的社会运行模式，"各自为政"，并没有统一的国家经济基础、文化基础与国家情感，也没有形成统一的民族心理。尼日利亚的形成"不是社会经济发展、民族一体化进程的结果，它是在还没形成统一的经济生活、没有形成统一的民族与文化的时候，就因为非殖民地化的完成而组成新的国家了"（刘鸿武，2014：130）。这就产生了很多问题。"昔日属于同一民族，现在被分割在不同的国家和地区；昔日在同一国家的不同民族，现在被分割在不同的国家和地区，相互变成外国人"（陆庭恩、彭坤元，1995：581）。因此，民族间的和谐相处变得十分困难。而且，短时期内，各民族的人民很难形成统一的国家认同。"由于这些边界是殖民大国任意划定的，没有考虑到已确立的文化或语言领域，因此，在尼日利亚 1960 年独立时，潜在的冲突已经显而易见"（Feldner，2019：39）。没有统一的国家认同，各民族间很容易爆发冲突。

20 世纪 50—60 年代，非洲民族解放运动高涨，民族主义政党如雨后春笋般纷纷涌现。仅在 1960 年就有喀麦隆、塞内加尔、马达加斯加、索马里和尼日利亚等 17 个非洲国家取得了独立，这一年也被称为"非洲年"（Birmingham，1995：1）。到了 1980 年，除了纳米比亚以外，非洲各国已经全部取得了独立。非洲国家独立之后出现了一系列的问题，如国家意识淡薄、政客对种族情绪的操纵、各层面的腐败、公共服务的缺乏、对已经建立起来的制度缺乏信心、阶级对立、城乡矛盾，等等（Michael，1984）。1966 年，以尼日利亚政府降低可可的收购价格为导火索，大批不满的农民以及在选举中失败的政党掀起反抗政府的运动，一批有预谋的伊博族军官趁机发动军事政变，联邦总理与财政部长等高官被杀。伊龙西将军担任尼日利亚国家元首，取消联邦制，建立中央集权政府。随后，政变与反政变频仍，民族矛盾日益激烈。1966 年 5 月，伊龙西政权颁布的"第 34 号政府法令"严重触犯了北方的保守势力，生活在北方地区的伊博族人遭到驱逐与屠杀，最后发展成大规模的军事暴动，伊龙西被杀。与此同时，东区的伊博族人开始对当地的豪萨-富拉尼族人进行还击。1966 年 7 月 29 日，北部豪萨族军官发动政变并很快控制了局势，选举戈翁担任国家元首，随即大肆杀害伊博族军官。

从身份认同这个层面来说，尼日利亚内部各民族间之所以爆发矛盾冲突，很大程度上是因为他们没有统一的国家认同，短时间内不可能形成对尼日利亚这个国家的国家认同，即他们并不认同"尼日利亚"这个现代国家。况且，民族矛盾由来已久。在各种力量的作用下，伊博族人必须自寻出路，那就是建构新的民族国家身份，成为"比亚夫拉人"。1967 年 5 月 30 日，东尼日利亚脱离联邦，成立比亚夫拉共和国。有论者指出，"比亚夫拉的独立标志着'非洲土著人民第一次掌握了自己的命运'，至少在非洲人无视欧洲殖民者留下的边界，试图划定自己的国家边界的时候是这样"（Coffey, 2014: 64）。划定自己的国家边界，很大程度上就是确立自己的身份认同，而身份认同就是民族意识高涨的表现。著名历史学家迈克尔·克劳德（Michael Crowder）指出，"尼日利亚内战及其余波增强了民族意识"（Crowder, 1984: 356）。东区领导人奥朱库宣布：

> 男女同胞们，东尼日利亚的人民……我庄严宣布，众所周知的东尼日利亚，被称为东尼日利亚的领土和地区，以及她的大陆架与领海，自此以后是一个独立的主权国家，她的名讳与称谓便是比亚夫拉共和国。（阿迪契，2017: 178）

听到这个消息，奥登尼博和奥兰纳兴高采烈，手舞足蹈。这是他们的新纪元，"这是一个新的开端，一个新的国家，他们的新国家"（阿迪契，2017: 185）。从这一刻开始，他们不再是尼日利亚人，而是比亚夫拉人。比亚夫拉共和国是他们自己的国家，他们有了自己认可的民族身份和国家身份。身份的确立必须得到他人的认同。伊博族自己宣布成立比亚夫拉共和国仅仅是一个方面，得到其他国家的认可同样非常重要。"奥登尼博！奥登尼博！坦桑尼亚承认了我们"（阿迪契，2017: 322）！奥兰纳从收音机中得到这一消息后异常兴奋。在庆祝比亚夫拉共和国成立的集会上，"比亚夫拉人"举行了一场身份转换的仪式，那就是葬送尼日利亚。"一些年轻人正在抬一副棺材，上面用白粉笔写着'尼日利亚'；他们佯装严肃，举起棺材。随后……在地上挖一个浅坑。他们把棺材抬进浅坑时，人群爆发出一阵欢呼"（阿迪契，2017: 179）。把写着"尼日利亚"的棺材埋进浅坑，就是葬送尼日利亚的象征，也意味着否认"尼日利亚"这个国家，否认"尼日利亚人"这个身份。除此之外，身份转换还有一些其他形式，比如更换货币。"奥兰纳在银行前的长队里站了四小时，躲闪着用笞鞭打人的男人和推推搡搡的女人，终于把尼日利亚币换成了更漂亮的比亚夫拉磅"（阿迪契，2017: 285）。货币的更换，是身份认同转变的一种体现，也是强化身份认同的一种方式。

由于东区领导人拒绝承认北方戈翁为首的政府，再加上戈翁的"建州计划"以及争夺东区的石油、森林、矿产等原因，1967年8月9日惨烈的尼日利亚–比亚夫拉战争（Nigerian-Biafran War）爆发了。"简单说来，这一仇恨的始作俑者是英国殖民实践中非正式的分而治之政策。这种政策操控部落间的差异，确保统一难以为继，从而实现对这样一个大国的轻松统治"（阿迪契，2017: 184）。成立比亚夫拉共和国并不仅仅是分离主义者的意图，还有一个推力，即豪萨族的驱赶。"伊博族人必须滚蛋。异教徒必须滚蛋。伊博族人必须滚蛋"（阿迪契，2017: 161）。对伊博族人来说，"大屠杀使得之前的尼日利亚人变成了热忱的比亚夫拉人"（阿迪契，2017: 224）。也就是说，大屠杀使那些身为伊博族的"尼日利亚人"下定决心，建立由单一民族构成的国家，成为比亚夫拉人。尽管那些伊博族人可能内心深处并不认可尼日利亚这个国家，但是不认可并不表明就要群起反抗，而很可能会忍气吞声。但是其他民族的大屠杀加快了伊博族人成为比亚夫拉人的步伐，使他们放弃了成为尼日利亚人的"幻想"。但是，伊博族成为比亚夫拉人的努力最终失败了。

比亚夫拉失败了，尼日利亚重新获得了统一。但战争结束之后并没有立刻迎来安宁的生活环境，尼日利亚士兵还在挨家挨户搜索，搜寻能够威胁尼日利亚统一的东西。两个士兵闯进了奥兰纳的家里，命令房间内的所有人都趴在地上，然后翻箱倒柜。士兵走后，奥兰纳从藏在鞋里的信封中取出比亚夫拉磅，试图焚烧这些钱币。"'你在焚烧记忆。'奥登尼博说。'我不是。'她不会把记忆寄托于陌生人可以闯进来抢走的东西上，'我的记忆在我心里'"（阿迪契，2017: 470）。对于奥兰纳来说，比亚夫拉磅就是比亚夫拉的象征。虽然，比亚夫拉共和国最终灭亡了，但是，奥兰纳私藏比亚夫拉磅，就是认可自己属于比亚夫拉人这一身份。奥登尼博也是如此。奥登尼博把比亚夫拉国旗叠好，藏在裤子的口袋里，也是对自我身份认同的一种体现。但是，私自保存比亚夫拉的"遗物"的行为并不安全和妥当，因为尼日利亚士兵仍在搜查。对于尼日利亚士兵来说，私自保存比亚夫拉的遗物就是仍旧对比亚夫拉共和国存有念想，仍旧期待比亚夫拉"死灰复燃"的可能性，就依然不会从心底里认可尼日利亚这个国家，也不会认可"尼日利亚人"这个身份，而这对于尼日利亚的统一和稳固是不利的。奥兰纳试图焚毁比亚夫拉币，并不是如奥登尼博所忖度的那样，是在焚烧记忆，或者主动放弃对比亚夫拉的记忆。奥兰纳此举是把对比亚夫拉的记忆藏在更私密、更隐秘的地方，即自己的内心里。奥兰纳的自我身份认同转入了更内在化的心灵层面。比亚夫拉的失败让伊博族感到羞愧，阿迪契称之为伊博族的耻辱。"在拉各斯长大的伊博人竭尽全力想要逃离他们的伊博人身份。如果你在公共场合遇到他们，并且用伊博语说话，他们不会用伊博语回应"（MacFarquhar, 2018）。比亚夫拉的失败是尼日利亚军队武力镇压的结果，伊博族不得不放弃比亚夫拉的身份，不得不承认尼日利亚这个身份，尽管在内心深处，他们还是认同比亚夫拉。伊博族人在内心深处认同比亚夫拉，就有重新建立比亚夫拉的可能性。对于尼日利亚来说，比亚夫拉也就有死灰复燃的那一天。从身份认同这一层面来说，尼日利亚-比亚夫拉之间的战争就是一场身份争夺之战。

3　回归国家认同：重做"尼日利亚人"

以奥登尼博和奥兰纳为代表的伊博族人建立比亚夫拉共和国的愿望落空了，尼日利亚重新得到了统一。与之相对，伊博族人成为比亚夫拉人的努力失败了，不得不重又成为尼日利亚人。但是，正如《半轮黄日》的结尾所暗示的，对比亚夫拉的记忆，对比亚夫拉人这个身份的坚守，已被奥兰纳等人藏在内心深处。这种记忆和认同虽被隐藏，但并没有消失。也就是说，伊博族成为比亚夫拉人的愿望依旧存在，当条件允许的时候，这种成为比亚夫拉人的冲动很可能会东山再起。如果成为比亚夫拉人的民族情绪重出江湖，尼日利亚很可能会再次陷入动乱的境地。由此看来，身份认同极为重要，它关乎民族、国家的生死存亡。如果以奥登尼博和奥兰娜为代表的伊博族人放弃成为比亚夫拉人的追求，而主动且心甘情愿地投入尼日利亚的怀抱，那么所谓的分离主义很可能就会偃旗息鼓，而不会再像一枚定时炸弹一般利剑高悬。问题是，如何让那些存有分离主义意愿的民族认同尼日利亚这个现代主权国家呢？重要的是让那些有分离主义倾向的民族建构起对尼日利亚这个国家的认同，而在流散的语境中，则有助于这种对现代国家身份认同的构建。

非洲许多国家在独立后并没有迎来期待已久的和平发展，而是陷入政变与反政变、腐败与反腐败、独裁与反独裁的斗争之中。因此，20 世纪 60

年代末至 80 年代，"政治幻灭"（politics of disillusionment）是非洲文学中的突出主题（Gikandi, 2003: 499）。与"政治幻灭"相伴而来的，是一大批作家的流亡。乌干达的著名诗人奥考特·普比泰克（Okot p'Bitek），剧作家约翰·鲁甘达（John Ruganda）和罗伯特·塞鲁马加（Robert Serumaga）等人就在独裁者伊迪·阿明（Idi Amin）统治期间离开了祖国。肯尼亚著名作家恩古吉·提安哥也在独裁者莫伊（Daniel Moi）执政期间流亡海外。阿迪契在《紫木槿》中借助奇雅库之口如此说道："受过教育的人都走了，有可能扭转时局的人都走了。留下来的都是孱弱的人。暴政将继续下去，因为软弱的人无法抵抗。难道你没看到这是个恶性循环？谁来打破它"（阿迪契，2016: 192）？面对令人如此绝望的局面，可行的办法就是离开自己的国家，前往一个遥远、未知却充满"希望"的地方。在《紫木槿》的结尾，伊菲欧玛虽然来到了美国，但对于其在美国的经历与感受并没有提及，她的故事在《美国佬》中通过伊菲麦露这个角色得到了详细的描述。

　　《美国佬》中的伊菲麦露和奥宾仔为了寻求更好的发展空间，离开尼日利亚，分别前往美国和英国。异邦流散者离开尼日利亚，来到英美等第一世界国家，不管这些流散者的主观意图是什么，在英美国家的"目光"中，他们首先是来自非洲或尼日利亚的人，是非洲人或尼日利亚人，不管这些被审视者，也就是这些异邦流散者愿不愿意。也就是说，自我身份的构建不仅需要自我的确认，还需要他者的认可。阿迪契在回顾自己刚到美国的感受时说道："我没有意识到自己是黑人，因为种族不是一种自我认同的方式"（Adichie, 2013）。异邦流散者的参照标准变了，不再是一个国家之内的其他民族，而是全球体系中的某个国家。参照标准的变化也影响着流散者的身份认同。但是，他们的原初身份得不到移居国的认可，新的身份的建构也需要移居国的承认。对伊菲麦露来说，"她的生活具有一种洗尽铅华的特质，一种激发人心的质朴无华，没有父母、朋友、家，那些使她之所以成为她的熟悉陆标"（阿迪契，2017: 112）。父母、朋友和家这些使伊菲麦露"是"其所"是"的熟悉陆标，到了美国之后统统失效了。"她突然感觉云山雾罩，一张她努力想扒住的白茫茫的网……世界如裹上了纱布。她能了解事情的大致轮廓，但看不真切，远远不够"（阿迪契，2017: 133）。这就是身份迷失带给伊菲麦露的感觉。身份迷失给伊菲麦露的侄子戴克带来更大的冲击。戴克是乌茱年轻时被尼日利亚的一位将军傲甲包养时所生的儿子。戴克周岁的时候，傲甲因政变而死。乌茱无奈之下，带着戴克来到了美国。戴克从小便脱离了尼日利亚这一母体文化，又跟随逐渐美国化的母亲生活，成长于新的环境中。戴克接受的完全是美国式的教育。他在地下室里吞了一整瓶泰诺，还服用了止吐药。幸好乌茱及时发现，把他送往医院。伊菲麦露认为，戴克之所以试图自杀，与他的身份迷失密切相关。

> "你记得吗，有一次，戴克在告诉你什么事，他说'我们黑人'，你告诉他'你不是黑人'？"她问乌茱姑姑，压低声音，因为戴克还在楼上睡觉……"你告诉他，他不是什么人，却没有告诉他，他是什么人。"（阿迪契，2017: 385-386）

处于青春期的戴克明明有着黑色的皮肤，来自尼日利亚，他的母亲却告诉他，他不是黑人。但是，在那些白人面前，戴克的黑皮肤无声地表明了一切。戴克只知道他不是什么人而不知道他是什么人。"身份就是一个个体所有的关于他这种人是其所是的意识"（钱超英，2006: 90）。在美国，戴克"是"其所不"是"。戴克尚未在尼日利亚的环境中建立起自我身份认同，便被带到了美国，而在美国，他又在自己到底是尼日利亚黑人还是美国人的身份认同困境中迷失。他的身份认同的同一性出了问题。"身份认同的同一性是指某一个体或群体身份的整一性、一致性、连续性、确定性、稳定性的状态，它表明一个个体或群体'是其所是'的意蕴，换言之，它表明一个个体或群体身份的时间和空间关系的动态一致性"（张其学：2017: 128）。所以他的这种身份认同的同一性、一致性是断裂的。戴克的身份认同是失落的、丢失的和尚未建立的。

经历了身份迷失的困扰，伊菲麦露等人接下来的工作就是努力建构新的身份，得到移居国的认可，但是身份建构之路何其困难。"身份确认对任何个人来说，都是一个内在的、无意识的行为要求。个人努力设法确认身份以获得心理安全感，也努力设法维持、保护和巩固身份以维护和加强这种心理安全感"（乐黛云、张辉，1999: 331）。在取得合法身份以前，奥宾仔和伊菲麦露一直过着提心吊胆的生活，所从事的工作也是十分低下和卑微的。奥宾仔在英国的第一份工作是在一家地产经纪人事务所打扫厕所。他的第二份工作是在一间洗涤剂包装仓库清扫宽敞的过道，但是没过多久就因为公司裁员而被辞退，接下来的工作是顶替别人当脚夫送货，一小时四英镑。身在美国的伊菲麦露也不例外，她冒充别人的身份应聘过家庭护工、服务员、招待员、酒吧侍者、收银员等工作。她逐渐囊中羞涩，但是接踵而至的基本消费令她日益惶恐。她的脑海中时常环绕着无法驱散的隐忧。她买不起教科书，付不起房租。她只得借别人的教科书，疯狂地抄笔记。那种不得不求人的感觉噬啮着她的自尊心。她在走投无路之际，给那位白人网球教练提供了肉体抚慰。她用那得来的一百美元渡过了难关。

> 在富裕的西方社会里被纳入了一种高度边缘化的社会分工，这种分工剥夺了他们几乎全部从其"原初联系"那里获得的社会资源和身份意义，把他们变成了"多元文化"社会构造中某个必要而晦暗的角落的填充物——只有一小部分幸运儿能够除外。（钱超英，2007:10）

初抵第一世界的第三世界移民有着相似的遭际，他们为了生存下来不得不从事十分低贱的工作，奥宾仔和伊菲麦露在尼日利亚虽不是大富大贵，但也算生活无忧。但在英美国家，他们被纳入了一种高度边缘化的社会分工，充当着西方社会中某个角落的填充物，而他们在尼日利亚的一切社会资源和身份意义统统失效了。在卡罗尔·博伊斯·戴维斯（Carole Boyce Davies）看来，奥宾仔和伊菲麦露等非洲流散者之所以前往英美国家，是由于全球性的经济结构不平等导致的，即20—21世纪的非洲移民是源于世界经济的失衡（Davies, 2008）。经济发达的英美国家对欠发达的非洲国家释放出一种诱惑力和吸引力，非洲国家的劳动力和知识分子源源不断地输入英美国家，而要得到西方国家的认可和接受，就必须符合他们的标准和要求，否则就是困难重重。但也有少数人除外。在阿迪契的另一部小说《半轮黄日》中，富家女奥兰纳和凯内内就属于这一小部分幸运儿，她们都曾留学英国，但从全书来看，她们并没有遭遇过《美国佬》中伊菲麦露和奥宾仔那样的经历，因为她们在国内有着雄厚的财力支撑，她们的父亲是当地的酋长，拥有半个尼日利亚。

流散者的空间位移打破了个体或群体身份的同一性、一致性、连续性和稳定性的状态，破坏了个体或群体身份在时间和空间方面的动态一致性。如果流散者在异域没有重新建立起新的身份认同，那就会一直处在焦虑之中。

> 身份的焦虑是一种担忧。担忧我们处在无法与社会设定的成功典范保持一致的危险中，从而被夺去尊严和尊重，这种担忧的破坏力足以摧毁我们生活的松紧度；以及担忧我们当下所处的社会等级过于平庸，或者会堕至更低的等级。（德波顿，2007: 6）

异邦流散者在移居国的身份追求，既是自我主动靠近移居国的过程，也是目标国主动认可的过程。如果移居国并未满足流散者的被认同期待，那么就会产生身份的焦虑。奥宾仔和伊菲麦露就时时处在这种身份焦虑之中。虽然身份不是固定不变的，而是根据时间、地点的转变而不断变化的，"从理论上说，有多少不同的时间、地点、身份的构造者，属于一个文化共同体的身份就有多少"（乐黛云、张辉，1999: 336）。但是，理论上的可行性往往忽略了人们身份变化时所导致的情绪变化和心灵创伤。所以，伊菲麦露、戴克和奥宾仔等人因为身份转变而遭遇的艰难困苦和悲欢离合是绝对不能忽视的。

奥宾仔最大的问题就是无法得到他者的认可，当然，这里的他者既包括个体层面的他者也包括国族层面的他者。"对他者的承认，只有在每个人都明确承认他者有权成为一个主体的条件下，才有可能实现。反过来说，主体如果不承认他者为主体，则主体本身也不能得到他人的明确承认，而且，主体首先就不能摆脱对他者的恐惧"（图海纳，2003: 230）。身为在英国的尼日利亚男性，奥宾仔是有权成为一个主体的，但是奥宾仔这个充满血肉的主体首先得得到英国这个抽象的主体的认同，然后才能得到具体的英国国民的认可。奥宾仔要做的是以一己之力对付庞大的英国。在获得合法身份之前，奥宾仔将被视为他者、异类、危险的制造者。他要努力获得英国及其国民这个他者的认同。"这就预示了自我的另一个关键特征。一个人只有在其他自我之中才是自我。在不参照周围的那些人的情况下，自我是无法得到描述的"（泰勒，2001: 48）。也就是说，身份找寻一方面要获得自我认同，另一方面也要获得他人认同。除却个人层面上的意义，奥宾仔寻求身份的努力还象征着其母国在第一世界找寻身份的艰难历程。因为在全球化时代，在国与国之间的政治、经济和文化相互影响的时代之中，任何一个国家都无法脱离其他国家，尤其是英美等第一世界的影响而独自存在，也就是说，每一个国家都镶嵌在全球化的权力关系网络中。那么，异域流散者在迁居国不仅仅与自身相关，他还代表着他的祖国。"一种人在某个社会里的景况，在很大程度上是其'原初联系'的背景社会在世界格局中所处的权力关系，被复制到一个新社会内部的结果"（钱超英，2006: 98）。所以，异域流散者在迁居国的处境就可以视为他的母国在全球化的国际权力关系体系中的境遇的象征。他们在寄居国所遭遇的种族歧视、身份迷失和边缘化处境等问题就是他们的祖国在国际权力关系格局中的遭遇的象征性体现。

　　奥宾仔最终被遣返回国，没能在英国站稳脚跟；伊菲麦露通过自己的努力，拿到了绿卡，成功在美国定居下来。但是，她在适应美国文化的过程中遭受了挫败和歧视。歧视"影响和创造了对祖国的归属感，并在她的内心产生了返回尼日利亚的冲动"（Janice & Paul X, 2019: 2780）。最终，伊菲麦露还是回到了尼日利亚。但这种返回并不是一种圆形循环，而是一种螺旋式的发展，她的回归并不表明回到了原点（Feldner, 2019）。她的脑海中已经存有双重意识。其实，伊菲麦露算是"新非洲流散"的代表性人物。"新非洲流散"的与众不同之处在于作品中的人物具有返回的可能性，并与故乡保持着密切的联系，而其他非洲流散者则很难返回故国（Feldner, 2019）。有趣的是，奥宾仔和伊菲麦露分别前往英国和美国之后，他们的"身份"自然而然地变成了"尼日利亚人"，或者是"非洲人"。在一次采访中，阿迪契表示她是在美国的非洲人，而不是非裔美国人（Terry Gross, 2013）。因为参照标准变了，变成了英国和美国。在《半轮黄日》中，人物的活动中心一直在尼日利亚，没有英美等西方国家的参照，他们的自我身份认同不是"国家"层面，而是"民族"的层面，他们认同自己的民族身份，正如奥兰纳和奥登尼博所表现的那样，一直强调自己的伊博族身份，甚至为建立由伊博族组成的国家努力奋斗，不惜牺牲性命。也就是说，个体的身份认同随着参照标准的变化而变化。

通过以上分析，我们可以获得如下结论。第一，从美国或英国的角度来看，伊菲麦露和奥宾仔等人的国籍就是尼日利亚，他们首先是尼日利亚人，而不是伊博族人。因为这是国家与国家之间的相互认可。第二，从伊菲麦露和奥宾仔等异邦流散者的角度来看，尽管他们个人有着强烈的融入英国或美国的意愿，但是必须要得到移居国的认可。就算奥宾仔和伊菲麦露的自我身份认同是伊博族人，但如果没有"他者"——英国和美国——的认可，他们也就无法把自我身份认同和移居国对他们的认同完美对接。第三，伊菲麦露和奥宾仔等人在移居国的遭遇，诸如身份迷失、种族歧视、失去家园和边缘化体验等问题，皆构成了一种"反推力"，即融入英美国家阻力重重，而返回尼日利亚则变得顺理成章。正是有了流散这种跨国界跨文化的生存经历，他们才接触到"西方"这个"他者"，那么在西方这个"他者"的目光中，他们才凸显了其国家的身份属性，也正是"西方"这个"他者"，才使得他们陷于流散的境地之中。可以说，尽管流散令他们身份迷失，纠结困惑，但有助于他们重新认同尼日利亚这个国家。

4 结语

阿迪契作为生活在美国的尼日利亚人，与其他非洲流散者一样，都生活在两种异质文化的张力之下。在异质文化的双重影响下，身份认同成为一个非常重要的问题。"由于他们的写作是介于两种或两种以上的民族文化之间的，因而，他们的民族和文化身份认同就不可能是单一的，而是分裂的和多重的"（王宁，2006: 172）。其实，这种分裂的和多重的民族、文化身份是在经历过异质文化的双重影响之后形成的结果，并不是一开始就是如此。也即是说，非洲流散者的身份认同经历了多重转变，即：（1）殖民者入侵之前，非洲原住民自有其原初的身份归属。殖民者到来之后，非洲原住民陷入了本土流散的境地，他们在"我是谁？"这个问题上纠结徘徊，犹疑不决。（2）后来，他们便寻求确定的身份认同，即殖民者到来之前的身份，并试图建立单一的民族国家。（3）流散到异邦之后，在异国他乡的衬托下，流散者的身份又经历了新的变化。第一，流散者完全融入移居国，认同他们的生活方式和价值观。第二，流散者完全拒斥移居国的文化习俗，无法适应那里的生活而返回祖国。第三，流散者受两种文化影响而在脑海中形成了一种双重意识，既不属于此也不属于彼，在其间徘徊、踟蹰，无法摆脱任何一方。但是这三种情况也并不是泾渭分明的，而且，前两种情况大都是"理论"化的推演，实际情况要复杂得多。比如，就算异邦流散者完全融入了移居国，他们在融合的过程中所遭受的苦难和创伤也是很难消除的，况且，在他者的眼中，是否真正认可他们的融入也是一个复杂的问题。那些最终返回故国的流散者，往往也携带着在异国他乡获得的眼光或标准，审视、衡量自己的祖国，结果便是对自己的祖国产生复杂的感情。而且，他们在异国他乡所遭受的不愉快经历也很难消弭。这些返回祖国的流散者尽管回到了自己的"国家"，他们是否真正认同了这个"国家"，而不是像奥兰纳和奥登尼博那样，把象征着"比亚夫拉"的国旗和钱币私自藏起来，或把对"比亚夫拉"的记忆潜藏于心？要知道，把对"比亚夫拉"的记忆深藏于心，"比亚夫拉"就会在一定的历史条件下重出江湖。这种复杂性使得我们很难对非洲流散者的身份认同做出一个毋庸置疑的判定，后事如何，还需对非洲流散文学的发展作进一步追踪。另外，在异国他乡，流散者的形象很大程度上就代表了其母国的形象，他人很容易把流散者个人的行为和特征跟其祖国的印象等同起来。况且，在全球化的语境中，个体也确实具有象征的意义。故而，流散者迷失身份、找寻身份和重建身份的过程也是个体所代表的国家在全球化的背景之下身份失落、身份找寻和身份重建的过程。最后，探讨非洲流散文学中的身份问题对于多民族国家，尤其是有着民族矛盾的国家来说具有重要的现实意义和参考价值。

参考文献：

ADEBANWI W, "Nigerian identity is burdensome" The Chimamanda Ngozi Adichie interview [EB/OL]. (2004-05-11) [2022-04-21]. http://www.

nigeriavillagesquare.com/book-reviews/nigerian-identity-is-burdensome-the-chimamanda-ngozi-adichie-interview.html.

ADICHIE C, 2013. Facts are stranger than fiction [EB/OL]. (2013-04-19) [2022-04-20]. https://www.theguardian.com/books/2013/apr/19/chimamanda-ngozi-adichie-stranger-fiction.

ANYA I, 2005. In the footsteps of Achebe: enter Chimamanda Ngozi Adichie [EB/OL]. (2005-10-15) [2022-04-19]. https://www.africanwriter.com/in-the-footsteps-of-achebe-enter-chimamanda-ngozi-adichie/.

BIRMINGHAM D, 1995. The decolonization of Africa [M]. London: Routledge.

COFFEY M. 2014. "She is waiting": political allegory and the specter of secession in Chimamanda Ngozi Adichie's Half of a Yellow Sun [J]. Research in African literatures, 45 (2): 63-85.

COHEN R, 2008. Global diasporas [M]. London: Routledge.

CROWDER M, 1984. The Cambridge history of Africa [M]. Cambridge: Cambridge University Press.

DAVIES B C E, 2008. Encyclopedia of the African diaspora: origins, experiences, and culture [M]. Santa Barbara: ABC-CLIO.

FELDNER M, 2019. Narrating the new African diaspora–21st century Nigerian literature in context [M]. London: Palgrave Macmillan.

GIKANDI S, 2003. Encyclopedia of African literature [M]. London: Routledge.

JANICE S D, PAUL X J, 2019. Negotiation of cultural identities in Chimamanda Ngozi Adichie's Americanah [J]. International journal of recent technology and engineering, 8 (3): 2780-2782.

MACFARQUHAR L, 2018. Chimamanda Ngozi Adichie comes to terms with global fame[EB/OL]. (2018-05-28) [2022-04-21]. https://www.newyorker.com/magazine/2018/06/04/chimamanda-ngozi-adichie-comes-to-terms-with-global-fame.

OJAIDE T, 2012. Contemporary African literature: new approaches [M]. Durham: Carolina Academic Press.

PATRICK M, 2009. The African diaspora: a history through culture [M]. New York: Columbia University Press.

RUSHTON A S, 2014. "A history of darkness": exoticising strategies and the Nigerian Civil War in Half of a Yellow Sun by Chimamanda Ngozi Adichie [C] // ROUSSELOT E. Exoticizing the past in contemporary Neo-Historical fiction. London: Palgrave Macmillan.

STREHLE S, 2008. The decolonized home: Chimamanda Ngozi Adichie's Purple Hibiscus, Transnational Women's fiction [M]. London：Palgrave Macmillan.

TERRY G, "Americanah" author explains "learning" to be black in the U.S. [EB/OL]. (2013-07-27) [2022-04-22]. https://www.npr.org/2013/06/27/195598496/americanah-author-explains-learning-to-be-black-in-the-u-s.

ZELEZA P T, EYOH D, 2003. Encyclopedia of twentieth-century African history [M]. London: Routledge.

阿迪契，2016. 紫木槿 [M]. 文静，译. 北京：人民文学出版社.

阿迪契，2017. 半轮黄日 [M]. 石平萍，译. 北京：人民文学出版社.

阿迪契，2017. 美国佬 [M]. 张芸，译. 北京：人民文学出版社年版.

艾杜，2017. 幽灵的困境 [M]. 宗玉，译. 上海：上海译文出版社.

博亨，1991. 非洲通史·第七卷：殖民统治下的非洲（1880—1935）[M]. 北京：中国对外翻译出版公司.

德波顿，2007. 身份的焦虑 [M]. 陈广兴、南治国，译. 上海：上海译文出版社.

乐黛云，张辉，1999. 文化传递与文学形象 [M]. 北京：北京大学出版社.

刘鸿武，2014. 尼日利亚建国百年史（1914—2014）[M]. 杭州：浙江人民出版社.

陆庭恩，彭坤元，1995. 非洲通史·现代卷 [M]. 上海：华东师范大学出版社.

罗伯茨，2019. 剑桥非洲史 [M]. 李鹏涛，译. 杭州：浙江人民出版社.

尼基福罗娃，1981. 非洲现代文学：东非和南非 [M]. 陈开种，等译. 北京：外国文学出版社.

钱超英，2006. 广义移民与文化离散——有关拓展当代文学阐释基础的思考 [J]. 深圳大学学报（人文社会科学版），（1）：97-101.

钱超英，2007. 流散文学：本土与海外 [M]. 深圳：海天出版社.

泰勒，2001. 自我的根源：现代认同的形成 [M]. 韩震，等译. 南京：译林出版社.

提安哥，2015. 大河两岸 [M]. 蔡临祥，译. 上海：上海文艺出版社.

图海纳，2003. 我们能否共同生存 [M]. 狄玉明、李平沤，译. 北京：商务印书馆.

王宁，2006. 流散文学与文化身份认同 [J]. 社会科学，（11）：170-176.

杨中举，2019. 帕克的"边缘人"理论及其当代价值 [J]. 山东师范大学学报（人文社会科学版），（4）：129-137.

袁俊卿，2021. 带你走进非洲流散者的困境 [J]. 明报月刊，（11）：56-60.

张平功，2013. 全球化与文化身份认同 [M]. 广州：暨南大学出版社.

张其学，2017. 文化殖民的主体性反思：对文化殖民主义的批判 [M]. 北京：北京师范大学出版社.

朱振武，2019. 非洲英语文学的源与流 [M]. 上海：学林出版社.

朱振武，袁俊卿，2019. 流散文学的时代表征及其世界意义——以非洲英语文学为例 [J]. 中国社会科学，（7）：135-158.

（编辑：赵磊）

现代斯瓦希里语小说的起源与发展 ①

魏媛媛

北京外国语大学非洲学院

摘　要： 19 世纪末 20 世纪初，东非地区沦为欧洲列强的殖民地，原有的社会政治经济秩序遭到严重破坏，长期的殖民统治给东非社会文化造成了极大的影响。在这种背景下，东非本土斯瓦希里语语言文学完成了历史上最重要的一次嬗变，即斯瓦希里语文字由阿拉伯字母过渡到拉丁字母，斯瓦希里语文学由以口传文学为主过渡到以书面文学为主，同时这一时期还诞生了新的文学形式和体裁——现代斯瓦希里语小说。本文将通过分析现代斯瓦希里语小说的起源和发展来探讨斯瓦希里语文学在这一时期的嬗变。

关键词： 现代斯瓦希里语文学；斯瓦希里语小说；起源；发展

The Origin and Development of the Modern Swahili Novels

Wei Yuanyuan

School of African Studies, Beijing Foreign Studies University

Abstract: At the end of the 19th and the beginning of the 20th centuries, East African countries became European colonies. The long-term colonial rule had a great impact on the society and the political, economic and cultural development of East African. In this context, Swahili language and literature in East Africa completed the most important evolution in its history. Swahili writing system was changed from Arabic letters to Latin letters; Swahili literature was transformed from oral literature to written literature. At the same time, a new literary form and genre—

① 本文系北京外国语大学基本科研业务项目“现代斯瓦希里语文学的起源与发展”（项目编号：2021JJ007）的阶段性研究成果。

收稿日期：2022-02-1

作者信息：魏媛媛，北京外国语大学非洲学院讲师，博士，研究方向为斯瓦希里语文学，电子邮箱：weiyuanyuan@bfsu.edu.cn。

modern Swahili novels—was born in this period. This article will discuss the evolution of Swahili literature in this period by analysing the origin and development of modern Swahili novels.

Keywords: Modern Swahili literature; Swahili novels; origin; development

1 斯瓦希里语文学简介

斯瓦希里语是非洲本土三大语言之一。斯瓦希里语文学是非洲本土文学的重要组成部分，在世界文学宝库中占有一定的地位。古代斯瓦希里语文学以口头文学为主，其形式和内容丰富多样，并且深入民间，其影响力和普及度都非常高。其主要形式包括神话传说、民间故事、动物寓言、诗歌、格言、谚语、谜语、对唱诗等。这些民间文学在斯瓦希里人的精神生活中占有极其重要的地位，反映了人们渴望认识和征服自然的意愿及惩恶扬善、以弱抗暴的精神。

斯瓦希里社会有着悠久的书写传统。斯瓦希里语是非洲本土语言中为数不多的较早拥有书面文字的语言。在阿拉伯民族与东非本土班图人民的交往过程中，阿拉伯字母也随之传入东非地区。早在公元 12—15 世纪，东非沿海地区就出现了以阿拉伯字母书写的斯瓦希里语文学作品。早期斯瓦希里语文学作品的体裁主要是长篇史诗和古体杂诗，内容多与伊斯兰教和阿拉伯地区的事物相关。除诗歌外，以书面形式出现和传承的斯瓦希里语文献还有相当重要的一部分是一些斯瓦希里城邦国家的编年史和王室文献。这些记载城邦国家兴衰过程的编年史著作，记载了这些城邦国王的名册和政治经济生活，为后人提供了了解这些城邦历史的珍贵史料。古代斯瓦希里语文学作品的普及和推广度不高，其作者和读者主要是受过教育的穆斯林贵族阶层。

19 世纪末 20 世纪初，东非地区逐渐沦为欧洲列强的殖民地，原有的社会政治经济秩序遭到了严重的破坏，长期的殖民统治给东非社会文化造成了极大的影响。在这种背景下，斯瓦希里人原有的社会秩序和文学传统被打破，斯瓦希里语书写的文字由阿拉伯字母过渡到拉丁字母，现代斯瓦希里语得到大规模的推广和传播，新的文学形式和内容传入东非地区，斯瓦希里语书面文学的受众也从少数贵族阶层推广到广大东非民众之中，东非本土斯瓦希里语语言文学由此完成了历史上最重要的一次嬗变，现代斯瓦希里语小说也随之诞生了。

尽管斯瓦希里语有着历史较久的书写传统，但斯瓦希里语小说是在 19 世纪末 20 世纪初欧洲殖民者入侵东非之后才慢慢发展起来的。随着标准斯瓦希里语的普及和东非教育事业的发展，斯瓦希里语小说发展迅猛，其影响和地位大大超过了历史悠久的诗歌。像其他所有文学形式一样，斯瓦希里语小说的发展不可避免地经历了一个从萌芽到成熟的过程。事实上，它的每一个发展阶段都同东非地区当时的社会、历史、政治、文化和经济状况息息相关。当然，斯瓦希里语小说艺术的发展与演变有其自身的规律和秩序。这种规律和秩序不能通过抽象主观的方法来解释，只能通过对各个时期斯瓦希里语小说文本的考察与研究来加以揭示和验证。我国目前对包括现代小说在内的斯瓦希里语文学的研究还仅仅停留在描述阶段，缺乏深入系统的研究。在深入探讨斯瓦希里语小说艺术的具体特征与艺术价值之前，需要对其历史发展和演变过程进行梳理和论述。

2　斯瓦希里语小说的起源

19 世纪欧洲殖民者到达东非以后，一些掌握了斯瓦希里语的欧洲传教士和受过教育的本土知识分子开始对斯瓦希里语口头文学形式进行搜集和整理，先后出版了一批神话传说故事集。早期这些作品大多是用英语或德语出版的。其中影响最大的是传教士爱德华·斯蒂尔（Edward Steere）于 1870 年整理出版的《桑给巴尔民间故事集》（*Swahili Tales as Told by Natives of Zanzibar*）（King'ei, 1999）。在之后的很长一段时间里，民间故事都是斯瓦希里语出版物最重要的主题。纵观古今中外各种语言文学发展的历史，小说最初都是以民间传说和寓言故事为其渊源的，斯瓦希里语小说也不例外。小说是通过完整的故事情节和具体的环境描写，塑造多种多样的人物形象，广泛且多方面地反映社会生活的一种文学样式。通俗地说，小说就是一种叙事的艺术。而构成民间传说和寓言故事的最主要要素是故事，这和现代小说的文学形式呈现出很大的相似性。因此，口头文学中的民间传说、寓言故事等形式对斯瓦希里语小说的产生和发展有着很大的影响。

早期的斯瓦希里语小说带有强烈的口头文学色彩。从内容上来看，作者们的创作题材与灵感很多都来自斯瓦希里人的古老传说与民间故事。这些本土斯瓦希里语作者将口头文学和民间传说收集起来，并将其转化加工成现代小说的形式。比如坦桑尼亚早期著名作家夏班·罗伯特（Shaaban Robert）的作品《阿迪力兄弟》（*Adili na Nduguze*）就是在一个家喻户晓的民间故事的基础上加工而成的。从语言形式和叙述风格上来看，口头文学中常用的讽刺和比喻的手法被大量地运用在现代小说的写作中。夏班·罗伯特在给小说中的人物和地点命名时会使用与他们的性格品质特点相符的抽象名词，这种写作手法几乎贯穿在他所有的作品之中，比如，"阿迪力"（Adili）代表"正义"，"乌吐卜萨拉"（Utubusara）代表"智慧"，"乌吐波拉"（Utubora）代表"善良"等。这些民间传说和寓言故事既是斯瓦希里社会传统文化遗产的一部分，也是现代斯瓦希里语文学的基础，是具有想象力的创造性写作的源泉。

3 早期斯瓦希里语小说的发展

小说是一种叙述性散文作品。早期斯瓦希里语叙述性散文作品大多是编年史或民族志性质（Bertoncini, 2009）。19世纪末，东非斯瓦希里社会已经出现了非常类似于小说的叙述性散文作品。1895—1907年出版的《基林迪人编年史》（*Habari za Wakilindi*）被誉为斯瓦希里语叙述性散文作品的开端，"这是一部关于基林迪人的非常好的作品，先不论其缺陷，这是斯瓦希里语文学史上第一部散文作品，从人物塑造和环境的渲染方面来看它已经非常接近现代小说了"（Bertoncini, 2009: 24）。这一时期出版的重要散文作品还有《帕泰编年史》（*Habari za Pate*）、《拉姆编年史》（*Habari za Lamu*）和《提普提普自传》（*Tippu Tip's Maisha*）（Bertoncini, 2009）。这些作品是斯瓦希里语小说的雏形，与历史紧密相连，可以作为史料的补充记载。这些作品已经具有小说讲求虚构的特点，但是同现代小说相比，它们的情节往往比较简单，语言的文学性也不高。随着时间的推移，这种历史叙述性散文作品逐渐失去了它的地位和热度，这种文学形式逐渐被新的现代小说的形式取代了。

上述这些叙述性作品有一个很重要的共同点就是它们都是用阿拉伯字

母书写的，推广和传播的难度非常大。在之后的很长一段时间内，小说都没有任何新的发展。直到 20 世纪 20 年代，斯瓦希里语标准化运动，也就是斯瓦希里语拉丁化运动开始以后，斯瓦希里小说才有了新的发展。现代斯瓦希里语学者认为斯瓦希里语拉丁化运动是现代斯瓦希里语文学与古代文学的分水岭，是 20 世纪斯瓦希里语文学嬗变的一个重要标志（Garnier，2013）。

斯瓦希里语拉丁化和规范化工作最初是由西方传教士来进行的。19 世纪中期，欧洲传教士进入东非地区时，意识到了斯瓦希里语在传播基督教过程中的重要作用。传教士们对早期斯瓦希里语语言学研究和规范化工作做出了巨大的贡献，他们致力于研究斯瓦希里语语法和词汇，搜集斯瓦希里语文学文本，翻译出版了大量宗教文本。这对早期斯瓦希里语小说的叙述风格产生了十分重要的影响（King'ei，1999）。

19 世纪末至 20 世纪 60 年代，坦桑尼亚曾先后被德、英两国殖民政府统治。德国殖民政府曾明确提出要使用拉丁字母来书写斯瓦希里语，实现斯瓦希里语的规范化和去伊斯兰化。第一次世界大战结束后，英国接管德属东非殖民地，将东非四国均纳入其管辖范围，使得斯瓦希里语在整个东非地区的标准化运动成为可能。1925 年，英属东非殖民政府决定正式开始实施斯瓦希里语标准化，其主要内容是统一斯瓦希里语的书写方式，并使用标准斯瓦希里语出版教科书和其他印刷品。随后，英殖民政府正式决定将斯瓦希里语确定为整个英属东非殖民地的行政和教育系统语言，并将桑给巴尔地区使用的温古贾方言定为标准斯瓦希里语的基础，对这一方言的字母、词汇、发音等进行一系列的标准化改革。同时，英殖民政府还成立了东非斯瓦希里语委员会和东非文学局等机构，以推动斯瓦希里语的标准化进程，促进斯瓦希里语的发展和推广。

英国殖民政府统治下的斯瓦希里文学是典型的殖民地文学，其主要目的是为了满足传播基督教和殖民地官办学校及教会学校的教育需求。这一时期，殖民地教育体制发展迅速，对基础教育阶段教科书的需求量激增，而东非当地又缺乏足够的有创作能力的本土非洲教师。为了满足英属东非殖民地教育发展的需求，殖民政府从英语书籍中翻译出版了大量斯瓦希里语读物。这些读物主要包括宗教、健康教育、行政事务、农业技术、历史知识、地理知识等读本，也有一些从欧洲学校的文学读本中翻译过来的文本。这些作品的译者大多是掌握了斯瓦希里语的欧洲官员或传教士，而非本土非洲人（Bertoncini, 2009）。其中，有些作品直到今天还在东非地区的小学教育系统中使用，如《所罗门国王的宝藏》（*Mashimo ya Mfalme Suleman*）、《金银岛》（*Kisiwa Chenye Hazina*）、《阿布努瓦斯的故事》（*Hadithi za Abunuwas*）、《一千零一夜》（*Alfu Lela Ulela*）、《伊索寓言》（*Hadithi za Esopo*）、《格列佛游记》（*Safari za Gulliver*）等（King'ei, 1999）。

除了翻译的文学作品之外，为了推广标准斯瓦希里语、鼓励本土非洲人使用标准斯瓦希里语进行文学创作，东非斯瓦希里语委员会从 1935 年起多次组织斯瓦希里语文学写作大赛。许多优秀的本土斯瓦希里语作家和作品从写作比赛中脱颖而出。比如，夏班·罗伯特的自传体小说《我的一生》（*Maisha Yangu*），风靡一时的通俗小说《祖庙》（*Mzimu wa Watu wa Kale*）和《库尔瓦和多托》（*Kurwa na Doto*）都是写作大赛的获奖作品。通过殖民地政府审核的斯瓦希里语书籍可以得到政府的资助，并在东非殖民地所有的官办学校中使用（Mbaabu, 2007）。这一政策使得东非地区的斯瓦希里语作家大受鼓舞，许多本土的官员和学者开始用标准斯瓦希里语进行创作。斯瓦希里语书籍一度大受欢迎，部分书籍的发行量甚至达到了近百万册（Mlacha & Madhumulla, 1991）。

本土作家的另一个发表渠道是英殖民政府在殖民地发行的斯瓦希里语报刊。这些报刊使用的都是非常简单的叙述性语言，旨在推广现代斯瓦希里语的使用，同时也会刊登一些原创故事，给用斯瓦希里语创作的非洲本土作家提供文学创作的机会（Mlacha & Madhumulla, 1991）。

一时间，大量新的非本土形式但具有本土内涵的斯瓦希里语叙述性作品出现并在斯瓦希里社会中广泛传播。欧洲殖民者带到非洲的这种新的文学形式引发了斯瓦希里语文学史上一场激烈的文学形式变革，新兴的现代斯瓦希里语小说迅速成为最受欢迎的文学形式之一。

学界公认的第一部斯瓦希里语小说是 1934 年出版的，即肯尼亚作家詹姆斯·姆博泰拉（James Mbotela）所著的《奴隶的自由》（*Uhuru wa Watumwa*）。这部小说被很多人认为是斯瓦希里语小说的开山之作，在斯瓦希里语文学史上的地位十分重要。这部作品还被译为英文，并多次再版。这部小说的出现标志着斯瓦希里小说的发展进入了一个新的发展阶段。此后，随着现代斯瓦希里语教育的普及，现代斯瓦希里语文学逐渐发展成熟起来，大批非洲本土作家开始涌现出来，如夏班·罗伯特、穆罕默德·萨勒·法尔西（Muhammed Saleh Farsy）和穆罕默德·赛义德·阿卜杜拉（Muhammed Said Abdulla）等。这些作家大多是传教士或政府公务员，与殖民政府的关系良好。其中，夏班·罗伯特是殖民统治时期最著名的一位用斯瓦希里语创作的作家和诗人，是 20 世纪东非文学史上一个最突出的人物。1926—1956 年，夏班·罗伯特曾在英殖民政府部门供职，同时也是东非斯瓦希里语委员会、东非文学局、坦噶尼喀语言委员会内部成员（Bertoncini, 2009）。尽管他只接受了 6 年的正规教育，但他一生笔耕不辍，在他 1962 年去世时，创作了 20 余部作品，被誉为斯瓦希里语文学史上最伟大的诗人和作家（冯玉培，2012）。夏班·罗伯特去世之后，他的作品被汇编成《夏班·罗伯特丛书》。他的主要作品是诗歌，他的小说作品共有 7 部，分别是《可信国》（*Kusadikika*）、《想象国》（*Kufikirika*）、《阿迪力兄弟》（*Adili na Nduguze*）、《农民乌吐波拉》（*Utubora Mkulima*）、《我的一生和五十年后》（*Maisha Yanguna Baada ya Miaka Hamsini*）、《西提传》（*Wasifu wa Siti Binti Saad*）和《全体劳动人民的日子》（*Siku ya Watenzi Wote*）。他的多部作品被译为英文、中文和其他语种，在斯瓦希里语文学中占有重要地位，对近代斯瓦希里语诗歌和小说的发展产生了极其重要的影响。鉴于他在文学创作方面所取得的成就，他曾被授予"玛格丽特纪念奖"和"不列颠帝国员佐勋章"，被誉为"东非的莎士比亚"（Bertoncini, 2009: 35）。

4　早期斯瓦希里语小说中的殖民性与民族性

我们在讨论现代斯瓦希里语小说的诞生与发展时，不得不将其与殖民者入侵东非的历史联系在一起。19—20 世纪，西方列强通过在东非地区的殖民统治对东非地区实施了影响深远的文化霸权，对这一地区的语言和文学的发展产生了强烈的影响。

从内容和主题上看，殖民时期的斯瓦希里语小说多是具有道德训诫和说教意义的小说，甚至不乏歌颂殖民统治的内容，而甚少有关于非洲民族解放运动的内容。比如，前文提到的《奴隶的自由》和夏班·罗伯特早期的大部分作品都是这类作品。《奴隶的自由》这部作品讲述了作者的父亲和族人被阿拉伯人贩卖为奴，最后被英国人解放的故事。该书作者姆博泰拉于1905—1906年在英国接受教育，之后回到肯尼亚定居，他曾经做过教师、传教士和翻译官。作者的教育和生活经历决定了其作品的局限性，这部作品纯粹是一部英国颂，对英国殖民者在东非的统治没有任何的责备或批评，甚至歌颂了英国政府在非洲的殖民统治。这部小说对英国殖民者在东非的所作所为极力称颂，认为非洲人只能依附殖民者生存，而这正是殖民政府巩固其统治所需要的。意大利斯瓦希里语文学评论家艾莱娜·贝托奇尼（Elena Bertoncini）指出："作为一种文学形式，姆博泰拉的这部作品用的是简单但是正确的标准斯瓦希里语书写的，但它的文学审美价值并不大。这部在艺术成就上并没有过人之处的作品在斯瓦希里语文学史上的地位如此重要，仅仅只是因为这是一部契合了殖民统治需要的、非民间故事主题的散文作品"（Bertoncini, 2009: 33）。另外，这一时期得到广泛传播的还有一些娱乐性较强的通俗小说，如《桑给巴尔的婚俗》（*Ada za Arusi katika Unguja*）、《库尔瓦和多托》（*Kurwa na Doto*）、《祖庙》（*Mzimu wa Watu wa Kale*）、《穆丽娜轶事》（*Kisa cha Mrina Asali*）等（King'ei, 1999）。

而反观同一时期的殖民地英语文学的情况则完全不同，用英语创作的东非本土作家发表了大量反殖民主题的作品，如恩古吉·瓦·提安哥（Ngugi wa Thiong'o）、穆戈·瓦·伽什卢（Mugo wa Gatheru）和姆旺吉·卡里乌其（Mwangi Katiuki）等（King'ei, 1999）。究其原因，这是英殖民政府实施文化霸权的结果，他们通过文化输出，将西方的价值观和意识形态强行灌输给非洲人民，认为斯瓦希里语是愚昧的、肮脏的、低级的、奴隶的语言，造成传统文化的边缘化。在殖民时期，用英语创作具有绝对的优势，英语作品更容易得到资助和出版，其地位和影响力远远超过斯瓦希里语作品。而斯瓦希里语作品如果要得到殖民政府的资助，其题材和内容就必须迎合殖民主义的需要。这种影响直到今天依然存在，传统文化一直被视为一种比西方文化劣等的文化，导致了民众文化自尊心的丧失。

从语言上来看，现代斯瓦希里语小说所使用的标准斯瓦希里语也深受西方语言和文化的影响。斯瓦希里语标准化运动普及了以拉丁字母书写的标准斯瓦希里语，将斯瓦希里语的口头语言和书面语言统一起来，用斯瓦希里语书写的图书和报刊在东非地区得到普遍推广，为斯瓦希里语文学作品的发表提供了机会和舞台。现代斯瓦希里语小说也由此逐渐发展繁荣起来。

但是，值得我们注意的是，斯瓦希里语标准化运动从头至尾都是由西方殖民者主导的，这项工作的初衷是为加强殖民政府的管理服务，而不是为了发展非洲的民族语言（Maganga, 1997）。负责斯瓦希里语标准化工作的东非斯瓦希里语委员会最初的组成人员均为白人教育官员，并没有吸收非洲人参加。直到 1939 年，殖民当局才允许非洲人进入该委员会（Mbaabu, 2007）。这种情况下，斯瓦希里语标准化工作一定会存在一些无法回避的问题。首先，选择何种方言作为标准斯瓦希里语的基础完全是出于欧洲人的喜好，并没有尊重斯瓦希里人自己的意见（齐拉格丁，1965）。其次，从事标准化工作的主要是英国人，而非斯瓦希里人，这使得现代标准斯瓦希里语的发音、结构、词汇和表达深受英语的影响。尽管每一种语言都会在与外来文明的交往中发生改变，得到新的发展，但是，人类文明史上的这种改变应是主动的，而不是强制推行的。甚至有学者认为，"标准斯瓦希里语是一种英语式的斯瓦希里语"（Mbaabu, 2007: 38）。另外，在推广现代斯瓦希里语的过程中，殖民政府出版了许多斯瓦希里语书籍，由于缺少原创作品，许多书籍都是由欧洲原本翻译而来的。因此，这些作品中的语言深受英语语法规则的影响，这些从欧洲语言逐字逐句翻译而来的斯瓦希里语书籍缺乏传统斯瓦希里语中的谚语、习语等生动的表达（齐拉格丁，1965）。这些作品对现代斯瓦希里语小说和散文的叙述方式产生了极大的影响。比如，部分学者认为《奴隶的自由》这部作品并不属于斯瓦希里语文学，因为书中的许多观点、想法和语言结构都是欧洲式的（Shariff, 1988）。

尽管如此，我们不能把现代斯瓦希里语小说这种文学形式简单地理解为就是西方的，而应理解为现代小说这种西方的文学形式适应了斯瓦希里社会的文化背景，满足了斯瓦希里社会的需求，因而为其所接受，并在这种特定的社会背景下获得了一些不同于西方现代小说的具体特征（Bertoncini, 2009）。

随着非洲民族独立运动的发展，斯瓦希里语作家的思想也变得越来越进步。夏班·罗伯特的《可信国》和《想象国》等作品中也出现了反抗的政治和哲学思想（King'ei, 1999）。他后期的作品，比如《农民乌吐波拉》和《全体劳动人民的日子》更是体现了理想主义和人道主义的特点，反映了迫切的社会问题。这两部作品的背景都设定于当代坦噶尼喀而不是像其他早期作品一样是一个想象中的国家。在《农民乌吐波拉》中，作者对资本主义殖民地社会及其黑暗，对非自然、非人性化的城市化进行了抨击。

另外，早期的斯瓦希里语小说家还擅长将传统的古代文学形式和现代小说结合起来，比如，在自传体小说《我的一生》中，夏班·罗伯特插入了两首教诲诗——正义史诗和道德史诗，这种形式是 19 世纪古代斯瓦希里语文学的主要形式之一。可以看出，面对西方殖民者的侵略和文化渗透，斯瓦希里语作家也在努力寻求民族文化之根，在对本土文化发掘、肯定的基础上，确立民族的尊严和自豪感。

殖民者利用文化来达到他们输出思维方式和文化价值观的目的，对独立后东非民族的身份认同和国家民族的构建都产生了持续的影响。相对于其他东非国家，坦桑尼亚的首位总统尼雷尔在民族融合的过程中充分利用语言和文学的力量，为促进斯瓦希里语的广泛使用做了很多工作。他曾用斯瓦希里语翻译了莎士比亚的几个剧本，引起了世界文学界的关注，极大地激发了坦桑尼亚人的民族自豪感和自信心。尽管殖民时期斯瓦希里语小说的数量以及影响力都远远不及同一时期的非洲英语文学，但这仍是现代斯瓦希里语小说发展史上一个非常重要的时期。斯瓦希里语小说的发展取得了长足的进步，其地位和影响在斯瓦希里语文学史上首次超过了诗歌，为当代斯瓦希里语小说的全面发展奠定了基础。经过无数斯瓦希里语作家的探索与实践，当代斯瓦希里语小说在艺术形式和创作技巧上与它早期的雏形已不可同日而语。

参考文献

BERTONCINI E Z, 2009. Outline of Swahili literature: prose fiction and drama [M].

Leiden: Bril.

GARNIER X, 2013. The Swahili novel: challenging the idea of minor literature [M]. Woodbridge: Boydell & Brewer Ltd.

KING'EI K, 1999. Historia na maendeleo ya Kiswahili [J]. Chemchemi: International journal of arts and social sciences, 1: 82-93.

MAGANGA C, 1997. Historia ya Kiswahili [M]. Dar es Salaam: Open University of Tanzania.

MBAABU I, 2007. Historia ya Usanifishaji wa Kiswahili [M]. Dar es Salaam: Taasisi ya Uchunguzi wa Kiswahili, Chuo Kikuu cha Dar es Salaam.

MLACHA S A K, MADHUMULLA J S, 1991. Riwaya ya Kiswahili [M]. Dar es Salaam: Dar es Salaam University Press.

SHARIFF I N, 1988. Tungo Zetu [M]. New Jersey: Red Sea Press.

冯玉培，2012. 一位杰出的民族主义者——坦桑尼亚著名作家夏班·罗伯特 [J]. 亚非研究，（6）：243-255.

齐拉格丁，1965. 斯瓦希利语在东非各国的民族意识、团结和文化上的作用 [J]. 当代语言学，（4）：1-4.

（编辑：马秀杰）

阿契贝的种族政治批评及其文化语境考察[①]

秦鹏举

长江大学人文与新媒体学院

摘　要： 现代种族主义的诞生，源于资产阶级的产生及其对海外殖民地的掠夺和侵略。种族主义产生于封建时代的阶级分层，鼎盛于19世纪垄断资本主义大肆扩张时期。西方的殖民主义与种族主义从反向上刺激了非洲的反种族主义与民族主义思潮的产生。阿契贝的种族政治批评表现为对西方中心主义和虚假"普遍性"的质疑与批判，蕴涵着共同的人性与包容辩证的人文精神。其种族政治批评的形成有着深刻的历史文化语境渊源，即独特的非—西混杂文化成长环境、独特的人生体验和对民族国家建设和文化的艰难探索。

关键词： 阿契贝；种族主义；民族主义

Achebe's Racial Political Criticism and Its Cultural Context Investigation

Qin Pengju

School of Humanities and New Media, Yangtze University

Abstract: Modern Racism stemmed from the birth of the bourgeoisie and its exploitation and aggression of overseas colonies. Racism originated from the class stratification in feudal times and flourished in the process of the wild expansion of monopoly capitalism in the 19th century. The colonialism and racism of the West stimulated the birth of the anti-racism and nationalism thoughts of the African people.

① 本文为2019年国家社科基金重大项目"丝路文化视域下的东方文学与东方文学学科体系建构"（项目编号：19ZDA290）、2019年国家社科基金重大项目"非洲英语文学史"（项目编号：19ZDA296）、2021年湖北省社科基金项目"非洲现代文学之父阿契贝小说的文化诗学研究"（项目编号：2021276）的阶段性研究成果。

收稿日期：2020-11-18

作者信息：秦鹏举，长江大学人文与新媒体学院，副教授，硕士生导师，研究方向为非洲文学与文化，电子邮箱：pengjuqin@yangtzeu.edu.cn。

Achebe's racial political criticism was manifested in questioning and criticizing Western centralism and false "universality", containing the common human nature and the humanistic spirit of tolerance and dialectics. The formation of his racial political criticism had a profound historical and cultural context, that was the unique growth environment of African-Western mixed culture, the unique life experience and the difficult exploration of the construction and culture of the nation-states.

Keywords: Achebe; racism; nationalism

1　种族主义与阿契贝的种族政治观

1.1　种族主义的诞生与发展

种族即"人种"，指的是"具有共同起源和共同遗传特征的人群"（中国社会科学院语言研究所词典编辑室，2019: 1100）。人种意义上的西方种族观来源于其人种志学和考古学的发现，并借此区分不同地域、血缘、肤色意义上的人种。西方早期的种族观是一个不断发展的过程。西方现代种族观的诞生，源于资产阶级的产生及其对海外殖民地的掠夺和侵略。奴隶贸易的巨大利润刺激了西方殖民者的野心，种族主义观因而变为他们开脱上述罪恶商贸的辩护词，进而扭曲价值观，并不惜歪曲历史，以助长其膨胀的白人至上的种族优越主义和强权政治。这里需要明晰的是种族主义与民族主义的区分。种族主义是根据生物学的人种辨别，而民族主义是根据民族共同心理的一种文化认同。换言之，种族是先天形成的，民族是后来形成的。但二者有着紧密关联，种族主义可能打着民族主义的旗号行事，如西方殖民者的种族歧视与非洲民族主义者的种族主义理论。

几个世纪以来，从事大西洋奴隶贸易的白人的种族逻辑是："非洲人民似乎由于生理特点，以及所谓智力和德性低劣，不仅没有能力创造高度的文化，而且还没有能力在自己的土地上当家作主，没有欧洲人的'帮助'，他们似乎没有能力管理自己的土地"（奥尔洛娃，1960: 12）。大批传教士随同商业殖民者进入非洲本土，他们手握《圣经》，以上帝的化身显现"真理"，向非洲人民播撒"文明"的种子，驱散"野蛮"和"无知"。当殖民统治建立后，殖民者需要一个稳固的统治秩序和俯首帖耳的顺民，于是种族主义又与殖民主义相勾结，共同变本加厉地制造了"文明"与"野蛮"分野的种族主义观。

种族主义产生于封建时代的阶级分层，鼎盛于 19 世纪资本主义在全世界殖民扩张的进程中。西方自近代的启蒙主义之后，人的理性和"人定胜天"的观念深入人心，资产阶级征服世界的野心膨胀，种族主义便是其极端典型表现。笛卡尔的理性原则逐渐演进为人类唯一的生存法则，宗教神学上"因信称义"的改革，因资产阶级的全面崛起，又将宗教观与世俗的进取结合起来。鲁滨孙的成功就充分证明了韦伯（Weber）在"信仰"与"世俗"之间的紧密配合与互动。而莎士比亚眼中"宇宙的精华、万物的灵长"的人类自我意识开始觉醒的自由理性已经一去不复返，取而代之的是一种"物竞天择"的达尔文式的丛林法则和不择手段的工具理性。"泰勒或者摩根的进化论，以及列维－布留尔傲慢又反动的种族中心主义是无法接受的。他们无法想象出'原始'社会的文化生活，只会承认'原始'社会代表单一文化过程中的初级阶段，而欧洲则代表其中的最发达阶段"（奥拉尼央、奎森，2020: 337）。与此同时，自莎士比亚开始的西方文学长廊也进入了种族主义蔓延的续写进程中，这批作家都呈现在东方学大家萨义德（Said）的笔下，无须一一列举。总之，从哲学、生物学、宗教观、考古学和文学方面，世界由此开启了一个种族主义弥漫的时代。

19 世纪非洲民族主义之父布莱登（Blyden）提出"非洲个性"[①] 的思想，此思想奠定了非洲种族论的基石。在他看来，"种族观念不仅是基于生物学意义上的判断，而且具有文化、宗教等人类精神的表征"（张宏明，2006）。实际上，种族观念从其诞生伊始，便内含着文化上的意识形态与野心，西方人眼中的自然种族观早已摆脱了人种观念的域限，实行其文明高下之野的"高贵"与"低贱"的人为区分。西方人的殖民野心和控制欲望正是助长种族主义话语的前提。但布莱登的种族理论却是种族平等与种族和谐互补，其种族特性论虽有翻转黑白对立的二元论意味，但其主体是种族的和谐平等与对话。可以说，"只有考虑到非洲各族人民发展所处环

---

① 主张非洲是"非洲人的非洲"，"非洲是人类文明的摇篮"，"非洲特性"思想延续了黑人奴隶贸易和殖民时期的种族主义思想，但其种族平等理论却扭转了种族达尔文主义的泛滥。

境的全部复杂性和特殊性，只有考虑到对他们有影响的地理、经济、历史和社会等方面的全部因素，才能理解他们的文化"（奥尔洛娃，1960：13）。布莱登的思想深刻启悟了后来的非洲民族主义者，黑人性、黑人精神、泛非主义、非洲中心主义、非洲民族主义等社会运动和文化思潮都或多或少受到布莱登思想的影响。尤其是塞内加尔的桑戈尔（Senghor）等人发起的"黑人性"运动与谢赫·安塔·迪奥普（Cheikh Anta Diop）的"非洲中心主义"理论就是直接受到了布莱登的深刻启发和影响。

西方的殖民主义与种族主义从反向上刺激了非洲人民的反种族主义与民族主义的思潮。如同西方一样，非洲人的民族主义与种族主义亦是相生相伴的。"非洲民族主义的动力并不是那种对一个力求保护和维护自身权利的独特的政治-文化统一体的归属感，而是一些具有种族意识的现代派的运动，这些人力图在欧洲主子强加的人为边界之内，由不同的民族建立起政治和文化的新民族"（博亨，1991：458）。简言之，非洲的民族主义在于其种族性即伴随着对整个黑人种族的认同（李安山，2004）。对黑人种族性的强调，就是对黑人民族主义和黑人文化复兴的强调，这在后来一系列的黑人社会运动和文化思潮中可以得到印证。这种种族性后来演变为一种整体性和宏观性的泛非主义和泛非精神，其在黑人民族国家建构和统一复兴道路中扮演了重要作用。当然，黑人没有经历现代民族国家的冶炼，在殖民者撤退后的非洲独立发展的进程中，并没有培育统一的国民文化和民族心理，而是直接跃步至殖民遗产的地域拼凑与政治混杂状态中，因而其公民对国家的认同心理薄弱、社会文化结构较涣散。而强调种族性的泛非运动很好地弥补了国家民族当中缺失的文化统一性与历史认同感。正是由于殖民主义与种族性的深刻勾联，阿契贝（Achebe）的创作凸显了对西方种族政治的强烈批判。

1.2　阿契贝的种族政治观

1974 年，阿契贝发表《殖民主义批评》（*Colonialist Criticism*），对西方意识形态包裹下的艺术样态尤其是小说给予了批判。他认为"普遍性"总是西方的代名词，西方总是自动地拥有普遍性和真理，而对于西方的对立面非洲而言，其"野蛮"和"不成熟"的一面自然要等待西方的"救赎"。对于身处后殖民时代的非洲人来说，要懂得一个道理："殖民地人民道德的堕落，是招致西方人镇压和惩罚的主要原因"（Achebe, 1990: 79）。因为在后殖民时代，要求非洲人对西方露骨的直接颂扬已显得不合时宜，那么，非洲人此刻应该自我贬抑，这在西方人看来是一种十分必要的"谦逊"和"感恩"的诚实品德。当代的非洲，已摆脱了西方直接的殖民统治与干预，走向独立发展的阶段。但殖民余毒却始终如影随形，西方利用极富隐蔽性的金融渗透、内含西方价值观和政治符码的舆论等手段对亚非拉国家进行新一轮的殖民扩张（谓之"新殖民主义"），并且这一过程延续至今，远未结束。

1975 年，阿契贝在美国马萨诸塞大学阿默斯特分校的讲座中对约瑟夫·康拉德（Joseph Conrad）的种族主义作了更为具体深刻的批评。在他影响巨大的文论《非洲的一种形象：论康拉德〈黑暗的心灵〉中的种族主义》（*An Image Africa: Racism in Conrad's* Heart of Darkness）中，阿契贝毫不客气地指出："康拉德是个彻头彻尾的种族主义者"（Achebe, 1990: 11）。平心而论，康拉德无论文笔还是思想，都称得上是世界文学史上少有的经典作家，但其整体思路，正如萨义德后来所分析的，康拉德的《黑暗的心灵》逃不脱帝国主义的整体叙事架构，"从政治和美学的角度来看，都是帝国主义式的"（萨义德，2003: 30）。这不是康拉德一个人的问题，而是所有西方作家都面临的困境。因为对"自我"的想象与定位，总是需要一个外在的"他者"。对非洲的种族歪曲，是"西方人心中的一种愿望，也可以说是一种需求，即把非洲看成是欧洲的陪衬物，一个遥远而又似曾相识的对立面，在它的映衬下，欧洲优点才能显现出来"（Achebe, 1990: 3）。

1990 年，阿契贝遭遇车祸后定居美国，并于 1993 年发表了评论《受英国保护的孩童的求学记》（*The Education of a British-Protected Child: Essays*）。评论中追溯了他的求学和成长经历，叙述中充满了对殖民主义的痛恨，同时他的思想也更为圆融包容，充满智慧。"殖民主义本质上就是一种对人的价值和尊严的否定……作为人的一个重要特征就是，通过拒绝被逆境定义、拒绝沦为其代理人或受害人来克服逆境的能力"（Achebe, 2009: 22-23）。此外，教育中的人文主义却时时显现出超越种族和民族国家的界限，人文精神可以抵抗对人性的剥夺。这一点，无论是非洲人，还是西方人，都显示了宝贵的精神价值与"合而为一"的人类愿景。

在"尼日利亚四部曲"《瓦解》（*Things Fall Apart*）、《再也不得安宁》（*No Longer at Ease*）、《神箭》（*Arrow of God*）、《人民公仆》（*A Man of the People*）中，阿契贝对种族主义提出了深刻的批判与文明反思。《瓦解》中的奥贡喀沃是一个类似希腊英雄的悲剧主人公，他在部落文明面临崩溃的时候，以不为他人所理解的方式结束了自己的生命。这里揭示的是现代西方殖民文化对传统非洲本土文化的摧毁和文明冲突交融的客观进程，作者固然没有价值观的显在表达，但字里行间明显的民族挽歌无疑凸显了西方殖民文化的种族主义高下之分。读者不免从中读出奥贡喀沃其情可悯、西方殖民者其行可鄙的深意。《神箭》中的伊祖鲁作为部落大祭司，是西方殖民者倾力培植的一位部落傀儡，但他有自己的价值观和情感倾向。他不愿当殖民者的提线木偶，而是利用手中的神圣权力（宣布收获节和种植节等）作为利箭，射向了殖民者和违背他意愿的本土居民，最终他的命运就像一位向神献祭的祭品一样，以疯癫的死亡高调地完成了他心中的复仇计划。伊祖鲁的权力论固然是他悲剧命运的主要原因，但别有用心的西方殖民者和不觉醒的部落民众也是悲剧制造者。令伊祖鲁尤其痛心疾首的是村民的背叛与不坚定，就像那个走向末世的英雄奥贡喀沃一样，他们都是生活的强者，但是都逃不脱殖民文化的侵袭。在我们看来，未必是他们看不清未来的路，而是不愿从英雄的幻境中醒过来，毕竟那是耗尽心血得来的勇士称号和积攒几辈子的祭司荣誉，这是比生命更高贵更值得珍惜的。而于此，献祭的英雄们所代表的本土文化便有了更深层的意义，他们用生命换来了后来所理所当然的一种民族主义式的同情与缅怀。

《人民公仆》中的萨马鲁、长篇小说《荒原蚁丘》（*Anthills of the Savannah*）中的伊肯就是这样的民族主义式的人物。萨马鲁的公正公平换来的是可耻的阴谋与欺骗，最终他以《圣经》的"以牙还牙"的方式走向共同"吃"的道路便暴露和讽刺了殖民选举文化的虚伪。伊肯与昔日当上总统的萨姆分道扬镳，并最终被其阴谋杀害。萨姆是西化派的典型代表，他俨然是西方殖民文化的急先锋，对本土人士充满种族主义式的仇恨，当然他自己的身份是一个悖谬。而《再也不得安宁》中的奥比，是一个摇摆在非洲传统与西方现代之间的"空心人"，最终走向失败的人生。阿契贝所倾心的理想人物是《荒原蚁丘》中的女主人公比阿特丽斯，她以种族和解和各阶层联合的方式实现了作者希冀化解民族仇恨、团结各级力量的理想。对于本土西化派的卖国行为和殖民主义者的种族主义歧视，作者在文本中是有着一贯的谴责态度与强烈批判力度的。

2 阿契贝种族政治批评的文化考察

2.1 独特的非－西混杂文化成长环境

　　阿契贝的种族政治批评受独特的历史文化语境的浸染与熏陶。阿契贝自小生活在一个双重宗教文化（基督教文化和非洲传统宗教文化）语境中，但却并不因文化的混杂而感到焦虑和矛盾。他的父母都是虔诚的圣公会基督教徒，而他的叔叔、父亲的舅舅和周围的邻居，都给他一种传统文化的实在感和无形的精神影响。"我知道我喜欢故事，在家中，我最先接触的是我母亲讲述的故事，其次是我的大姐讲述的故事，如乌龟的故事。当父亲有访客进行闲聊时，我能够从他们的谈话中获得无限的故事性灵感"（Lindfors, 1997: X）。母亲给阿契贝讲的故事大都来自伊博族的神话故事、民间谚语。姐姐的教诲和哥哥的引导，也都奠定了他的传统文化底子。阿契贝在英国殖民政府举办的公学里就读（飞利浦氏中央小学、乌穆阿希亚中学、伊巴丹大学），体验到不同宗教文化和民族习俗的碰撞，尽管它们有差异和冲突，但人类人文主义的精神主题都是相通的。"我们在树林里捡的每一颗棕榈仁都能买到希特勒棺材上的一根钉子"（Achebe, 2009: 18）。这是对违反人类人道主义与人性的共同抵制，同时也说明种族歧视的观念还并未在年幼的阿契贝心里扎根。

　　但种族主义终究会刺破人类的道德底线。母亲因教沃纳小姐伊博语而发出的善意"嘲笑"却换来殖民贵妇的一顿棍棒，这在阿契贝幼小的心灵里蒙上了一层阴影。基督教崇尚宽容的品德，父母也并未因基督徒身份而获得更多的实际权益，相反，实际生活中却招致本地民众与殖民者的双重排斥与不满。殖民公学里并不是每一位白人教育者都充满了人类的公平与良知，许多的教育制度和语言学习条款都充满着"文明"与"野蛮"的二元敌对。这些对作为黑人学生的阿契贝而言，以他对文学和生活的敏锐感知，并非没有深切体味。

最终触发阿契贝拿起笔进行反抗种族主义的是他读到了英国作家康拉德的《黑暗的心灵》与爱尔兰作家乔伊斯·卡里（Joyce Cary）的《约翰逊先生》。如上分析，康拉德的小说彻底暴露了他种族主义的观点。而卡里的小说中的主人公约翰逊，是一位对白人主子讨好献媚的人格低贱的黑人，他悲剧性的命运激怒了阿契贝，"它激发了阿契贝变成一个小说家以致他能够'从内部'讲述尼日利亚的故事"（Innes, 1990: 2）。而后，他创作的以尼日利亚独立前后为背景的"尼日利亚四部曲"，通过几代人的文化痛苦选择和悲剧性命运书写了非洲人的非洲。凭借这些作品，他重新定义了非洲，刻画了非洲人心目中的英雄，以充满人道主义的人性之笔和大悲悯情怀揭露了一个客观而又真实的非洲。

2.2　独特的人生体验

1960 年，阿契贝获得洛克菲勒奖学金，并去非洲各国访学，然而他的访学热情很快就被种族主义的阴影所击退。他冷静思索：独立后的非洲并不是一块净土，殖民主义带来的种族主义毒害影响深远。1966 年发表的《人民公仆》以新独立的国家部长南加和人民教师奥迪里之间的竞选展开，深刻揭露了一场荒唐的政坛闹剧，它是对非洲现实的深刻透视和无情揭露。"我的本意是借小说谴责后殖民时期的尼日利亚及 20 世纪 60 年代许多其他国家的所谓独立，我想讲述一个可怕的警世故事，提醒国人约束自己的行为"（Achebe, 2009: 43）。没曾想阿契贝一语成谶，就在小说发表后的第二年，尼日利亚内战爆发了。美国《时代周刊》认为它是一部伟大的非洲政治寓言，比成千上万的新闻纪录更有价值，比一切政治家和记者更具智慧。小说中被誉为"人民公仆"的人，其实只是一群"你吃，大家也吃"的人民蛀虫。导致这场政治丑闻的不仅有国际势力的操控，更有国内对狭隘的部族主义的固守与种族主义的贻害。

1962 年，"非洲英语作家大会"在新独立的乌干达首都坎帕拉的马凯雷雷大学举行，阿契贝受邀参会。会上，他结识了美国非裔大作家兰休斯（Hughes），休斯的直率和抗争精神深深鼓舞了阿契贝。后来，阿契贝在评论中写道："受害者要了解自己，要意识到压迫的存在，意识到自己从充满荣耀或希望的地位跌落到如今所在的深渊；然后，受害者必须清楚谁是敌人，他需要清楚压迫者真正的名字，而非别名、化名或者笔名"（Achebe,2009: 57）！正视现实，而不是逃避，才是非洲人的责任和使命。但"黑人也无须为了证明他们如今的存在与尊严的正当性而编造一个伟大的过去。他们该做的是重获本就属于他们的东西——他们的历史——并亲口讲出来"（Achebe, 2009: 61）。阿契贝意有所指，非洲历史上桑戈尔等人提倡的"黑人性"运动确实恢复了黑人的历史与尊严，但其"反种族主义的种族主义"（萨特语）意味也非常明显。他指出："你们都听说过非洲个性，听说过非洲民主、非洲特色社会主义，以及黑人性运动等。这些都是我们在不同时期创造出的支柱，帮助我们重新站立起来。而一旦我们站了起来，就不再需要这些支柱了。但是目前，我们理所当然需要用让–保罗·萨特所谓的反种族主义的种族主义，来对抗种族主义，来宣告我们不仅和其他民族一样出色，而且比他们更优秀"（奥拉尼央、奎森，2020: 132）。而文学之"富有想象力的生活是我们整体特质的关键要素，如果缺少滋养或受到污染，我们的生活质量就会下降，或被玷污"（奥拉尼央、奎森，2020: 140）。这正好是种族主义者所缺乏的。从反种族主义的种族主义，到富有想象力的文学创作，看来阿契贝是充分相信文学能修复人心并能改变世界这一文学意义上的政治信条。

1967—1970 年，尼日利亚内战即比夫拉战争爆发，彻底揭露了阿契贝所言的腐朽的国内政治生态。"严重的区域仇恨和无效的中央权力使得尼日利亚联邦存在了六年就分崩离析了"（Achebe, 2009: 42）。殖民主义者以其对非洲全方位的政治和经济的剥夺和分割来维持后殖民时期的继续操控，形成非洲对外来势力的"依附"。阿明指出："非洲经济灾难的根源是资本主义的全球扩张……处于依附地位的非洲国家不会出现一种成熟、自主的资本主义前景"（阿明，2003）。在此期间，阿契贝担任比夫拉政府的外交部官员，为国家前途积极奔走。比夫拉共和国最终失败了，但阿契贝认为是"国家没能履行对公民应尽的最基本的义务，最终导致东尼日利亚脱离联邦政府"（Achebe, 2009: 44）。伊博人一再忍让，但贪婪无耻的北方邦腐败政府毫无道德底线，战争终将置几百万生灵于涂炭。无论后来者如何评论这一段历史，对生命的伤害和残杀无疑是需要谴责的，双方都要为这一历史罪行负责，在种族仇恨和教派仇杀面前，没有人是无辜的。但历史的前提是，种族主义并不是非洲人与生俱来的，它是西方人的"新发明"。

　　肯尼亚作家恩古吉（Ngugi）认为，70年代的非洲作家，"他们的斗争不只是肤色和种族的问题。他们的敌人是帝国主义。在独立的非洲国家内部，政变开始呈现出更为鲜明的反帝和反殖民特征"（奥拉尼央、奎森，2020: 204）。对于自己的祖国尼日利亚，阿契贝认为它曾经也是一个受到神恩眷顾的国家，处处充满了拥有特殊才华的人和创造的奇迹。但如今，尼日利亚的"人们挥霍在进口的琳琅满目的无用消费商品上面，这些商品充斥着世界的每一个角落。"而"受膨胀的合同使得贪污不断在党派忠诚主义者的队伍中生长，这些人既没有希望，也没有能力执行这些合同"（Achebe, 1998: 4）。机构办事人员过多，效率低下已经蔚然成风。阿契贝不无担忧："我们已经失去了20世纪，我们还能决心看着我们的下一代也失去21世纪吗？"（Achebe, 1998: 4）阿契贝希望创造一个清明廉洁的社会和政治环境，拥有一个智慧超群、意志坚定、全身心为人民服务的政府管理者，一个没有腐败和贪污、政治清明、办事效率高、作风正派而严谨的政府。不得不说，这仅是阿契贝的一个良好祝愿和美好的乌托邦幻想，现实的残酷使他的期冀破灭。从阿契贝的急切盼望因而显得有些激愤的声音中，我们看到的是作为一个有良知的知识分子对社会的担忧和深沉思索。他直指社会病痛却不失冷静客观，在他指责领导者的过错和失误的同时，也指出了社会的整体麻木和不觉醒。而要想改变这一切，并非易事，对于灾难深重和顽疾缠身的尼日利亚而言，任何一点改变都是十分困难的。

2.3　民族国家建设和文化的艰难探索

　　阿契贝认为，按照学者的理解，部落主义就是"因为出生地方的不同而产生的对公民的一种歧视"。部落主义曾经是我们对付殖民主义的制胜法宝，"尽管部落和语言不同，但我们如兄弟般紧紧相连"。然而如今，"我们却在同族相残的土地上苟延残喘"。我们先前如此看重的这个词汇，在此时此刻，却幻想从眼前擦除。但无论如何，任何幻想擦除部落影响的观念和行为都是"不成熟的"，"没有经过认真思考的"，也是"不诚实的"。无疑，部落文化值得尊重，每一个民族都有它独特的文化信条和规则。但这不能成为偏见的借口。"偏见和固执破坏进步和文明，尽管我们不能以法律的形式要求人人都能够消除它们，但我们的国家和社会机构不必实践、认可或宽恕像这样的习惯"（Achebe, 1998: 9）。

然而，地方民族主义并不等于真正的爱国主义，无论是一个地区的民族主义①还是国家整体意义上的民族主义。"虚伪的爱国主义是尼日利亚特权阶层的标志之一，对于他们而言，面临突如其来的权力和财富以及这种不劳而获的地位，真正的爱国主义显得不切实际。他们所谓的爱国主义是为了安放他们不安的灵魂。他们的爱国主义仅仅停留在嘴边，爱国主义从来不在这些人的心中或头脑里，当然更不在他们的手头实践上"，而真正的"爱国主义是一种为批判的理性所主导的爱的情感。真正的爱国者总是以最高的标准期待祖国，他从人民那里接受最好的东西，并且也把最好的东西奉献给人民。他坦率直陈祖国的弊病，毫不屈服于迷信、绝望与讥嘲"（Achebe, 1998: 18）。

阿契贝认为，造成独立后非洲发展困境的原因有很多，其中最为典型的是国家领导人的腐败、独裁和无能。"尼日利亚的问题在于领导者不愿意或没有能力承担责任，真正的领导者在于挑战私人利益"（Achebe, 1998: 1）。但与其谴责非洲和非洲人，不如思考非洲的客观现实处境。"帝国霸权需要一种新的语言来描述它所缔造的世界及征服的民族……非洲作为欧洲帝国主义政策的首要目标，几乎没有哪块地方逃脱了被占领的命运，自然会受到全方位的负面定义"（Achebe, 2009: 159）。作为非洲人，阿契贝首选的不是抱怨和一味地谴责，而是"献祭"自己。正如他小说中的主人公伊祖鲁，一位发疯的大祭司那样，如果不去考虑他觊觎权力的野心，他的行为似乎完全是为了献祭神灵和社会，非洲彼时正需要这样的献祭者。即使在当代的非洲，虽然社会已经进步了，但非洲人依然被人瞧不起。正如神学家施韦泽所言："非洲人的确是我的兄弟，不过是小兄弟"（Achebe, 2009: 158）。在当代西方，非洲人想被当作人类中的平等一员并获得承认，这依然是一个问题。这显示了部分西方人虚伪的人道价值观与人性的双重标准。

多年前，马丁·路德·金（Martin Luther King）呼喊："对黑人来讲，

---

① 李安山先生认为非洲"部落主义"（tribalism）应为"地方民族主义"。笔者赞同此观点。

'解放'就是获得饥饿的自由，获得风吹雨打的自由，获得无片瓦遮顶的自由。这是没有面包果腹的自由，这是没有土地耕种的自由。这是自由与饥饿的并存"（Deacon, 2018）。"种族问题不再是会议室里可见的存在。它蛰伏在我们的潜意识里，只是我们看不见……当我们轻松自在、漫不经心的时候，可能会无意间做出严重的不公之举"（Achebe, 2009: 95）。就此而言，世界消除种族主义的道路依旧漫长。

3　结语

1987 年，阿契贝发表了最后一部小说《荒原蚁丘》，他在小说中表达了各阶层人民大团结的良好愿望。"阿玛琪娜"意谓道路永远不会完结，"这个世界属于全世界的人民，而不是属于一个小小的团体"（阿契贝，2009: 273）。

从懵然无知地接受西方教育，到深切体味种族主义的伤害，阿契贝正是在接受殖民教育中吸取了反抗的资源，批判种族主义和殖民主义相互结合的罪恶阴谋。当然，人文主义作为人类共同的道德底线，不应该在殖民主义和种族主义的扩散以及与之抵抗的事业中被抛弃和遗忘。非洲文学作为一种想象性的事业，或许它没有其他民族的风花雪月和浪漫多姿，但对种族良知和公平正义的追求，却是人类的共同选择。正如阿契贝所言："正是故事，而不是任何其他的东西，才能使我们的后代免于像瞎眼的乞丐一样撞进尖尖的仙人掌栅栏。故事是我们的向导；没有故事，我们便成为瞎子"（阿契贝，2019: 148）。书写非洲的故事，正是阿契贝这样一批拥有良知的知识分子的文学政治期待。

参考文献

ACHEBE C, 1990. Home and impediments: selected essays [M]. New York: A Division of Randow House.

ACHEBE C, 1998. The trouble with Nigeria [M]. Engue, Nigeria: Fourth Dimension Publishers.

ACHEBE C, 2009. The education of a British-protected child: essays [M]. New York: Alfred A. Knopf Press.

DEACON R G, 2018. Martin Luther King Jr. saw three evils in the world [EB/OL]. (2018-02-08) [2020-04-22]. https: //www. theatlantic. com/magazine/archive/2018/02/martin-luther-king-hungry-club-forum/552533/.

INNES C L, 1990. Chinua Achebe [M]. Cambridge: Cambridge University Press.

LINDFORS B, 1997. Conversations with Chinua Achebe [M]. Starkville：University Press of Mississippi.

阿明，2003. 非洲沦为第四世界的根源 [J]. 何吉贤，译. 国外理论动态，（2）：26-30.

阿契贝，2019. 荒原蚁丘 [M]. 朱世达，译. 重庆：重庆出版社.

奥尔洛娃，1960. 非洲各族人民—文化、经济和生活概况 [M]. 莹石，译. 北京：世界知识出版社.

奥拉尼央、奎森，2020. 非洲文学批评史稿 [M]. 姚峰，等译. 上海：华东师范大学出版社.

博亨，1991. 非洲通史：殖民统治下的非洲 1880—1935 年（第七卷）[M]. 屠尔康，等译. 北京：中国对外翻译出版公司.

李安山，2004. 非洲民族主义 [M]. 北京：中国国际广播出版社.

萨义德，2003. 文化与帝国主义 [M]. 李琨，译. 北京：生活·读书·新知三联书店.

张宏明，2006. 爱德华·布莱登关于种族的论述 [J]. 西亚非洲，（7）：52-80.

中国社会科学院语言研究所词典编辑室，2019. 现代汉语词典（第 7 版）[M]. 北京：商务印书馆.

（编辑：赵磊）

非洲身份认同的艰难建构

——《马永贝森林》中的"部落主义"[①]

解冬珵

北京师范大学历史学院

摘　要:《马永贝森林》是安哥拉作家佩佩特拉的重要作品之一，主要讲述了安哥拉人民解放运动成员通过游击战抗击葡萄牙殖民者、争取民族独立的故事。在本文中作者着重展现了"部落主义"思想对于安哥拉身份认同建构的负面影响，并提出了相对理想主义的解决方法。本文试图通过文本细读分析的方式，结合对作品历史背景的研究，分析作者对于"部落主义"的认识，探究"部落主义"的含义、原因及影响，并说明在现实中解决"部落主义"的困难性。

关键词: 佩佩特拉;《马永贝森林》; 部落主义; 身份认同

The Difficult Construction of African Identity: "Tribalism" in *Mayombe*

Xie Dongcheng

School of History, Beijing Normal University

Abstract: *Mayombe* is one of the most important works of Angolan writer Pepetela. It mainly tells a story of the members of the Angolan People's Liberation Movement who fought against Portuguese occupation through guerrilla warfare, for the liberation of the nation. In this work, the author shows especially the negative effect of "tribalism" on the construction of Angolan identity and proposes a relatively idealistic solution. This article attempts, by the methods of text analysis and the study of the historical context, to analyse the author's understanding of

---

① 收稿日期：2020-11-20

作者信息：解冬珵，北京师范大学历史学院世界史专业硕士生，研究方向为国际关系史，电子邮箱：xiedongcheng@pku.edu.cn。

"tribalism", to discuss the meanings, reasons and impacts of "tribalism", and to explain the difficulty of its resolution in reality.

Keywords: Pepetela; *Mayombe*; tribalism; identity

1 引言

《马永贝森林》（*Mayombe*）是安哥拉作家佩佩特拉（Pepetela）的代表作之一，讲述了安哥拉解放战争时期，安哥拉人民解放运动（以下简称安人运）的一群游击战士在马永贝森林中对抗葡萄牙殖民军队的故事。故事的内容主要取自作者亲身参与安人运游击战争的经历，因此在很大程度上真实地反映了当时安人运游击队员们的思想与行动。在展现安人运游击队英勇抗击葡萄牙殖民者的同时，《马永贝森林》也着力反映斗争中存在的问题。其中，作者尤其重视游击队员之间影响团结的矛盾与冲突，对其进行了详细的描写和深入的思考。《马永贝森林》中所描绘的游击队员人物形象出身各异，主要有出身于刚果族的游击队指挥官"无畏"、出身于金邦杜族的政委若昂、黑白混血的随军教师"理论"、出生于卡宾达的游击队员卢塔莫斯，以及出身于姆班杜族的游击队员伊奎奎等。虽然游击队员们团结在安人运的马克思主义纲领之下，共同抗击葡萄牙殖民者，但也经常会根据出身结成小团体，维护本族游击队员的利益，打压他族游击队员，甚至出现分裂主义的思想倾向，作者将这种思想称为"部落主义"。事实上，作者对于"部落主义"的思考不仅局限于安人运内部，也扩展到了整个安哥拉社会，并得到了时任安哥拉领导人内图（Neto）的关注。据说，内图总统的遗愿推动了该部小说的出版。在内图看来，本书关于"部落主义"的讨论，对于在去殖民化背景下争取民族独立的非洲国家有着积极的意义（Pepetela, 1983）。

2 后殖民主义语境下的非洲"部落主义"

若要探讨《马永贝森林》中的"部落主义"，首先需要了解"部落主义"一词的含义与起源。目前学界对于"部落主义"一词的使用普遍持批判态度，认为非洲"部落主义"这一概念是欧洲殖民主义的产物。从词源上来看，欧洲语言中的"部落"大多源于拉丁语"tribus"，在古罗马时期用于描述血缘相近的群体所组成的共同体。自欧洲进入近现代以来，这一词汇便成了一个历史概念（Fried, 1975）。但当欧洲殖民者踏上非洲大陆之后，这一词汇便被赋予了新的含义。在欧洲对非洲进行殖民统治的过程中，欧洲的传教士和人类学家往往用欧洲中心主义视角来审视非洲的民族、传统和文化，认为相比于欧洲"先进"的社会形态，非洲的社会形态是"落后"的，因此将"部落"这一描述欧洲早期社会形态的词语套用到非洲社会形态的叙述中。而殖民政府的统治者也乐于运用这样的观点来"塑造"非洲社会，用"部落"来划分非洲的政治单元。例如，英国殖民者要求殖民统治下的非洲人在填写各类申请表时填写自己的"部落"，并采取"分而治之"的策略，强化自身的殖民统治，进而造成了非洲人之间的不平等乃至歧视现象（李安山，2004: 227-228）。更广为人知的是比利时殖民者对于图西族和胡图族的划分，成为日后卢旺达种族灭绝的根本原因。因此，在非洲赢得了对抗欧洲殖民主义的斗争后，不断有非洲学者质疑用"部落"及"部落主义"来描述非洲社会的做法，认为这些词语带有明显的欧洲中心主义和殖民主义偏见。这样的质疑最终得到了学界的广泛认可。在由联合国教科文组织编辑出版的《非洲通史》中，主编布基纳法索史学家约瑟夫·基-泽博（Joseph Ki-Zerbo）写道："如有可能，'部落'这一词，除了北非的某些地区外，在这本书里将不再使用，因为这个词含有诬蔑和许多错误的思想内容"（基-泽博，1984: 16）。肯尼亚作家恩吉吉·瓦提安哥（Ngugi Wa Thiong'o）也在他的文章中批判道：

> 毫无疑问，部落、部落主义和部落战争是殖民主义的发明，这些术语通常用来解释非洲的冲突。大多数非洲语言都没有英语单词"tribe"的等同词，在18世纪和19世纪，由于欧洲人在非洲的探险活动，其贬义的含义在人类学词汇的发展中迅速涌现。这些词与其他殖民地概念相伴，如原始、黑暗大陆、落后种族和武士社会。（Thiong'o, 2009: 20）

尽管"部落主义"这一概念作为欧洲中心主义和殖民主义的产物理应遭到批判，但必须承认的是，这一概念所描述的现象并非不存在。欧洲殖民者在殖民统治中对于"部落主义"思想的实践，对于非洲反殖民斗争后形成的新生国家依然有着深远的影响。自柏林西非会议以来，欧洲殖民者忽视非洲历史实际，通过签订一系列条约对非洲进行瓜分，因此很多本属同一民族的居民被划分到了不同国家的殖民地，而本不属于同一民族的人群又被聚合在同一国家的殖民地，这导致许多争取独立的殖民地实际上并没有统一的民族基础。正如科特迪瓦首任总统乌弗埃-博瓦尼（Houphouet-Boigny）所言，"我们没有继承一个民族，继承的只是一个由于殖民化而人为产生的国家"（李安山，2004: 220）。这在很大程度上加深了非洲各民族之间的矛盾，导致许多非洲国家从殖民统治下解放后，还必须面对民族矛盾所导致的动荡乃至分裂。为了避免这种情况，它们就必须将传统的民族身份认同与基于殖民边界产生的国家所带来的新身份认同区别开来。这其中也不乏欧洲话语体系的影响，因为在欧洲的话语体系中，民族基本上可以与国家画上等号，然而在非洲乃至世界上的大多数国家却并非如此。因此在许多非洲新生国家的政治话语体系中，传统的民族主义被贬斥为"落后"的"部落主义"，以区别于新生国家的民族主义认同（Ekeh, 1990: 688-690）。对此，非洲学者维克托·奥罗伦索拉（Victor Olorunsola）主张用"国家-多种民族主义"来描述新生的非洲国家，而中国非洲研究学者李安山则用"地方民族主义"来形容这种传统的民族主义（李安山，2004: 4）。

综上所述，佩佩特拉在《马永贝森林》中对于"部落主义"一词的使用，既应当认识到其存在的问题，也应当理解其合理性。从佩佩特拉本人的出身来看，他是生于安哥拉的葡萄牙后裔，祖父曾在葡萄牙军队中担任少校。佩佩特拉虽然生活在安哥拉，但实际上是受到了欧洲家庭环境的熏陶。而且，佩佩特拉的中学和大学时光都是在葡萄牙度过的，直到大学期间才接触了安人运，确立了自身的反殖民斗争理想。这样长期生活在欧洲文化之中的经历，使他不可避免地在一定程度上受到了欧洲中心主义思想的影响。这在《马永贝森林》开篇的献词中也有所体现，例如，佩佩特拉将约鲁巴神话中的主神"奥贡"比作"非洲的普罗米修斯"，实际上他还是从欧洲视角出发去审视非洲文化。但从安哥拉的社会现实上看，当时的安哥拉同许多其他刚刚从殖民统治下解放的新生非洲国家一样，在独立后面临着民族矛盾导致分裂的威胁，需要强有力的政治话语去批判分裂主义。在这种情况下，"部落主义"是对欧洲话语的一种"借用"，本质上还是要批判这一词语背后所反映的问题，是出于现实的政治需要，而不是对"部落主义"这一概念本身的认同。因此，《马永贝森林》中所描写的"部落主义"对于研究安哥拉乃至整个非洲身份认同的建构都有重要的参考价值，不能因为词语和概念本身体现了殖民主义和欧洲中心主义思想而对其价值避而不谈。但本文中的"部落主义"均加引号，以示本文并不认同"部落主义"这一概念本身，而仅仅是将其作为研究对象进行研究。

3 《马永贝森林》中的"部落主义"

在《马永贝森林》中，佩佩特拉较为详细地展现了安哥拉各民族间存在的"部落主义"矛盾。这样的矛盾既集中在金邦杜族和刚果族两个民族之间，同时也有二者对姆班杜族和卡宾达人的"部落主义"歧视。从地理分布上来看，金邦杜族分布于安哥拉的中西部偏北，是安哥拉的主体民族之一，而刚果族则分布于安哥拉西北部与刚果共和国的交界处，可以称得上是一个跨界民族。从历史上来看，刚果族是古代刚果王国的后裔。刚果王国曾经统治了刚果河流域的大部分地区，包括金邦杜族在内的许多部落都曾臣服于刚果王国。16世纪初，葡萄牙人在到达西非沿岸时，曾经试图与刚果王国建立友好关系，但随着葡萄牙人不断侵占刚果王国的领土，并将其臣民贩卖为奴隶，刚果王国与葡萄牙的关系逐渐恶化。随着荷兰人的到来，刚果王国与荷兰人联手对抗葡萄牙人，并一度占领了罗安达等重要沿海城市，但最终还是被葡萄牙人驱逐。葡萄牙人对刚果王国展开报复，双方战争不断。17世纪，葡萄牙人彻底击溃了刚果王国，刚果王国爆发了争夺王位的内战，此后王国中各族之间征伐不断，为日后的民族仇恨埋下了种子。

在小说中，故事主要在被马永贝森林覆盖的卡宾达地区展开，因此包括指挥官"无畏"在内的许多游击队员都是刚果人，但安哥拉主体民族之一的金邦杜人同样也有不少。通过作者在作品中的描写，读者能看到这种民族差异对于游击队员的影响。小说还多次提到了另一个活跃于安哥拉北部的反殖民武装组织——安哥拉人民联盟。其前身为安哥拉北方人民联盟，后发展为安哥拉民族解放阵线，创建人为刚果王室的后裔罗贝托

（Roberto）。与以阶级认同团结群众的安人运不同，这一组织是以刚果民族主义认同将群众团结起来的。从安人运的角度来看，安哥拉人民联盟坚持的"部落主义"思想是落后的，因此在作品中，安哥拉人民联盟通常是作为批判对象或反面教材出现的。

《马永贝森林》对于故事情节的叙述主要是第三人称视角的线性叙事，但在一些段落中作者会插入一些人物的内心独白和回忆。这样的叙事方式让读者不仅可以用客观的、全知的视角来审视"部落主义"，而且还可以从个体的视角出发，去体会人物的"部落主义"心理。总体而言，作者的描写主要通过安人运游击队员的视角来展开，试图以"以小见大"的方式来展现"部落主义"的影响，通常带有一定的主观性和理想主义色彩。

"部落主义"在《马永贝森林》线性叙事中的首次登场，是在第一次军事行动后。政委若昂和随军教师"理论"在对被游击队员抓捕的工人做思想工作时，指挥官"无畏"注意到游击队员们很自然地根据自己所属的部落形成了不同的意见。

> "无畏"在一旁听着，但也注意着其他游击队员的评论。他们大致分为两类：金邦杜人为一组，以行动负责人为中心；另外一组则是非金邦杜人，即刚果人、姆班杜人以及"去部落化"的穆阿提安瓦——他生于罗安达，父亲是姆班杜人，母亲是刚果人。另一个来自罗安达的游击队员，代号"新世界"，虽然是金邦杜人，但或许是因为他在非洲留学的经历使他从"部落主义"中解放了出来。他独自一人借着火光擦拭武器。（Pepetela, 1993: 21）

这一段描写展现了游击队内部"部落主义"与"反部落主义"之间的冲突。根据作者的叙述，虽然游击队纲领禁止"部落主义"思想，但对于许多游击队员而言，"部落主义"依然是一种很强的思维定式。甚至在游击队的核心领导层中，指挥官"无畏"、政委若昂与行动负责人三人的立场也并不完全一致。尽管政委与行动负责人同属金邦杜族，指挥官属于刚果族，但在面对"部落主义"的问题上，指挥官与政委是一致反对"部落主义"的，而行动负责人则会或多或少偏袒本族的游击队员。这样的叙述主要聚焦于"部落主义"的外在表现。

通过在线性叙事中插入人物内心独白，作者向读者进一步展示了"部落主义"的深层原因。在不同角色的内心独白中，可以看出不同角色因出身和经历的不同，对于"部落主义"也有着不同的认识。对于黑白混血的随军教师"理论"而言，"部落主义"意味着排斥与痛苦，使他在黑人身份与白人身份之间纠结与迷茫。

> 　　我出生在加贝拉，那里是咖啡之乡。在那里，我从母亲身上继承了咖啡的黑，从我父亲，一位葡萄牙商人身上，继承了枯槁的白。我内心中这两股势不两立的力量是我动力的源泉。在这是非分明、非黑即白的世界中，我代表了"也许"。"也许"，对于想听到"是"的人来说代表了"否"，而对于想听到"否"的人来说代表了"是"。如果人们要求纯粹而拒绝二者的结合，这是我的错吗？我是否应该把自己转变为"是"或"否"呢？还是人们应当接受"也许"？
>
> 　　当我还是个孩子的时候，我想成为白人，这样白人就不会叫我黑人。当我长大成人，我又想成为黑人，这样黑人就不会讨厌我。（Pepetela, 1993: 7）

"理论"的独白体现了"部落主义"身份认同"非友即敌"的二元对立性，即：要么是"黑"，要么是"白"，而不认可"也许"这样一种中间形态。在后殖民主义理论中，这种"也许"成为对抗殖民主义的积极力量。后殖民主义理论家霍米·巴巴（Homi K. Bhabha）将其称为"混杂性"。霍米·巴巴认为，"混杂性"虽然是殖民主义的产物，但是却模糊了殖民者在"自我"与"他者"之间的界限，产生出了新的文化和身份认同，进而形成对于殖民主义的颠覆（Bhabha, 1994: 111-112）。然而，对处于反葡萄牙殖民主义战斗中的安人运而言，为了强化游击队员之间的团结，必须"同仇敌忾"，必须明确斗争的目标，因此"非友即敌"的二元对立具有必要性。在这种语境下，葡萄牙人乃至欧洲白人不可避免地被划定为"他者"，进而导致像"理论"这样的黑白混血处于尴尬的地位。这或许也反映了佩佩特拉本人作为葡萄牙后裔在参与反殖民斗争中所面临的困境。

另一角色"奇迹"的独白则体现了"部落主义"因民族矛盾而不断深化的原因。"奇迹"是一名金邦杜族游击队员的军事代号,他在游击队中负责操控火箭筒。1961年,"奇迹"的父亲遭到了刚果民族的种族仇杀,而带领他加入安人运的叔父,则因为反对刚果人的领导而遭到开除。这在很大程度上导致了"奇迹"对安人运反"部落主义"政策的不满。

> 1961年的时候,我还是个小孩。但我依然记得那些场景:在树下被射杀的孩子,被埋在土里的男人,头露在外面,拖拉机经过,用耕犁把头割下……指挥官并不在意,因为他1961年的时候也许并不在安哥拉,或者,即使他在,也没有遭受任何不幸。他在罗安达,大概是学生,对此一无所知。而政委呢?在这件事上政委感情用事,他想用好话来劝服这些卡宾达人,这些叛徒。只有行动负责人……但他在指挥上排在第三位,没什么权力。（Pepetela, 1993: 19-20）

在"奇迹"的内心独白中,突出了反对"部落主义"的指挥官"无畏"在面对民族仇杀这一场景时的"缺席",从而强调了自己在面对这一创伤时的"在场",而"在场"则意味着真实。正如后现代主义理论所指出的那样,"在场"使得"话语被历史化,与个人和集体的经历重新联系在一起,构成了对于现实的必然表现"（Zapf, 2016: 229）。"奇迹"内心的真实想法也反映了安人运队伍中的普遍现象,即队员们接受反"部落主义"政策并非真心实意地认识到"部落主义"的问题,而是受到权力的压制。这样的压制日积月累,反而会导致"部落主义"情绪的反弹。

"奇迹"本人的"部落主义"情绪终于在一次与一名来自刚果族的军医的争吵中爆发。争吵的缘由是政委对指挥官的一次批评。指挥官因为一名新入队的刚果族队员用亲戚的身份接近自己而大发雷霆,而政委认为领导人不能用那样的态度与队员交流。在政委和指挥官看来,这次争执与"部落主义"并无关联,但由于二人不同的部落身份,被其他的游击队员解读为"部落主义"矛盾。争吵中"奇迹"与军医激烈对峙，争论点从当时的民族矛盾一路上升到历史上刚果王国的统治。虽然这一争论最终被教师"理论"和政委制止，但依然对游击队员之间的关系产生了很大的影响。作者借一位姆班杜族游击队员之口对这种矛盾作出了总结："当产生部落矛盾的时候，没必要去判断错误在谁。今天的新怨，一定是因为昨日的旧仇。鸡和蛋谁先出生？这就是部落主义"（Pepetela, 1993: 67）。这意味着，"部落主义"的矛盾无法追溯最初始的缘由，而仇恨却在报复行为中不断累加。当矛盾再次产生时，这种仇恨就会成为激化矛盾的催化剂，陷入矛盾不断加深的恶性循环。

4 《马永贝森林》中关于"部落主义"的理想与现实

在《马永贝森林》中，佩佩特拉对于应对"部落主义"的思考可以归结为两个方面。一方面是从精神层面，瓦解"部落主义"的话语体系，进而消除游击队员乃至安哥拉人民的"部落主义"思想。另一方面是从物质层面，建设安哥拉的社会主义社会，用经济的发展来推动思想上的进步。同时，佩佩特拉也认识到，这两个方面的应对方法也都存在不足。

在精神层面上，话语即权力，"部落主义"思想与语言的运用有着紧密的联系。这在《马永贝森林》中一个为新入队的刚果族队员选取军事代号的情节中有着很好的体现。一名来自姆班杜族的队员想出了一个姆班杜语代号"蛇"，却即刻遭到了指挥官的反驳，讽刺他为"姆班杜帝国主义"。

> "别用你的姆班杜语。"无畏打断道："要么用他自己的语言为他起名，要么用我们都会说的葡萄牙语。但不能用你的……这要开始搞姆班杜帝国主义了！还有，他没给我留下任何关于蛇的印象。"（Pepetela, 1993: 43）

"命名权"是话语权中相当重要的一环，这体现了"部落主义"思想强调本族话语权的现象。"无畏"所说的"姆班杜帝国主义"可以视为是对列宁"帝国主义论"的一种戏仿，用以批判"部落主义"思想对于话语权的垄断。指挥官的两种建议体现了作者对于解决这一问题的思考即：既尊重各族语言的独特性，但同时又要找到一种通用性的语言，对于安哥拉而言，这个语言就是葡萄牙语。在理想上，作者希望，如同反殖民斗争团结了安哥拉各族人民一样，安哥拉人民也可以用殖民者的语言来实现思想上的团结。但作者同时也意识到，在实际中，团结还需要强调各族语言的独特性。在一段描写中，来自卡宾达游击战士卢塔莫斯，用卡宾达地方语言费奥特语与工人们交流，很快便赢得了工人们的好感，方便了政委对工人展开政治宣传（Pepetela, 1993）。指挥官也因此认为"部落主义"有时对工作有所助力，但此举却招致了行动负责人的不满，认为这是对"部落主义"的庇护。从这一角度来看，"部落主义"作为一种建立在共同语言、文化、血缘等基础上的身份认同，具有强大的力量，难以简单地从思想上消除。

在物质层面上，经济发展固然可以推动思想上的发展，但经济很难无限发展下去。对此，作者借指挥官之口表达了对安人运未来发展的忧虑。在游击队基地中发生"部落主义"的矛盾时，指挥官敏锐地指出，这种矛盾实际上是由于基地缺少给养的现实状况所导致。资源的缺乏导致人们精神紧张，退回到一种所属部族互相抱团取暖的心理状态，去寻求一种情感上的认同，在游击队中便体现为"部落主义"。在给养到达后，这样的矛盾便自然减轻了。指挥官由此联想到反殖民斗争胜利、安哥拉独立后，安人运执掌权力的未来。

> 建设（社会主义）将花费 30 或 50 年。但 5 年后，人民就会开始说：这种社会主义并没有解决这样或那样的问题。这是事实，因为在落后的国家中，有些问题不可能在 5 年内解决。你们将如何应对？人民会被反革命分子煽动！……客观上，有必要提高党内的警惕性，加强纪律，搞肃反。客观上是这样。但是，野心家会利用肃反运动，将反革命分子与批评自己野心和错误的人们混为一谈。所谓必要的警惕性成了独裁的借口，掩盖所有的批评。极权政治加强，民主消失。戏剧性的是你无法避免这种事情的发生。（Pepetela, 1993: 74）

　　诚然，用社会主义思想去改造安哥拉会为社会带来进步，但这不能解决现存的所有问题。在安人运构建的阶级认同中，葡萄牙殖民者作为"他者"，是建构这一认同的重要基石之一。在赢得独立以后，葡萄牙殖民者的"他者"形象被削弱，以反殖民为基础的认同便难以维系。因此在面对新的社会问题时，很难阻止人们回头拥抱"部落主义"。如果通过政治力量去压制人民的意愿，则会导致独裁与暴力，使得民主政治名存实亡。

　　对于这一问题，佩佩特拉在书的结尾给出了一个颇为理想化的解答。在对阵葡萄牙殖民军的最后一场战斗中，卢塔莫斯和指挥官在战斗中为了保护政委而战死，这给其他队员很大的触动。行动负责人在最后表达了自己的感慨："卢塔莫斯，一个卡宾达人，为救一个金邦杜人而死。'无畏'，一个刚果人，为救一个金邦杜人而死。这对我们是很重要的一课，同志们"（Pepetela, 1993: 170）。从这里我们可以看出作者对于解决"部落主义"问题所提出的方法，即通过抗击葡萄牙殖民者的共同战斗和在战斗中游击队员的献身精神，来消除"部落主义"的负面影响。这种方法富有理想主义色彩。

　　然而，这种理想主义色彩，最终会与现实产生冲突。葡萄牙殖民者由于对安哥拉人民的殖民压迫统治，成为安哥拉人身份认同中重要的"他者"形象，但在葡萄牙政府教育政策和同化政策下，这一形象是比较单薄的。殖民者在面对不同民族时采取分化瓦解的政策，基于与不同民族合作程度的不同，压迫程度也有不同，这使得各民族很难建立一种像抵抗侵略者一样"同仇敌忾"的反殖民认同。而这也正是导致安哥拉在独立后立刻陷入内战的原因之一。在安哥拉南部，由萨文比（Savimbi）领导的争取安哥拉彻底独立全国联盟（以下简称安盟）在美国与南非的支持下，与安人运展开了十余年的内战。这其中诚然有国际政治的因素，但安盟的群众基础也不可忽视。安盟以奥文本杜人为主体，还包括乔奎人、隆达人、恩冈格拉人和其他一些安哥拉南部的族群。他们自古以来就对北方的金邦杜人缺乏信任，认为北方的安人运以金邦杜人为主体，可能对自己不利，因此要武装保卫自己的权益（刘海方，2006）。这正是殖民者这一"他者"形象无法解决的问题。

　　卡宾达分裂主义也是《马永贝森林》中未能讨论清楚的问题。在小说中，来自卡宾达的卢塔莫斯用生命的牺牲证明了自己对安人运的忠诚，揭掉了自己"卡宾达叛徒"的标签，然而在现实中，卡宾达飞地解放阵线（以下简称卡解阵）这一反政府武装力量却威胁着安哥拉的统一。在葡萄牙殖民时期，卡宾达原为一个独立的海外省，1956 年被并入葡属西非殖民地，卡解阵就在此时诞生并逐渐发展壮大，甚至在 1967 年成立了流亡政府。但在 1975 年葡萄牙承认安哥拉独立的《阿沃尔协定》中，卡宾达被划为安哥拉的一部分，此后安人运与卡解阵爆发了多次武装冲突，甚至还有安人运的卡宾达士兵叛逃至卡解阵的事件。时至今日，卡解阵依然通过恐怖袭击等方式与安哥拉政府军战斗，例如，在 2010 年非洲杯期间，卡解阵袭击由安哥拉政府军护送的多哥国家队，从而造成了严重的国际影响。而卡解阵要求卡宾达独立的理由，正是刚果族的地方民族主义（邓延庭，2012）。

而用无产阶级的阶级认同取代"部落主义"认同的方法，似乎也难以成功。正如小说中政委和指挥官二人之间存在的理想主义和现实主义的矛盾一样，安人运内部既有马列主义和苏联模式的坚定拥护者，也有提出在经济上向西方靠拢的实用主义者。内图在执政时期，便有意不再强调意识形态的斗争，而仅仅把马列主义视为团结安哥拉的"工具"，例如，安哥拉 1975 年的宪法明白无误地提出"承认、保护和维护私有财产"的原则。内图政府还与美国海湾石油公司合作开发卡宾达地区的石油资源（刘海方，2016: 52-53）。曾经的"他者"，即生产资料的占有者，成了自己的一部分，势必导致重新定义"他者"的形象。但如今，像殖民者那样强力的"他者"已然不存在了，安哥拉人民必须反求诸己，寻找内在的自我认同，即建立以安哥拉国家为核心的国家民族主义认同。无论是单一民族国家还是多民族国家，其民族利益、国家利益既有不一致、矛盾甚至冲突，但它们往往有着共同的、一致的地方。只要民族国家存在，民族国家利益就是客观存在的，并且具有历史的继承性（李兴，1995）。在《马永贝森林》中，这种认同被定格在卢塔莫斯和指挥官"无畏"为保护政委而牺牲的结局中。一个卡宾达人和一个刚果人，为救一个金邦杜人而死，或许这就是书中作者对"如何建立安哥拉国家民族主义认同"这一问题给出的答案。但这种理想主义的想法或许很难接受现实的考验。地方民族之间的相互奉献与牺牲，最终挡不住内战的历史车轮。卡宾达的地方民族主义分裂势力，至今依然困扰着安哥拉。在建立国家认同的问题上，安哥拉乃至许多非洲国家，依然有很长的路要走。

5　结语

作为早期加入安哥拉反殖民独立运动的知识分子之一，佩佩特拉在歌颂游击队员斗争精神的同时，也敏锐地发现了安哥拉社会中存在的种种问题，这是非常难能可贵的。在《马永贝森林》中，他通过角色的对话和内心独白，较为全面地展现了安哥拉"部落主义"问题的历史原因和社会影响，使得这部作品在具有文学研究价值的同时，也具有相当的社会研究价值。从某种程度上来说，安哥拉独立后内战的爆发，印证了佩佩特拉在《马永贝森林》中借游击队员之口表达出的忧虑。因此，对于安哥拉乃至全非洲民族身份认同问题而言，《马永贝森林》都有着非常重要的意义。

当然，不可否认的是，在如何解决"部落主义"这一问题上，佩佩特拉依然存在着一定的理想主义色彩，而安哥拉近三十年断断续续的内战，证明这种理想主义是难以实现的。从世界范围来看，演变为美苏"代理人战争"的安哥拉内战只是 20 世纪"美苏争霸"的冰山一角。在国际大背景下，国内的社会矛盾很难不被国内外的政治势力所利用，从而由社会问题演变为政治问题，进而变得更加难以解决。这在一定程度上反映了非洲在后殖民时代所面临的困境，也是安哥拉在建立民族身份认同过程中不可避免的问题。

参考文献

BHABHA H, 1994. The location of culture [M]. London: Routledge.

EKEH P, 1990. Social anthropology and two contrasting uses of tribalism in Africa [J]. Comparative studies in society and history, 32 (4): 660-700.

FRIED M, 1975. The notion of tribe [M]. Menlo Park: Cummings Publishing Company.

PEPETELA, 1983. Mayombe [M]. Trans, WOLFERS M. London: Heinemann.

PEPETELA, 1993. Mayombe [M]. Lisboa: Publicações Dom Quixote.

THIONG'O N, 2009. The myth of tribe in African politics [J]. Transition, 101: 16-23.

ZAPF H, 2016. Literature as cultural ecology: sustainable texts[M]. London: Bloomsbury Academic.

邓延庭，2012. 卡宾达危机：下一个南苏丹？——浅析安哥拉的卡宾达问题 [J]. 亚非纵横，（3）：22-29.

基-泽博，1984. 非洲通史第一卷：编史方法及非洲史前史 [M]. 北京：中国对外翻译出版公司.

李安山，2004. 非洲民族主义研究 [M]. 北京：中国国际广播出版社.

李兴，1995. 论国家民族主义概念 [J]. 北京大学学报（哲学社会科学版），（4）：74-80.

刘海方，2006. 多元政治传统碰撞 多种政治势力交锋——安哥拉现代政治发展分析 [J]. 北京大学非洲研究丛书第四辑——亚非葡语国家发展研究：37-76.

（编辑：赵磊）

Self-Inscription: Writing and the Debunking of the Myth of Race in Lewis Nkosi's *Mating Birds*①

Phomolo Mosito

Department of Education, Durban University of Technology

Abstract: *Mating Birds* (1986) by Lewis Nkosi deals with many themes that affect the communities and individuals in the text. The thematic concerns such as forced removals, writing (self-inscription), land and ownership, inclusion and exclusion in marked spaces, racial divisions and education seek to foreground Lewis Nkosi's literary shrewdness. However, it is the theme of self-inscription and writing that appropriately shows an attempt by Lewis Nkosi to allow the protagonist, Ndi Sibiya, to tell the story of an individual faced with the vicissitudes of racial divisions in South Africa. In *Mating Birds*, Ndi is given the platform to write while he is waiting to be hanged as he is given a life sentence in jail. In this instance, writing in prison offers him an opportunity to choose the themes of his own narrative while it also imbues him with the responsibility to form and mould characters. To a certain extent, to Ndi and to Nkosi, writing serves multifarious functions; as such, it assists the protagonist to make sense of his situation. Firstly, it calls for self-reflexivity in which Ndi as a writer is able to reflect and gets the events of his own life which lead to his incarceration into perspective. Writing affords Ndi an occasion to make

① **Date of reception:** 2022-01-31

Author: Phomolo Mosito, Lecturer of English Language and Literature with a focus on postcolonial studies at Department of Education, Faculty of Arts and Design of Durban University of Technology; Research fields: postmodernism, schizoanalysis and poststructuralist theory; Email: phomolomosito@gmail.com.

sense of these experiences and orders them into a coherent narrative that has a beginning and an ending. Secondly, writing allows the writer (Ndi) to record his abhorrence and derision of the injustices of racial division. On the same breath, he is able to debunk the specific myths levelled against his own people especially about writing. This myth perpetuates the stereotype on writing and orality. As a bird of gallows that is sentenced to be hanged in prison, Ndi uses writing to liberate and transcend the racial boundaries set by the apartheid regime and retrieve the narrative of his people that is marginalised in the colonial historiography.

Keywords: self-inscription; writing; self-reflexivity; narrative; colonial historiography

自题：刘易斯·恩科西《交配的鸟》中种族故事的写作与其真相的揭露

波莫洛·莫斯多

德班理工大学教育学院

摘　要： 刘易斯·恩科西的《交配的鸟》（1986 年）涉及许多影响当时社会和个人的主题，如强制迁移、写作（自题）、土地和所有权、在特定区域的纳入与排斥，以及种族隔离和教育等主题，凸显了刘易斯·恩科西文学作品的厚重性。其中，自题和写作的主题恰如其分地展现了刘易斯·恩科西试图通过小说中的主人公恩迪·斯比亚来讲述个人所面临的南非种族隔离制度的兴衰变迁。在《交配的鸟》中，恩迪被判终身监禁。在等待执行绞刑期间，他获得了写作这样一种方式。狱中写作给恩迪提供了一个可以自主选择写作主题的机会，也赋予他塑造人物的责任。在某种程度上，对于恩迪和恩科西来说，写作具有多重功能，有助于主人公理解他的处境。首先，写作使恩迪以作家的身份，对他生活中发生的一系列事件进行自我反省，从而得以清楚地认识他入狱获刑这一事件。写作为恩迪提供了认识他过去经历的机会，并使这些经历成为一个有始有终的故事。其次，写作使恩迪记录下了他对种族隔离不公平性的憎恶与嘲讽。同时，他能够揭穿那些针对他的族人而编造的谎言，尤其是在写作方面。这种谎言使书面和口头上的刻板印象永久化。作为绞刑架上被判绞刑的鸟，恩迪通过写作脱离并超越了种族隔离制度设定的种族界限，重新找回了原本属于他的族人而在殖民史学被边缘化的叙事方式和故事。

关键词： 自题；写作；自我反思；叙事；殖民史学

1   Introduction

Mating Birds (1986) by Lewis Nkosi, is a novel set in the temporal space
defined by apartheid, and its narrative threads depict Nkosi's endeavor to move
beyond the fixed and easy associations of race, land and identity by showing how
diverse races relate to each other. While empowering his protagonist, Ndi Sibiya,
with the urgency to challenge the apartheid system, Nkosi significantly uses
the theme of writing to debunk the myth of race that projects the black race
as incapable of self-inscription. Spatially, the novel is set in different fictional
places in KwaZulu-Natal. The depiction of places such as Mzimba (fictional
rural place occupied by black Africans in Natal), the prison (a place where the
narrator and protagonist, Ndi is awaiting death by hanging), Durban beach (a
place that embraces barriers that separate blacks and whites, as there is a whites-
only side preserved for whites), the university (a place of higher learning where
dominance is sought and gained through mastery of the Afrikaans language to
the exclusion of those who do not speak it), highlights the racial divisions in the
country. This paper aims to examine how Lewis Nkosi uses writing and self-
inscription by the protagonist in the text to salvage the story of an individual
immersed in the vicissitudes of a system which seeks to efface the unique history
of his people, and submerge it in the apartheid discourse. Thus, Nkosi strives
to debunk the racial myths about blacks in the colonial historiography. The text
further illustrates that the methods of access to landscape and movement onto it
are determined by race, highlighting that race is a significant organizing trope
that animates the narrative. The black people in the text are marked by constant
movement and/or migration from one rural place to the next and are denied
access to the resources because of this mobility; therefore, they do not have a
permanent place of abode. This condition perpetuates the idea of homelessness;
it also interrogates the ludicrous nature of apartheid. Nkosi himself is also a
victim of homelessness and mobility without permanence, as Emily Gall argues,
"Nkosi had no true physical spaces of home, and his literary exploration also

failed to provide a home for him" (Gall, 2014: 4).[①]

2 The absurdity of race and characterisation

The characterisation of Ndi, the protagonist in *Mating Birds*, underscores the effects of race and modernity on the individual. Ndi as an educated African figure finds himself holding a position located in the rim or border of two opposing cultures. He is in a situation of one who is shunned by his community because he has inherited the ways of the white man (through education and socialisation) and is excluded from the white world because of his race, as a black educated native. Ndi's position and segregation calls to attention what Homi Bhabha calls the "exclusionary imperialist ideologies of self and other" (Bhabha, 2005: 29) where the white imperialist is considered superior and pure, much to the marginalisation and segregation of the black race. Ndi is an intellectual trapped by the rigors of education and the alienating effects of education force him to roam the city of Durban without any purpose. Ndi, a prisoner awaiting death by hanging, finds himself at the "rim of an in-between reality"[②] (Bhabha, 2005: 19). He is distinctively empowered to be able to inscribe himself through writing and this process helps him confront issues of racial stereotypes that depict black people as victims of racial oppression, and as people with no history. Nkosi may be arguing that there is not only one version of apartheid history especially about black people but that there are other contending histories that stemmed out of this painful past that may have been ignored, marginalised or erased in the apartheid discourse. This line of argument recalls a beautifully argued essay by Iain Chambers and Lidia Curti (2008), titled

---

① Gall (2014) shows the way that the space and mobility are contested in the text as mirrored in Nkosi's own life. Perhaps lacking a permanent place of abode is symptomatic of the forced removals experienced by the black majority.

② Bhabha (2005) argues for the precarious position that individuals who were forced to leave their countries (through slavery as well) of origin and those who took voluntary exile find themselves in; as they neither belong to any of the countries they traverse hence they experience inclusion and exclusion from them.

"Migrating Modernities in the Mediterranean" in which they contest:

> Putting slavery back in the picture, taking those abandoned
> black bodies and reinserting them back into history, implies not only
> confronting the limits of a reason, and an aesthetics to consider the
> other side of history (the negated Black Atlantic), it also means to
> register the limits of such reasoning, and its political and cultural
> manner of narrating the world, in order to suggest that there are other
> histories, other modernities, to narrate. (Chambers & Curti, 2008: 388)[1]

Not only is it significant to salvage or "consider the other side of history"
but also it is absolutely necessary to confront and refute the myth of race in the
Mating Birds. Self-inscription through writing becomes an act and a tenuous
process which require profound focus. Ndi observes "a great discipline, writing."
He continues to assert that it "furnishes him with the occasion to form characters
while refining his own, and [o]ne might even say it is character-forming" (Nkosi,
1986: 23). However tenuous a process writing proves to be, it is essential in
the text because it becomes a vehiculated practice that allows him as an author,
a narrator to choose his themes or perhaps these themes choose him given his
position. This exercise further bequeaths him to negotiate the terms and manner
he tells in his own story. Thus, it reminds the reader that it is not only about the
temporal and spatial settings of his story, but also it is imperative to acknowledge
that there are other alternative histories, other modernities to narrate when one
is narrating the self (Chambers & Curti, 2008). Writing becomes the tool of
reflection on his life. Through writing Ndi is able to reimagine the absurdity
of apartheid in policing and controlling where people like Ndi and Nkosi live,
where they go to school, who they should fall in love with and many other
aspects of control.

---

[1] Chambers & Curti (2010) contend for the reinsertion of the black bodies into history and
ensuring that existing history is confronted by the presence of the Black Atlantic.

There is no denying the distinction of *Mating Birds* as a literary work of art that represents the story of an individual confined by the apartheid regime, and also one in which a nation is saturated in the absurdity of specific laws and events under the apartheid in South Africa—laws such as the immorality act, race relations or separate development laws and how these affected both the black and white races in different ways. In *Mating Birds,* the search and fight for land is overshadowed by the individual search for meaning because Ndi Sibiya seeks to be recognised as a human being in a country divided and defined by race. It may also be argued that Ndi further uses writing to project a being that is not stereotyped by the prescriptions and proscriptions of modern psychiatry and skin colour (race). This point is gleaned from the verbal exchange between Ndi (patient) and Emile Dufré (doctor), where the former uses the power of speech to prove that the latter is guilty of the crimes of which he is accused. By employing various stylistic-narrative techniques, such as psychiatry, writing and storytelling and others, *Mating Birds* seeks to move beyond the fixed and easy associations of land and identity illustrating that the modes of access to landscape and movement onto it are determined by the binaries of race and gender. Low & Lawrence-Zúñiga (2003) remind us of the symbolic connotation of place and landscape, highlighting the importance of people's attachment to their environment. They argue that landscape as a concept is often utilised to imbue meaning on the physical place and turns it into a meaningful social environment.[1][2] It follows that individuals input diverse meanings to different places and sites. For instance, the beach in the text is a place divided according to race where there is black side of the beach, and Ndi observes that he should have stayed within the bounds of his side of the beach instead of being too close to what is known as the "whites-only" bathing area (Nkosi, 1986: 04) because that is what makes him get into trouble in the first place.

---

[1] This recalls the laws in the painful past of South Africans, the excluded others, such as blacks who do not enjoy the same opportunities as whites.

[2] Low & Lawrence-Zúñiga (2003) highlight the importance of place and the meaning that the individuals input on it.

To Ndi as to other black people, the "whites-only" side of the beach is a marked and policed area in which they are denied for entry. Therefore, access to this side of the beach is granted based on one's racial orientation. This phrase "whites-only" which is often displayed on notice boards and in other public spaces is also iconic of what Phomolo Mosito calls the "general callous response to the black body" (Mosito, 2011: 157)[1]. This further signals that the apartheid ideology designed to control, police and monitor people's movements in the public spaces incriminates those who transgress the boundaries and makes it difficult for blacks to be near whites because of the law of Separate Development Act. Nkosi as an exile, may be using space and place to argue that they are not important tropes of one's identity. Nkosi's novels are all set generally in South Africa, showing the impression his country's landscape left in his becoming. His characters are familiar to South Africans but share various aspects of rootlessness and homelessness with him. Nkosi was born and raised in Natal, the landscape of his narrative in *Mating Birds*, and worked in Johannesburg for *Drum* magazine before he accepted a one-way exit scholarship to study at Harvard University under Nieman Fellowship. This one-way exit scholarship meant that he could not return to the country of his birth. Nkosi's life was marred by mobility, as he moved from one country to another, holding various teaching positions.

3   Writing and the challenging of racial stereotypes

As a writer of fiction and literary critic, Nkosi privileges writing over speech in *Mating Birds*. In the text, Ndi as an university educated writer has been empowered to choose his own path and whom he wants to love. Thus, Ndi is breaking the ridiculous and false barriers erected by the apartheid regime where black people are prohibited to have relationships with whites, and vice versa. In the court of law and generally in the way Ndi's case is handled, it is

---

[1] Mosito (2011) comments on the othering of the black body.

demonstrated that law favours colour (race) despite the efforts of Ndi's lawyer to present the facts of the case to which the prosecutor, Kaakmekaar, remains immune. What Kaakmekaar supposes as crime is allegedly committed by a native with a "smattering of education" (Nkosi, 1986: 12) that actually allowed him to have a glimpse into white paradise from which the majority are forbidden for entry and are excluded. *Mating Birds*, is not a narrative about a nation (country) defined by segregation, but it is a narrative about one individual's experience in a country defined by race under the harsh laws of the apartheid regime. Furthermore, it captures a concerted effort by this individual to oppose the social engineering of apartheid. It is may also be read as Lewis Nkosi's attempt to highlight the significant fact that the apartheid did not affect all black people in the same way given his harsh experience and reality of departure (exile) without the promise of return. The consequence of this is dislocation and displacement. Ndi is in prison facing life sentence and Nkosi is in exile with no opportunity for return. To this end, Fetson Kalua argues, "colonial dislocation has left people like him racked with anxieties, either with complete loss or of being completely lost in the space of the other" (Kalua, 2015: 04).[①]

In the text, Ndi dreams of becoming a truly great African writer and he is encouraged by Emile Dufré and prison officials to write the story of his life. Dufré, a great German-Swiss criminal psychologist, is dispatched to enquire, to prod and to probe Ndi's behaviour as rape accused prisoner. He is eager to trace the origins of the obsession of "a native who in order to gain a glimpse of a white paradise, of that heaven from which many blacks are excluded, tore up barriers, trampled down fences, ignored the race laws and defied custom and convention to sleep with a lily-white 'virgin' woman" (Nkosi, 1986: 12). This is important for Ndi because it is where he attempts to inscribe himself as someone who defied custom and convention in need of acceptance, and as a person defined not by his race, class, or to a certain extent, his gender. He

---

① Kalua (2015) highlights the significance of exile perpetuated by colonialism and to some extent apartheid.

ignored and disregarded the false barriers and fences erected by apartheid to assert his individuality and chart the history of his people that would otherwise remain untold and peripheral. Ndi understands this very well, as he hazards, "I try to describe to him [Dufré] the impulse that drew me to the English girl in a country where even to look at a white woman is to court daylight beatings and worse" (Nkosi, 1986: 25). This may also be interpreted as Lewis Nkosi's attempt to assert that sexual crimes involving blacks and whites attracted more attention than if it was a black on black or white on white crime. Therefore, sexual tendencies of blacks merited scrutiny and investigation, as the "other".

Nkosi employs the first-person narrative technique to explore the role of writing in the life of an individual prisoner who is facing death by hanging, for a supposed crime of violating a white woman. As Ndi, the protagonist suggests, "I hope to preserve these fruits of self-scrutiny for posterity on cheap, unimpressive notepaper with which I have been provided by the authorities in order, as many have urged me, to write the story of my life" (Nkosi, 1986: 16). Ndi, as the narrator of his own story, uses the act of writing to relieve and relive the disdainful experiential and existential burden and confines of prison to inscribe himself in an endeavor to share his individual experiences. In the same breath, the questions that Dr Dufré, Ndi's constant visitor, interrogator and confessor, asks him (Ndi) to recall and reflect on some of his experiences of youth, school and education, family life, meeting whites for the first time, eventually led to his incarceration. Although Dr Dufré has already made up his mind about Ndi's obsession with Veronica Slater (a white woman he has allegedly violated), Ndi on the contrary is eager to prove to him that there is something deeply human that drew them together. Nkosi in equipping Ndi with the necessary skills to be a writer also makes a strong point about the absurdity of racial segregation. Writing and language in the text play an important role as they are used to depict speech types (deduced from the conversations between Ndi and Dr Dufré) meant to show racial divide, different worldviews and to reconcile the ever-widening gap separating the present and past. The narrator observes that he engages in writing when he is not talking to Dr Dufré.

> I am engaged in writing my life story. It helps to pass the time. A great discipline, writing. One might even say it is character-forming were the observation not likely to sound a trifle odd in the mouth of one already condemned to die for the crime of raping a white woman. All the same I derive great satisfaction from writing. I write all the time. The thought of death, the horror of departing from this world before my time is served, so to speak, puts a new zeal into my pen. (Nkosi, 1986: 23-24)

Writing offers him an opportunity for reflection, and he further attempts to re-enacts the fragments of the events that led to his incarceration and takes the reader including his interlocutor (Dr Dufré) back in time to the specific moments of his past. In this context while narrating and writing about his past, Ndi has an opportunity to come to terms with his present situation while also confronting the past and putting the puzzles of his life together; however they may be fictitious. More importantly, the narrator is aware of the significance attached to the process of writing. He suggests that writing is a process that requires great discipline from the writer, and he further perceives it as character-forming. One also identifies the flaw of the first-person narration technique in which the action of the story is subjected to the view of the narrator. The other blank is that other characters are mocked because the reader is unable to hear their side of the story. This may also be Nkosi's argument against writing in which readers must be given the balanced view of events without playing into the apartheid and psychiatry script in which linear story telling approach is preferred.

To Ndi and to some extend Nkosi, writing becomes an act of creation and a tool that is used to interrogate the fixed assertions and understanding of race. Mieke Bal makes a useful point as he maintains, "the moment of writing down one's adventures is never the moment of experiencing them" (Bal, 2006: 5)[1]. Bal's argument further highlights the temporal and spatial distance that exists between an experience as it took place in the past and when it is recalled in the present. And therefore, such an experience undergoes changes and modifications as a consequence of time and other experiences. The point that Ndi's interlocutor, Dr Dufré, misses is that the linear mode of narration that clearly marks the beginning and end of an event is not possible as far as memory and experience are concerned. Dufré quips, "Shall we start at the beginning, Mr Sibiya?" (Nkosi, 1986: 290) Dufré facilitates this process of reflection by asking him questions about his life — his youth, his parents and family, his community and his education. Dufré centres his interrogation on his profession and psychiatry as he seeks confession from Ndi. This is emphasised by his strong belief in "talking cure". The aspect of "talking cure" is contrasted with Ndi's preference of writing in which he can revisit and alter the portrayal of characters and events as opposed to speech where one does not have such luxury. Nkosi through Dufré's assertions reminds the reader that a human life or experience is constantly open for interpretation, as Widdershoven (1993: 2)[2] further notes, "Human life is a process of narrative interpretation", and it is so autonomous and precedes any narrative examination. This assertion resonates with what Bhabha argues on the profound examination of the third space, as he suggests:

> It is that Third Space, though unrepresentable in itself, which
> constitutes the discursive conditions of enunciation that ensure that
> the meaning and symbols of culture have no primordial unity or fixity;
> that even the same signs can be appropriated, translated, rehistoricized

---

[1] Bal (2006) emphasizes that the moment of recall is different from the moment when the experience happens.

[2] Following the interpretation by Mosito (2011) on the callous treatment of the black body as a text, Widdershoven (1993) contests that it is imperative to note that any life of a human being calls for interpretation.

and read anew. (Bhabha, 2005: 55) [①]

Bhabha argues for the possibility that certain things, situations, behaviour and/or cultural artefacts may have different connotations to different people depending on who is interpreting and why. This means things/signs lose their original "unity or fixity" when they are scrutinised closely through the act of interpretation, and the same may be argued of a person's experiences as they may be adopted, interpreted, rehistoricised and read differently when recalled. The question the reader grapples with is: How much of what Ndi is forced to remember actually happened?

Moreover, when Ndi tells the story of his life, he also narrates his other selves and experiences, and fashions himself in language. Not only does he use language to narrate and fashion himself but he also uses it to debunk the myth of race through the mastery of this language. Ndi's mastery of the colonial language leads to the destabilization and undermining of the colonial power, as Dehdari, Darabi and Sepehrmanesh (2013: 2) [②] argue, "Language is among the powerful means through which the colonizer applies his authority". Ndi is acutely aware that writing offers him the chance to reflect on his other roles and positions, for instance, as a student, a son to his parents and as a black person in South Africa. All these aspects of the self and experience are organised in language, which is problematic. In explaining Homi Bhabha's concept of "liminality", Fetson Kalua (2009: 24) [③] contends that the life of an individual is defined by "liminality" which constantly questions the assumed and settled assumption about identity because there are fissures in the moment of telling and the actual time the event took place, and this is also exacerbated by the "inherent contradictions

---

① Bhabha (2005) argues that the experiences or cultural signs can be reinterpreted differently from their moment or place of origin. Therefore, meaning is never fixed.

② Dehdari, Darabi and Sepehrmanesh (2013) argue that language is often used by the colonizer to assert his authority. The same tool that the Swiss doctor applies in the text, *Mating Birds*.

③ Kalua (2009) observes the important fact about identity as it is marred by internal contradictions in which one cannot speak of identity without questioning these instabilities.

and instabilities that often come to haunt the subject". Therefore, Ndi finds it convenient to represent himself in writing as opposed to answering Dufré's questions. Dufré wants to trace the root of his (Ndi's) obsession, which may stereotype him and his race. Consequently, Ndi questions Dufré's understanding of African identity because there are always "inherent contradictions and instabilities" (Kalua, 2009: 24), which Psychiatry does not accommodate. Ndi also comes to understand this fact as he hints at the difficult position occupied by blacks who will never be part of any landscape in their own country, except as servants and/or slaves.

Dr Dufré is interested in Ndi's childhood and the relationship of his parents because he is looking for a flaw that can confirm his theory that Ndi did not have a good childhood and that he lusted after every white woman, hence he is guilty of the crime for which he is accused. If he is to relate his childhood, Ndi is aware that he is to coax his memory as he contends, "When Dufré is gone, I write down what I have been relating to him while it is still fresh in my mind. I write it down rapidly in longhand, with a steady and sober accumulation of details, coaxing the memory, which at best is unreliable, or at the very worst treacherous" (Nkosi, 1986: 26). As Stack-Adler contests, "The tales of childhood, however, can only be processed through an emotional, subjective memory" (Stark-Adler, 2006: 95)[1]. Ndi relies on his memory as a tool to recall and recount the fragments. And this reliance on memory also helps him with the process of self-inscription and writing.

4 Self-inscription

Ndi's reflection, and to a certain extent his self-inscription, as the narrator shows the eagerness to engage intellectually with his own social and political environment and situation or space, and to asset his identity as a black inmate and writer. Therefore, the place or space he is in at the time of writing — in

---

[1] Stack-Adler (2006) acknowledges the role of memory in telling one's childhood story and that this narrative may be coloured by emotions and other experiences.

the notional "present" — determines the way he looks back at the past and narrativises it. Ndi draws a picture of himself as a lone figure in the world or environment in which, as a person, he is judged by his race. "What beefy, red-faced Afrikaner farmers from the platteland come down to the coast to see a 'Kaffir Boy' who had the temerity, the audacity to seize a 'respectable' white woman in her bungalow and insert his horrible, oversized 'black thing' into her *Here my nadir*" (Nkosi, 1986: 12). The above quotation shows the exaggerated features that these "beefy, red-faced Afrikaner farmers ..." give to the "Kaffir Boy" or the "other". Ndi's biological features are anatomised, racialised and exaggerated as animalistic and atavistic ... insert his horrible, oversized "black thing". This further asserts that apartheid was not only a political ideology that caused and enforced divisions among blacks and whites in the country but it also sought to infiltrate the social and the biological aspects of their human existence. With the portrayal of Ndi's "horrible, oversized black thing", Nkosi posits a stereotype that assumes that all the biological attributes of black people are the same and equal in size and that these attributes are abnormal. Ndi is not naked for everyone to analyse his private parts, and as such he is harshly judged by his race and gender. As Bhabha (2005) maintains that it is important to move away from the concepts of "class" or "gender" as primary conceptual and organisational categories that inform how people view themselves and are viewed by others. Moreover, he acknowledges that it is significant to recognise that one's claim to identity is informed by the "subject positions informed by race, gender, generation, institutional location, geopolitical locale, sexual orientation — that inhabit any claim to identity in the modern world" (Bhabha, 2005: 2)[1].

Ndi's situation has attracted the attention of important and influential personalities from within the country and the world in general. He observes, "After all, it is my crime, as well as my presence in this nondescript jail, that has drawn attention to the governor and his staff and has brought observers

---

[1] Bhabha (2005) outlines the elements that most inform the subject positions of identity.

from international organisations and news correspondents from some of the best papers in the world" (Nkosi, 1986: 13-14). The attention that he attracts also shows the seriousness of his supposed crime, and a number of inferences may be drawn from it. First, it is inconceivable for two people of different colours to be consummately involved in sexual activities with each other even when it is consensual; and second, the supposed crime is misrepresented by the media, controlled by the white minority and misconstrued by the audience who flock in their numbers to witness the phenomenon in which a black man has crossed the man-made and illusory apartheid boundaries to sleep with a "lily white" woman. According to Mosito, this public consumption of the image of the black prisoner "perpetuates the objectification of the black body and the aestheticisation of violence against it because it transfigures the real to the imagined" (Mosito, 2011: 157). As Ndi observes, "They come and peer through the grill as I take my turn at physical exercises, and at their first glimpse of the ravisher I can see first surprise, then doubt, and finally disappointment on their faces" (Nkosi, 1986: 12). Following this argument Nkosi empowers his protagonist, Ndi at so many levels but to state the obvious; he elevates him above his peers in both black and white communities by being given the urgency to write which is itself an instance of subversion of the racial myths about blacks given how "the ritualised psychological and physical torture of the black body castrates, dehumanises and silences it" (Mosito, 2011: 157)[1].

Ndi is a writer and therefore endowed to record his thoughts, feelings, experiences and those of others around him. He is at the vintage point where he is able to provide social commentary on his situation and in the same breath, is able to twist and manipulate others' views. As Bhabha argues, Ndi's narrative is likened to "a mode of contradictory utterance that ambivalently reinscribes" (Bhabha, 2005: 96) relations of power between the colonizer and colonized. Furthermore, it may be argued that the essence of a person is not captured by where he or she comes from (origins or "initial subjectivities") but it is more

---

[1] Mosito (2011) contends that the violence visited on the black body deforms and dehumanizes it.

complicated than we are wont to admit, as it may include those traits that are one's own and those inherited in the process of interaction with people from other cultures.

For Homi Bhabha, the moment one leaves one's space and occupies another, more different world, then the terms from which identity is asserted become complicated. These terms include the negotiation of the "present and past, outside and inside, and exclusion and inclusion" (Bhabha, 2005: 2) [1]. For Bhabha there is a point in the telling in which the direction of the narrative is disrupted and disturbed and the thoughts of the teller are disoriented, particularly in claims to the originary cultural orientation. Bhabha acknowledges that one may be part and be excluded in the assertion of cultural belonging. For instance, in the novel, having consumed the cultural artefacts of the white world through education and interaction, Ndi notices that his white visitors insult and judge him openly while his African visitors just come and "sit in the visitors" room talking of matters far removed from sexual crimes for which, he is accused and imprisoned. "They talk of the weather, of the drought, and of the ruined countryside after last year's spring rains have carried the soil off into the ocean. After that they stop and let me talk while they listen" (Nkosi, 1986: 19). The black Africans unlike their white counterparts prefer to read the truth from what is not expressed verbally, and interactively let Ndi "talk while they listen" before they make up their minds about the verity of his facts. Writing in this instance depicts the different worldviews represented by both black and white visitors.

Bhabha maintains that identity is not a coherent and accomplished entity of a person or a group but that it is always in process, and this point he makes succinctly as he argues that identity is never an a priori, nor a finished product instead it is "always spatially split — it makes present something that is absent —

---

[1] Bhabha (2005), argues for the complicated nature of modern identities as it is difficult for people to remain in one place for a long time so that traversing different geographical spaces highlights how people gain "other" experiences.

and temporally deferred: it is the representation of a time that is elsewhere, a
repetition"[1] (Bhabha, 2005: 72). Significantly, in remembering and recalling
all the characteristics of the self, the subject always thinks in terms of origins
or past and somehow incorporates these into the present hence he recalls those
experiences that are "spatially split" and therefore eradicating the present at
the moment these experiences are recalled. Ndi says that as children, they
were protected from knowing the greater cruelties that black people generally
experienced in the rest of the country (Nkosi, 1986: 43). He remembers a time
that is "absent and temporally deferred" thereby merging the past with the
present experiences and recalling the past in the present; what may be called the
presence of the absent of the event or experience.

It is therefore the emblem of the apartheid regime to exaggerate and reify
the myth of the features of Africans as barbaric and ravenous, always ready to
attack and violate. Africans are portrayed as second-hand citizens whose features
are marked as animalistic, as Ndi observes, "[M]y white scrutinizers seem to
suspect that a subtle joke is being played on them. My size is too small and
unimpressive, my member is not hard and permanently erect for everyone to
see" (Nkosi, 1986: 13). The above point recalls the argument that Frantz Fanon
makes about negroes in Paris as he argues, "He is forced to inhabit an alienating
and fragmented reality as soon as the white man calls this 'other' being who
is 'battered down by tom-toms, cannibalism, intellectual deficiency, fetishism,
racial defects'" (Fanon, 1967: 166)[2].

5 Issues of identity and the juxtaposition with freedom

Ndi's story of how he came to face the charges that brought him to prison

---

[1] Bhabha (2005) makes an important point that telling a story of an event is different according
to the time this event takes place, and such telling is disrupted by other competing discourses and
viewpoints.

[2] Fanon (1967) argues racial disparities are always clear when a white man meets a black person.

is juxtaposed with the larger plight of Black Africans under the harsh laws of apartheid, and further expresses how the majority tried to oppose it. The freedom songs that other prisoners sing and chant epitomise the greater problem — *pars pro toto* — of marginalisation faced by black people outside prison, as Ndi observes, "Outside my prison cell door I can hear African prisoners singing freedom songs in loud defiant voices: 'Indod,' 'emnyama,' 'u-Voster!' 'Thina Sizwe'" (Nkosi, 1986: 75)[1]. Moreover, the difference between Ndi and other prisoners is that he is given urgency by the officials to assert his subjectivity while others are brutally beaten up for voicing their defiance and asserting their need for freedom, as he further maintains, "We can hear the hard thump of fists against a defenceless body, the dismal sound of bones crushing against a concrete wall. These beatings go on and on, every day, every week" (Nkosi, 1986: 75). According to Mosito, racial violence against black people is not a new phenomenon, as he argues, "[M]any writers have also written about this violence, some of whom sought to recuperate the black body from the claws of white racist violence and by attempting to do so, indexing the incomprehensible violation of the black body" (Mosito, 2011: 157)[2]. Given this point, Ndi's crime appears to be the fact of him being black and African because the law in his country (proverbial South Africa) does not protect people of his race, or rather, it seeks to protect and defend the rights of the white minorities. The point highlights the racial division in the country. Hence, the blacks deem it fit to protest by singing freedom or struggle songs — even in prison. These freedom songs are sung with emotion and the message reverberates beyond the prison walls, as Ndi maintains, "While these freedom songs are being sung, no one moves, no one talks, even the wind seems completely still as though the world were listening

---

① Although Ndi is telling his story from prison, his narrative is given legitimacy by the struggle songs sung in prison, and intimating that people may be imprisoned as a result of their skin colour. The song is roughly translated: Black man (Indod, emnyama). John Voster(u-Voster!)! We the nation (Thina Sizwe). It shows that what was happening in the country impacted the treatment of prisoners in jail.

② Mosito (2011) points out that the violence perpetrated on the black body is unimaginably deep and irreversible.

breathlessly to some universal chant of freedom" (Nkosi, 1986: 76).

The freedom songs are sung with emotions, and wherever they are sung people show solemn focus that one observes when Christians sing their religious hymns. The narrator also notes that even the natural aspects such as the wind seem to listen because these songs are sung with such respect, "no one moves, no one talks, even the wind seems completely still as though the world were listening breathlessly to some universal chant of freedom" (Nkosi, 1986: 76). It is also imperative to note that regardless of being jailed and persecuted, people still stood firm in their demand for freedom and relentlessly opposed the apartheid regime: "Only those who understand the words are moved to join in until the very prison walls seem to shake and vibrate with the volume of voices united in the sentiment of unspoken demand for liberty" (Nkosi, 1986: 76). It is important to note that it is not all prisoners who sing freedom songs are political prisoners, however, most are affected directly by derisive permutations of the apartheid legacy. For instance, Ndi and others whose crime is to pursue the passions of white women, which is an act prohibited by law. This further complicates the concept of racial divisions and conflicts, which on their own are based on unstable footings. As Paul Gilroy cogently argues that most conflicts that are racial in nature may spring from irreconcilable differences between cultures and contradictory identities (Gilroy, 2000)[1]. It is deduced from Gilroy's argument that terms of identity are used to arrive at selfish and indicting conclusions. However, Gilroy further posits that the term identity is normally used when races collude and two cultures come together, as he argues, "This diagnosis sets up or perhaps confirms the even more widespread belief that the forms of political conflict with which the racial division has been associated are somehow unreal or insubstantial, secondary or peripheral" (Gilroy, 2000: 5).

Ndi and Dufré are at the centre of two opposing sites. On one hand, Ndi is a writer who is aware of the merits of writing while on the other hand, Dufré prefers a talking cure, which is at the heart of modern psychoanalysis and

---

[1] Gilroy (2000) argues that cultures are responsible for the differences in identities.

psychiatry. Ndi is mindful of this complexity between psychiatry and writing. Hence, he prefers to write as opposed to talking, thus questioning the merits of the practice of psychoanalysis because it fundamentally requires an individual to speak and does not encourage writing. Trying to raise awareness of this fact of the selfish nature of psychiatry, Ndi observes, "[N]othing is more offensive to me than the distant objectivity in a social scientist who is more concerned with proving hypotheses than with discovering the true character of one man's passion for another human being" (Nkosi, 1986: 75). Nkosi through the character of Ndi, interrogates the applicability of the ready-made Western psychoanalytic theoretical hypotheses that are universally used without taking into account the contexts and nature of people who are deemed to require them. As Bhabha (2005) contests that we find ourselves in the moment of transit where space and time cross to produce complex figures of difference and identity, past, present, inside and outside, inclusion and exclusion. The difference is problematically and inherently induced by mobility, location, race, gender and other issues such as organising categories that most influence the definition of a modern man and woman in their understanding of issues such as cultural difference and national affiliation.

Bhabha understands identity as a problematic feature of the postcolonial being in this extract worth quoting at length.

The move away from the singularities of "class" or "gender" as primary conceptual and organizational categories, has resulted in an awareness of the subject positions — race, gender, generation, institutional location, geopolitical locale, sexual orientation — that inhabit any claim to identity in the modern world. What is theoretically innovative, and politically crucial, is the need to think beyond narratives of originary and initial subjectivities and to focus on those moments or processes that are produced in the articulation of cultural differences. These in-between, spaces provide the terrain for elaborating strategies of

identity, and innovative sites of collaboration, and contestation, in the
act of defining the idea of society itself. (Bhabha 2005: 2)[1]

Bhabha (2005: 72) maintains that identity and self-inscription are not
the accomplished and readily-available entities of a person or a group but that
they are always in process, and this point he makes succinctly as he argues that
identity is never an a priori, nor a finished product ... and its representation is
always spatially split — it makes present something that is absent and temporally
deferred. It is the representation of a time that is elsewhere, a repetition. Bhabha
sustains that in representing oneself in discourse one's identity is never a
"finished product" because it is always being formed or in process. Furthermore,
in the moment of telling one finds him/herself straddling between the past
and the present or "temporally deferred", which may also differ because one
recalls an event situated in "time or moment that is elsewhere". Significantly, in
piercing together all the characteristics of the self, the subject always thinks in
terms of origins or past and somehow incorporates these into the present. Hence,
he recalls those experiences that are "spatially split" and therefore eradicating
the present.

Bhabha's argument above does not simply mean identity is fluid, but it
highlights the complex nature of identity because, in defining oneself one relies
on memory, which is always unreliable and fragmented. As Dufré denotes in the
text, "shall we start at the beginning Mr Sibiya" (Nkosi, 1986: 290), he assumes
that identity is made up of ordered memories and that identity pre-exists the
individual, ignoring the fact that it is possible only through language or discourse
and fractured memories. Ndi, through the process of writing sets to reconcile all
the various versions of himself in his attempt to inscribe himself. Dufré makes
an assumption that Ndi's experiences are ordered and that they are readily
available for recall; hence he asks Ndi to start from the beginning. This contrasts
Ndi's idea of telling a story, as he writes, "I write not in an orderly fashion, not

---

[1] Bhabha (2005) proposes a move away from issues of origins in tackling issues of identity.

even chronologically, but randomly, setting down what memory thrusts to the forefront of my diseased mind, with a hasty if confined sense of relief. Relief, if I may say so, not unlike sexual release" (Nkosi, 1986: 24).

To Ndi, writing provides some "relief", which one can also call the act of aesthetic pleasure that comes with this self-inscription. The aesthetic dimension of the ordinary act of writing brings pleasure, a sense of "relief" (exaltation/ purgation) that he compares to "sexual release". This aesthetic ability to form characters — to breathe life into them, as well as to appreciate writing and the pleasures that come with it — sets Ndi apart from others of his race, class and gender. This further highlights the problems that are associated with identity and self-inscription. Stuart Hall (1990) captures the gravity of this situation, as he cautions about easy associations of identity.

> Perhaps instead of thinking of identity as an already accomplished fact, which the new cultural practices then represent, we should think, instead, of identity as a 'production', which is never complete, always in process, and always constituted within, not outside, representation. (Hall, 1990: 222)[①]

Stuart Hall makes a significant interjection that helps us to comprehend the complex nature of self-inscription and identity they possibly become subjects and an elements of discourse. Hall further frames self-inscription as a problematic concept that is "a production, which is never complete". In Ndi's narrative there is a competing story that intrudes and chooses for his story a place and space where it is told, and this story does not only intrude but to some extent influences Ndi's. In other words, his narrative is layered with other narratives — the narrative of the community and the narrative of power and segregation shown by the legal system and the prison officials.

---

① Hall (1990) makes a compelling argument about identity. He maintains that identity is always in production and it is never finished.

6 Conclusion

The danger in self-inscription is always that one is likely to miss subtle, yet important dimensions of himself and his life, especially in the context of exile and entrapment that the protagonist Ndi finds himself in. As Ndi suggests, "I hope to preserve these fruits of self-scrutiny for posterity on cheap, unimpressive notepaper with which I have been provided by the authorities in order, as many have urged me, to write the story of my life" (Nkosi, 1986: 16). Self-inscription through writing, and largely narrating the story, allows Ndi to inscribe himself and fashion himself anew in order to relive his individual experiences and project a positive image of himself. As Ndi himself asserts, he is writing to "preserve the fruits of self-scrutiny for posterity", then identity must surely crystallise into something more enduring than we are wont to admit, something that can be passed on — which takes us to the point that Brubaker and Cooper (2000) make, as they maintain that ways of understanding may harden, congeal and crystallise, and are beyond their nebulous conceptions of identity as soft, fluid and unfixed.

Ndi as a narrator is encouraged and given the resources to write, and merge and weave the scattered fragments of his past into a coherent narrative. As an aspiring writer, Ndi observes something subtle and rhythmic in the words or language that Dufré uses. This underlines the great attention and thought that he attributes to language, and to him language is not a mere tool of communication. However, it may also be used to portray human emotions. Ndi also draws our attention as readers, to how language may also be used to dominate, control and exclude. He is, through language, forced to recall and reflect on some of his experiences through questions asked by his constant visitor, interrogator and confessor, Dr Dufré. Dufré comes to visit Ndi in order to enquire, to prod, and to probe concerning the facts about his supposed rape of a white woman. Heinen and Sommer (2009: 10) contends that a narrative "seems to be a kind of vortex around which other discourses orbit in ever closer proximity".

Ndi's narrative is indicative of the fact that one man's story is interspersed with others' stories. In his case, these stories are told in various geographical locations such as in prison, in court and in the environment divided according to colour or race, for instance, the beach, and that it largely projects a trajectory through which a story of a nation divided by colour (race) is told. It is Masemola and Rafapa in their exploration of identity as shaped in the post-apartheid texts, who remind us that "what counts as common in the post-apartheid novel necessarily ranges itself against rigidities of both nation and identity" (Masemola & Rafapa, 2014: 89). Their argument demonstrates what Nkosi seeks to achieve in the text regarding the rigid conceptualisation of fluid concepts such as identity. Masemola and Rafapa do not only remind but they tacitly caution us on the cross cultural and racial influence, in which when two people of different cultures collude they learn the cultural traits of another and this impacts on how they frame themselves, as Bhabha cogently argues, "Now minority-status has generalized into a paradoxical condition where the distinction between the minority and majority becomes frequently blurred" (Bhabha, 1998: 123). It may be concluded that in Ndi's self-inscription, Nkosi has debunked the myth of race that portrays blacks as victims of apartheid, and people who are unable to tell meaningful stories about their lives, thereby failing to inscribe themselves in the annals of history.

References

BAL M, 2006. A Mieke reader [M]. Chicago: University of Chicago Press.

BHABHA H, 1998. The commitment to theory [J]. New Formations, 1: 5-23.

BHABHA H, 2005. The location of culture [M]. London: Routledge.

BRUBAKER R, COOPER F, 2000. Beyond 'identity' [J]. Theory and society, 29: 1-47.

CHAMBERS I, CURTI L, 2008. Migrating modernities in the Mediterranean[J]. Postcolonial studies, 11 (4): 387-399.

DEHDARI A, DARABI B, SEPEHRMANESH M, 2013. A study of the notion of Bhabhasque's hybridity in V.S Naipaul's in A Free State [J]. International journal of humanities and social sciences, 3 (3): 135-144.

FANON F, 1967. Black skin, white masks [M]. New York: Grove Atlantic.

GALL E, 2014. Lewis Nkosi: a fragile soul's quest for home [J]. English studies in
    Africa, 39 (3): 65-80.

GILROY P, 2000. Against race: imagining political culture byond the color line [M].
    Harvard: Havard University Press.

HALL S, 1990. Cultural identity and diaspora [C] // RUTHERFORD J. Identity:
    community, culture, difference. London: Lawrence and Wishart: 222-237.

HEINEN S, SOMMER R, 2009. Introduction: narratology and interdisciplinarity
    [C] // HEINEN S, SOMMER R. Narratology in the age of cross-disciplinary
    narrative research. Berlin: Walter de Gruyter & Co: 1-10.

KALUA F, 2009. Homi Bhabha's third space and African identity [J]. Journal of
    African cultural studies, 21 (1): 23-32.

KALUA F, 2015. You can't go home again: reading the shifting idea of "home"
    [C] // RUPERT I. The healing land: a Kalahari journey, Scrutiny 2, Vol. 20.
    London: Penguin (1): 54-62.

LOW S, LAWRENCE-ZÚÑIGA D, 2003. The anthropology of space: locating
    culture [M]. Oxford: Blackwell.

MASEMOLA K M, RAFAPA L, 2014. Representation of the national and trans-
    national in Phaswane Mpe's Welcome to Our Hillbrow [J]. Alternation, 21 (2):
    83-98.

MOSITO P, 2011. Re-reading, re-configuring and contesting the black body in
    the 21st century: Jackson S, Demissie F, Goodwin M, Eds (2009) imagining,
    writing, (re) reading the black body [J]. Imbizo: International journal of African
    literary and comparative studies, 2 (1): 158-161.

NKOSI L, 1986. Mating birds [M]. London: Constable and Company Limited.

STARK-ADLER A, 2006. Psychoanalysis and apartheid: the image and role of the
    psychiatrist in selected works of Lewis Nkosi [C] // STIEBEL L, GUNNER
    L. Still beating the drum: critical perspectives on Lewis Nkosi. Johannesburg:
    Wits University Press: 93-102.

WIDERSHOVEN G A, 1993. The story of life. Hermeneutic perspectives on the
    relationship between narrative and life history [J]. The narrative study of life,
    (1): 1-20.

（编辑：马秀杰）

新时代中非人文交流与合作：成效与挑战①

吴传华　卫白鸽

中国社会科学院大学国际政治经济学院

摘　要： 人文交流与合作是新时代中非合作的重要内容，是中非全面战略合作伙
伴关系的重要组成部分，也是中非命运共同体的重要支柱。在中非双方
共同努力下，中非人文交流与合作的内容越来越丰富，形式越来越多样，
领域越来越宽广，渠道越来越畅通，成效越来越显著，使得中非关系的
社会民意基础不断扩大和巩固。但是，与快速发展的中非政治关系和经
贸合作相比，中非人文交流与合作还是显得相对滞后和薄弱，依然被认
为是中非关系的"短板"，具体表现在：中非间相互直接了解还不够充
分，中非思想文化交流亟待加强，中非合作的舆论环境有待改善，中非
合作的国际影响因素日趋复杂。2019 年以来，新冠肺炎疫情肆虐全球，
也给中非人文交流与合作带来很多困难和挑战。着眼于未来发展，中非
要进一步健全人文交流与合作机制，充分调动各方积极性；进一步扩大
中非思想文化交流，着力推动中非语言互通；进一步提升中非合作话语
权和传播能力，防止和消除西方干扰与破坏；进一步讲好中国故事、非
洲故事和中非合作故事，推动国际社会形成正确的中国观、非洲观和中
非合作观。

关键词： 中非人文交流与合作；中非思想文化交流；中非命运共同体

① 本文系中国非洲研究院与南非联合研究课题"人文交流与中非命运共同体构建研究"（项
目编号：CAI-J2021-11）的阶段性研究成果。

收稿日期： 2022-7-20

作者信息： 吴传华，中国社会科学院大学国际政治经济学院副教授，《中国非洲学刊》常务
副主编、编辑部主任，研究领域为非洲政治、中非关系，电子邮箱：wuch@cass.org.cn。卫白鸽，
中国社会科学院大学国际政治经济学院博士研究生，研究领域为国际新闻传播、中非跨文化交
流，电子邮箱：weibaigemailbox@126.com。

China-Africa People-to-People Exchanges and Cooperation in the New Era: Achievements and Challenges

Wu Chuanhua　Wei Baige

School of International Politics and Economics, University

of Chinese Academy of Social Sciences

Abstract: People-to-people exchanges and cooperation are important parts of China-Africa cooperation in the new era, important components of China-Africa comprehensive strategic cooperative partnership, and important pillars of the China-Africa community with a shared future. With joint efforts of both sides, China-Africa people-to-people exchanges and cooperation have become increasingly rich in content, diverse in form, broad in scope, unimpeded in channel and remarkable in result, which has continuously expanded and consolidated the social public opinion base of China-Africa relations. However, compared with the rapid development of China-Africa political relations and economic and trade cooperation, China-Africa people-to-people exchanges and cooperation appear relatively backward and weak, which are considered to be the "short boards" of China-Africa relations. China-Africa people-to-people exchanges and cooperation in the new era are faced with many difficulties and severe challenges: the direct mutual understanding between China and Africa is not sufficient, the ideological and cultural exchanges between China and Africa need to be strengthened, the public opinion environment for China-Africa cooperation remains to be improved, the international influence factors of China-Africa cooperation are becoming increasingly complex. Since the COVID-19 pandemic has ravaged the world, focusing on future development, we should further improve the mechanism of China-Africa people-to-people exchanges and cooperation, and fully mobilise the enthusiasm of all parties. We should further expand China-Africa ideological and cultural exchanges, and especially work hard to promote language exchanges. We should further enhance the discourse and communication ability of China-Africa cooperation, and prevent and eliminate Western interference and sabotage. We should further tell the real stories of China, Africa, and China-Africa cooperation, and promote the international community to form a correct view of China, Africa, and China-Africa cooperation.

Keywords: China-Africa people-to-people exchanges and cooperation; China-Africa ideological and cultural exchanges; the China-Africa community with a shared future

国之交在于民相亲，民相亲在于心相通。人文交流是国与国、民与民之间增进了解、建立互信的桥梁，是各国对外交往的重要组成部分，对国家对外关系发展、国家形象塑造、国家软实力提升都具有重要意义。党的十八大以来，以习近平同志为核心的党中央高度重视对外人文交流工作，以元首外交引领中外人文交流和文明互鉴不断发展。2017 年，《关于加强和改进中外人文交流工作的若干意见》出台。该意见对进一步做好中外人文交流与合作作出全面部署，成为新时代我国对外人文交流工作的纲领性文件。

中国与非洲虽然相距遥远，但是双方的友好交往源远流长，历来是休戚与共的命运共同体。2000 年，中非合作论坛成立，此后中非全方位合作进入快车道。党的十八大以来，中国特色社会主义进入新时代。与此同时，非洲国家在谋求联合自强、自主发展的道路上也取得显著进展，非洲大陆一体化进程迎来加快发展的新阶段。中国与非洲国家发展任务相同、发展优势互补、发展战略契合。双方在政治互信、经贸合作、人文交流等领域的合作持续扩大深化，通过平等互利合作实现共同发展，为南南合作树立了典范。

其中，人文交流与合作是新时代中非合作的重要内容，是中非全面战略合作伙伴关系的重要组成部分，是构建高水平中非命运共同体的重要支柱。在双方共同努力下，中非人文交流与合作内容越来越丰富，形式越来越多样，领域越来越宽广，渠道越来越畅通，成效越来越显著，日益成为中非友好合作的新亮点，从而使中非关系的社会民意基础不断扩大和巩固。但是不可否认，与快速发展的中非政治关系和经贸合作相比，中非人文交流与合作还是显得相对滞后和薄弱，被认为是中非关系的"短板"（吴传华、郭佳、李玉洁，2018: 2）。2019 年以来，新冠肺炎疫情肆虐全球，深刻改变和影响着人类社会，给中非合作也带来很大冲击，尤其是人员往来受到疫情阻碍，正常的人文交流与合作难以开展。在新形势下，如何进一步扩大中非人文交流与合作、促进中非民心相通、深化中非文明互鉴，成为中非双方需要共同应对的重要课题。

1　国内关于中非人文交流与合作的研究现状

国内外学者对"人文及人文交流"的概念有诸多不同的定义，对人文交流所涵盖的范围界定不同，对人文交流与文化外交、公共外交、民间交流之间的关系有不同的理解。邢丽菊认为，"人文交流主要是以人员交流、文化交流和思想交流为主要内容，以国家间民众的互动、互识和互知为目的，直接感受相互间思想文化的交汇、碰撞和吸引"（邢丽菊，2021：64）。俞沂暄在《人文交流与新时代中国对外关系发展——兼与文化外交的比较分析》一文中，对人文交流的内涵和外延及其在国际关系中的意义进行了梳理探讨（俞沂暄，2019）。庄礼伟的《中国式"人文交流"能否有效实现"民心相通"》一文，对人文交流的概念内涵和观念差异进行了辨析（庄礼伟，2017）。张骥、丁媛媛在《中国民间外交、地方外交与人文交流70年》一文中认为，人文交流是在民间外交基础上发展起来的内涵更加广泛的外交形式，基本上除了政治、经济、军事、安全等领域以外，其他所有领域的交流几乎都可以纳入人文交流范畴（张骥、丁媛媛，2019）。本文所指的人文交流是较为广义上的人文交流，涵盖文化、教育、科技、卫生、体育、旅游、媒体、智库等诸多方面。

与政治互信、经贸合作相比，人文交流是中非关系的"短板"，国内学界对中非人文交流与合作的研究亦显薄弱和滞后。迄今为止，国内还没有一部全面系统地梳理并呈现中非人文交流与合作历史及现状的专著，相关研究大多散见于各类研究报告和学术论文中。吴传华等人著的《中非人文交流与合作》智库报告，主要分析了中非在文化教育、医疗卫生、媒体等领域交流合作取得的成效、面临的挑战及未来发展路径（吴传华、郭佳、李玉洁，2018）。张宏明主编的《非洲发展报告（2014～2015）：中国在非洲的软实力建设：成效、问题与出路》，阐述了中国在非洲软实力建设所取得的成效、面临的问题及发展思路（张宏明，2015）。徐薇、刘鸿武主编的《中国—南非人文交流发展报告（2018—2019）》，较全面地梳理了近年来两国人文交流，尤其是中南高级别人文交流机制运行情况（徐薇、刘鸿武，2020）。关于人文交流与人类命运共同体关系的研究，邢丽菊在《人文交流与人类命运共同体建设》一文中指出，加强中外人文交流既是构建人类命运共同体的重要途径，也是构建人类命运共同体的重要支柱（邢丽菊，2019）。王战等在《人类命运共同体理论的构建与践行——以中法非人文交流为中心》一文中提出，人文交流是构建人类命运共同体的加速器（王战等，2019）。侧重于中非人文交流理论、机制等方面研究的论文有：李安山的《中国与非洲的文化相似性——兼论中国应该向非洲学习什么》、刘鸿武、林晨的《人文交流推动中非合作行稳致远》、刘天南、蔡景峰的《中非人文交流：机制、局限与对策》等（李安山，2014；刘鸿武、林晨，2020；刘天南、蔡景峰，2018）。关于中国与非洲国家双边人文交流研究的论文有：古萍的《中国与摩洛哥人文交流合作机制建设研究》、单思明的《中国与埃及人文外交研究》、孙晓萌的《南非新闻出版业现状与中南人文交流的拓展》等（古萍，2017；单思明，2018；孙晓萌，2017）。关于人文交流不同领域研究的论文有：朱伟东的《文化交流助力中非合作行稳致远》；姜洋的《中非高等教育合作与交流探究》；刘官元的《中非体育互动60年历史演进与现代意义》等（朱伟东，2018；姜洋，2013；刘官元，2019）。非洲孔子学院的研究成为近年来学术研究的热点和重点，其中有代表性的著述为徐丽华主编的《非洲孔子学院：回视与前瞻》，以及徐丽华、包亮主编的《非洲孔子学院探索与研究》（徐丽华，2018；徐丽华、包亮，2020）。学术论文有数十篇甚至更多，如李红秀的《非洲孔子学院建设与汉语文化传播》，高莉莉的《非洲孔子学院人才培养和可持续发展的思考》，胡登全、王丽平的《非洲孔子学院研究述评（2006—2019年）》等（李红秀，2015；高莉莉，2019；胡登全、王丽平，2021）。此外，一些博士或硕士学位论文也从不同角度研究非洲孔子学院。

综上所述，虽然国内学界关于中非人文交流与合作的研究日趋丰富，但是仍然跟不上中非关系快速发展的现实需要。学界加强对中非人文交流与合作的理论与实践进行深入研究，对中非人文交流与合作取得的成就和面临的挑战进行综合评估，对中非人文交流与合作未来发展进行思考探讨，具有重要的理论意义和现实意义。

2　新时代中非人文交流与合作取得的巨大成效

新时代，随着中非关系全面快速发展，中非人文交流与合作亦呈现持续扩大深化之势，领域大幅拓展，内容不断丰富，形式趋于多样，机制日益完善，层次逐步提升，成效日趋明显。在元首外交的引领下，在双方的共同努力下，中非人文交流与合作取得前所未有的成就，极大地促进了中非民心相通，深化了中非文明互鉴，为中非关系行稳致远和中非命运共同体构建作出重要贡献。

2.1　以元首外交引领中非人文交流与合作

习近平高度重视、亲自擘画并推动中非人文交流和文明互鉴，促进中非民心相通，增进中非人民友谊，为扩大深化中非全方位合作创造有利条件。习近平在担任国家主席后，首次出访便选择了非洲，并先后4次踏上非洲大陆，访问了坦桑尼亚、南非、刚果（布）、津巴布韦、埃及、塞内加尔、卢旺达和毛里求斯8国，其中访问南非3次。习近平以元首外交引领对非外交，大力推动中非人文交流与合作。2013年，习近平访问坦桑尼亚时强调，中非关系的根基和血脉在人民，中非关系发展应该更多面向人民。中非人民有着天然的亲近感，只要不断加强人民之间的交流，中非人民友谊就一定能根深叶茂。我们要更加重视中非人文交流，增进中非人民的相互了解和认知，厚植中非友好事业的社会基础（习近平，2014）。在刚果（布）议会演讲中，习近平主席指出，中非关系发展既需要经贸合作的"硬"支撑，也离不开人文交流的"软"助力。人文交流将为中非关系发展提供丰富的文化营养，注入强大的精神动力（习近平，2013）。2018年，在中非合作论坛北京峰会上，习近平表示，我们都为中非各自灿烂的文明而自豪，也愿为世界文明多样化作出更大贡献。我们要促进中非文明交流互鉴、交融共存，为彼此文明复兴、文化进步、文艺繁荣提供持久助力，为中非合作提供更深厚的精神滋养。我们要扩大文化艺术、教育体育、智库媒体、妇女青年等各界人员交往，拉紧中非人民的情感纽带（习近平，2020）。习近平主席作出的一系列重要论述，提出的一系列重要理念、倡议和举措，为促进中非人文交流和深化中非文明互鉴提供了重要的思想和行动指南。

2.2 中非人文交流与合作机制日趋完善

与其他国家对非合作相比，机制保障是中非合作的特点和优势所在。中非合作论坛已走过 20 多年历程，成为引领中非合作乃至国际对非合作的一面旗帜，人文交流与合作是历届中非合作论坛的重要内容。2015 年，中非合作论坛约翰内斯堡峰会确定将中非关系提升为全面战略合作伙伴关系，其中文明交流互鉴是"五大支柱"之一，并且将"中非人文合作计划"列为"十大合作计划"之一。2018 年，中非合作论坛北京峰会提出携手打造"责任共担、合作共赢、幸福共享、文化共兴、安全共筑、和谐共生"的中非命运共同体，并且将"人文交流行动"列为"八大行动"之一。2021 年，中非合作论坛第八届部长级会议提出中非合作"九项工程"，其中"人文交流工程"被列为第八项。中非合作论坛历届会议发布的行动计划，包括《中非合作论坛—约翰内斯堡行动计划（2016—2018）》《中非合作论坛—北京行动计划（2019—2021）》《中非合作论坛—达喀尔行动计划（2022—2024）》等。这些计划均明确列出人文领域的具体目标、计划和项目等，为中非人文交流与合作的持续发展提供强有力的机制保障。

与中非合作论坛相得益彰，"一带一路"倡议提出近十年以来，日益成为造福中非人民的共同繁荣之路。习近平指出，非洲是共建"一带一路"的历史和自然延伸，是重要参与方。中非共建"一带一路"，是造福中非人民的共同繁荣之路，是言必行、行必果的务实合作之路，是敞开胸怀拥抱世界的开放包容之路，是推动贸易和投资便利化的自由通畅之路（新华网，2018）。这一重要论述明确了非洲在"一带一路"的重要地位，为中非共建"一带一路"指明了方向。"一带一路"建设秉持"共商、共建、共享"的原则，着力推动实现"五通"，即政策沟通、设施联通、贸易畅通、资金融通、民心相通。"把基础设施'硬联通'作为重要方向，把规则标准'软联通'作为重要支撑，把同共建国家人民'心联通'作为重要基础，推动共建'一带一路'高质量发展"（中国政府网，2021）。迄今，"一带一路"合作在非洲基本上实现了全覆盖，"一带一路"倡议的理念、精神和原则已完全融入新时代中非人文交流与合作。"一带一路"倡议为中非关系发展注入新的活力和动力，它既是经贸合作之路，也是人文交流之路，为扩大中非人文交流与合作提供了重要的历史机遇。

2017年，中国—南非高级别人文交流机制正式建立。这是中国同南非以及非洲国家之间首次建立高级别人文交流机制，也是迄今为止中国对外建立的八个高级别人文交流机制之一，旨在构建中非人文交流与合作新格局，推动中非人文交流与合作向全方位、高层次发展。

2.3　中非人文交流与合作主体不断增多

人文交流归根结底是人与人之间的交流、心与心之间的沟通，以此促进相互理解，增进彼此友谊，推进双方合作。随着中非关系快速发展，中非人员交往持续增多，中非人文交流与合作的主体不断扩大。越来越多的中国人前往非洲，他们一类是国家公派人员，包括外交人员、医疗队员、孔子学院教师和志愿者、农业专家以及少量留学生等；另一类是企业员工、私营业者、务工人员等。以援非医疗队为例，截至2021年，中国累计向非洲派出医疗队员2.3万人次，诊治患者2.3亿人次。目前，中国在非洲派有医疗队员近千人，共98个工作点（国务院新闻办公室，2021）。中国医疗队员在非治病救人的过程中，直接进行人与人之间的交流，他们的医德医术、义举善举获得非洲各界人士交口称赞，在当地被誉为"白衣使者""最受欢迎的人"。美国皮尤研究中心的调查显示，很多非洲国家对中国的好感与日俱增，而中国在非洲获得这种成就的方式之一就是提供公共医疗援助（吴传华、郭佳、李玉洁，2018）。放眼至孔子学院，至今中非合作共设立61所孔子学院和48所孔子课堂。自2004年以来，中国共向非洲派出中文教师和志愿者5,500余人次（国务院新闻办公室，2021）。经过多年发展，孔子学院已成为中非教育合作与人文交流的一张闪亮名片。经贸领域投融资合作方面，截至2020年，中国企业累计对非直接投资超过430亿美元。中国在非洲设立各类企业超过3500家，民营企业逐渐成为对非投资的主力，聘用非洲本地员工比例超80%，直接和间接创造了数百万个就业机会（国务院新闻办公室，2021）。随着大量中国企业"走出去"，赴非企业人员、经商人员大幅增长。他们虽然不是专门从事人文交流的专业人士，但是他们直接面对当地政府、企业、民间等各界人士，与当地人直接接触沟通，互动合作非常频繁，因此他们成为直接或间接参与中非人文交流最基层、最活跃的力量。此外，在每个非洲国家都有数量不等的华侨华人，少则几百人，多则数万人，具体数量难以准确统计。他们长期工作生活在非洲，熟悉当地国情民情，与当地社会的融入度较高，在促进中非人文交流方面有得天独厚的优势。

近年来，越来越多的非洲人来到中国，主要包含两类群体：一类是经商人员，另一类是留学人员。中国已经成为非洲青年学生重要的留学目的国。根据中国教育部数据，2018 年非洲来华留学生人数为 81,562 人，占来华留学生总数的 17%，仅次于亚洲（占 60%）（中国教育部网站，2019）。无论是留学人员、经商人员还是其他人员，他们都通过来华的亲身经历从而更了解中国，在中非人文交流与合作中发挥重要作用。

2.4 中非人文交流与合作领域持续扩大

新时代，中非人交流与合作的领域不断扩大，包括文化、教育、科技、卫生、旅游、媒体、智库等诸多方面，呈现出全面开花之势。

在文化方面，截至 2020，中非签署并落实了 346 个双边政府文化协定执行计划。2013—2020 年，中方组派艺术团赴非 140 国（次）举办演出。自 2013 年以来，中国邀请非洲 28 国的艺术团来华演出。自 2016 年以来，中方为非洲国家举办数百个文化领域研修班，非方参与人员累计近 1,500 人。中国在毛里求斯、贝宁、埃及、尼日利亚、坦桑尼亚、摩洛哥六国设有中国文化中心。作为派驻非洲国家的官方文化机构，中国文化中心常年开展各类丰富多彩的文化活动，在促进中非文化交流、增进中非友谊方面发挥了重要作用。2014—2015 年，中国与南非互办"国家年"活动，这是中非之间首次互办"国家年"活动。2016 年是中埃建交 60 周年，中国与埃及互办"文化年"活动。中埃文化年是中国与阿拉伯国家举办的首个文化年，实现了真正意义上的"两个伟大文明之间的对话"。"欢乐春节"活动在非洲已举办十多年，影响越来越大，成为中国节日文化走向世界的一个代表。

在教育方面，中非在留学生教育、孔子学院建设、高校交流合作、职业技术教育合作、教育领域援助等方面取得显著成果。中国大力支持非洲教育发展，帮助非洲培养急需人才，为非洲国家提供了大量政府奖学金，支持非洲青年学子来华留学。2012 年，"中非高校 20+20 合作计划"开始实施，为中非高校交流合作搭建平台。中国在联合国教科文组织设立信托基金项目，累计在非洲国家培训 1 万余名教师。自 2018 年以来，中国在埃及、南非、吉布提、肯尼亚等国共建"鲁班工坊"，为当地培养高素质技术技能人才。中国支持 30 余所非洲大学设立中文系或中文专业，配合16 个非洲国家将中文纳入国民教育体系，在非洲合作设立了 61 所孔子学院和 48 所孔子课堂。孔子学院以推广汉语、传播中国文化为己任，是中国对非文化交流与合作的一张闪亮名牌。

在科技方面，中非合作建设了一批高水平联合实验室，创建了中非联合研究中心、中非创新合作中心，帮助非洲国家培养了大量科技人才。中非在空间和航天合作方面取得新突破，双方利用中国遥感数据开展防灾减灾、射电天文、卫星导航定位和精准农业等领域合作。中国在埃及援建卫星总装集成及测试中心项目，还分别为阿尔及利亚、苏丹两国发射首颗人造卫星。

在卫生方面，中国派遣援非医疗队已有近 60 年的历史，是中非开展时间最长、涉及国家最多、成效最为显著的合作项目之一。"光明行"义诊活动在非洲实施 34 次，帮助近万名当地白内障患者重见光明。中国帮助 18 个非洲国家建立了 20 个专科中心，涉及心脏、重症医学、创伤、腔镜等专业，同 40 个非洲国家的 45 所医院建立了对口合作机制。2014 年，中国大力支持非洲国家战胜埃博拉出血热疫情。2019 年新冠肺炎疫情暴发以来，中非共克时艰、相互支持、团结抗疫，谱写了中非友好合作的新篇章，大大增进了中非人民之间的友谊。

在媒体及影视方面，中非在互设新闻机构、互派记者、互换信息、联合采制、人员培训、新媒体发展等方面的合作不断加强，举办了中非媒体领袖峰会、中非媒体合作论坛等大型交流活动，有 30 家非洲媒体加入了"一带一路"新闻合作联盟，42 个非洲国家参加了"一带一路"媒体合作论坛。中国支持非洲广播电影电视产业发展，积极落实"万村通"项目，使非洲一万个村落能够收看卫星电视节目，实施"中非影视合作工程"，将约200部中国优秀视听作品进行多语种译制，在非洲国家播出，成为当地民众了解中国的一个重要渠道。

在智库方面，双方支持智库、研究机构、高等院校开展课题研究、学术交流、著作出版等多种形式的合作。中非智库论坛创立于2011年，迄今已举办11届会议，成为中非学术界进行交流的一个重要平台，中非合作论坛框架下的一个机制化分论坛。2013年，中非智库"10+10合作伙伴计划"正式启动，旨在推动中非学术机构建立一对一的长期合作关系。中非联合研究交流计划实施十多年来，已有80余家中非智库学术研究机构参与该计划，旨在鼓励中非学者开展联合研究，为中非合作提供知识和智力支持。2019年，中国非洲研究院在北京成立，成为新时代促进中非人文交流与文明互鉴的一项重要举措。

在民间交流方面，自2011年以来，中非举办了6届中非民间论坛、5届中非青年领导人论坛、4届亚非青年联欢节和3届中非青年大联欢活动。中国已与53个非洲国家的100多个妇女机构（组织）建立联系和交往，在毛里求斯、莱索托、吉布提、津巴布韦和苏丹等国建立中非妇女友好交流（培训）中心。越来越多的民间组织参与中非人文交流与合作，如中国非洲人民友好协会、中国民间组织国际交流促进会、中国扶贫基金会、中国青年基金会等。

2.5　中非人文交流与合作成效非常显著

人文交流与合作在促进中非政治互信、深化中非经贸合作、扩大中非民心相通方面发挥了非常重要的作用。首先，人文交流与合作是中非全面战略合作伙伴关系的重要一环。平等相待是中非人文交流的精神内核，开放包容是中非人文合作的重要基石。通过人文交流与合作，中非人民增加了对彼此的认知和了解，减少了误解和偏见，并且有效防止了第三方抹黑挑拨中非关系、阻碍破坏中非合作，从而为中非开展各领域合作创造良好的社会条件和民意基础。其次，人文交流与合作以促进中非民心相通和文明互鉴为宗旨。缺乏民心相通，合作的成本将大大提高，甚至根本无法进行。缺乏文明互鉴，世界将会黯淡无光，甚至陷入冲突动荡。习近平强调，要尊重世界文明多样性，以文明交流超越文明隔阂、文明互鉴超越文明冲突、文明共存超越文明优越（习近平，2020）。中非人文交流与合作体现了对世界文明多样性的尊重，促进了中非文明互鉴，超越了"文明冲突论""文明优越论"等西方种族主义文明观，为世界不同文明之间的交往树立了典范。最后，人文交流与合作是构建中非命运共同体的重要途径。从中非命运共同体到更加紧密的中非命运共同体，再到新时代中非命运共同体，人文交流与合作都发挥了不可替代的作用。只有中非人文交流与合作不断扩大，民心相通不断加强，文明互鉴不断深化，构建中非命运共同体的社会民意基础才会愈加夯实巩固，从而更好地为构建人类命运共同体树立典范。

3　新时代中非人文交流与合作面临的困难与挑战

如上所述，新时代中非人文交流与合作不断扩大深化，取得非常显著的成效。但总体来说，相较于中非政治互信与经贸合作，中非人文交流与合作仍显滞后。如果把政治、经济和人文比作中非关系中的"三轮驱动"，那么"人文驱动"相对薄弱落后。中非之间相互直接了解还不够充分，中非思想文化交流亟待加强，中非合作的舆论环境有待改善，中非合作的国际影响因素日趋复杂，这些都给中非人文交流与合作带来很多困难和严峻挑战。

3.1　中非思想文化交流不足制约中非人文交流与合作

思想文化交流是人文交流最核心、最重要的部分。但是，受历史和现实等多重因素影响，中非对彼此思想文化的了解还不够深入，双方在思想文化上的交流和相互影响还较为薄弱。一方面，非洲人民对中国思想文化的了解还非常有限，一般民众仅限于知道或听说中国武术、杂技、春节等文化元素或符号，缺少对中国博大精深思想文化的全面认知、学习与研究。相对而言，西方思想文化虽然属于殖民主义遗产，但是对非洲的影响已经根深蒂固。非洲在语言、文化、宗教、意识形态、价值观等方面与西方更为接近，尤其是年轻人"西化"倾向严重，受西方思想文化影响很深。对此，有非洲人士就曾指出，非洲人已经被西方思想文化"洗脑"，本地文化被忽视，日益边缘化，对包括中国文化在内的世界其他文化更是知之甚少（伯高亚，2018）。另一方面，中国人民对非洲思想、文化、历史、哲学、文学、艺术等方面也是了解甚少，可以说非常欠缺。相对于政治经济影响力而言，思想文化影响力一旦形成之后，则是更为持久深远的。因此，要推动中非人文交流与合作向纵深发展，必须全面加强中非思想文化交流与互学互鉴。

3.2 中非经贸关系及人员往来存在的问题影响中非人文交流与合作

近年来中非经贸合作发展迅速，成为中非关系发展的主要推动力。但是，随着越来越多的中国企业和人员前往非洲，一系列问题不断凸显。一方面，有些在非中国企业存在急功近利、不正当竞争、不遵守当地劳动法、不注重履行社会责任等情况。有些在非洲的中国人存在不了解当地文化、不尊重当地习俗、不积极融入当地社会等现象。这些问题如果长期得不到解决，容易诱发不良甚或恶性事件，给中国形象和中非关系造成负面影响，非常不利于中非人文交流与合作。另一方面，随着越来越多的非洲人来到中国，"三非"问题（非法入境、非法居留、非法就业）较为凸显，由此给中非关系带来一些困扰，影响中非友好交往和民心相通。自新冠肺炎疫情发生后，中非之间正常的人员交往严重受阻，使中非人文交流与合作面临前所未有的新挑战。

3.3 舆论环境复杂对中非人文交流与合作造成不利局面

总体而言，非洲国家对华友好，非洲人民对华友善，非洲涉华舆论环境总体客观积极。但是，随着时代变迁和形势变化，影响中非关系的因素趋于复杂化。非洲老一辈领导人陆续退出历史舞台，新生代政治精英和青年人对中国的认识及对中非关系的看法趋于复杂化。非洲普通民众对中国的了解仍十分有限，渠道也不够畅通。非洲新闻传媒业落后，媒体欠发达，国际传播能力较弱。西方媒体在非洲占据重要地位，它们从西方立场、以西方视角、按西方价值观来向世界报道非洲。也就是说，非洲故事都是由西方媒体来讲述的，非洲形象也是由西方媒体来刻画的。最典型的例子就是英国《经济学人》杂志先是在 2000 年将非洲称为"无望的大陆"，后来又在 2011 年将非洲称为"崛起的大陆"。这种 180 度的大转变，很典型地体现了西方对国际话语权的操控。近年来中非媒体交流与合作不断加强，但是还难以从根本上改变和打破西方话语霸权。西方媒体和非洲当地媒体上时常出现一些涉华消极负面报道，中非合作面临的舆论环境非常复杂，给中非人民带来误解甚或偏见，干扰甚至破坏中非关系。这一方面给中非人文交流与合作带来困难，另一方面又说明中非人文交流与合作的必要性和重要性。

3.4　西方国家的干扰破坏给中非人文交流与合作带来负面影响

中非关系快速发展让西方国家深感忧虑，认为其在非洲的利益受到威胁，遂千方百计地诋毁抹黑中非关系，干扰破坏中非合作。西方一些政客、媒体和智库充当了反华主力军，处心积虑地炮制了所谓的"中国威胁论""新殖民主义论""债务陷阱论"等一系列不实论调，并且利用自身话语霸权，大肆进行渲染炒作。对于孔子学院、中国文化中心等项目，美西方则扣以"文化殖民主义"的帽子，试图阻止中非人文交流与合作顺利开展。美西方一方面加大对非洲的关注、投入和干涉，一方面竭力阻挠和破坏中非友好合作，由此产生的一些负面影响在所难免，对中非关系造成一定程度的干扰和破坏。长时期内，中非关系中的西方因素和中西关系中的非洲因素成为绕不开的议题。

4　进一步加强新时代中非人文交流与合作的建议

新时代，如何进一步加强中非人文交流与合作，促进中非民心相通和文明互鉴，让非洲了解真实的中国，让中国了解真实的非洲，让世界了解中非友好合作的真实故事，显得十分紧迫且必要。

4.1　进一步健全中非人文交流与合作机制，充分调动各方积极性

中非人文交流与合作要有规划、有设计、有方向地开展，坚持走出去和引进来相结合，不断健全多层次、全方位、广覆盖的人文交流机制；充分发挥中央与地方、政府与社会各自的功能作用，充分调动各地方、各部门、各类组织和群体的积极性，做到人文交流与合作重心下沉并贴近民众；着力推动人文交流理念深入人心，将人文交流寓于中非洲民众的日常交往

中。中方支持在非洲的中资企业积极履行社会责任，坚持经贸与人文并行，开展多种形式的交流活动，成为中非人文交流与合作的主动践行者。中方鼓励和引导在非洲各国的华侨华人组织起来，成立各类社团，独立或者与当地组织团体合作开展活动，实现中非人文交流与合作的本地化与常态化。此外，中非要充分发挥来华非洲留学生的桥梁作用，鼓励他们通过各种方式参与或开展中非人文交流活动，以此促进中非长期友好。

4.2 进一步扩大中非思想文化交流，着力推动中非语言互通

鉴于思想文化在人文交流中的核心地位，中非要进一步加强思想交流，弘扬"和平、发展、公平、正义、民主、自由"的全人类共同价值，倡导不同文明交流互鉴，推动构建中非命运共同体和人类命运共同体。中方要进一步推动中国文化走进非洲，既包括博大精深的中国优秀传统文化，也包括彰显新时代中国特色社会主义伟大成就的现代先进文化，从而让非洲人民更客观全面地了解中国、认识中国。与此同时，中方也要把具有代表性的非洲文化引到中国来，实现文化交流"走出去"与"引进来"相结合，改变人们对非洲只有"贫穷、落后、战乱、疾病"的刻板负面印象，认识了解一个真正的、丰富多彩的非洲。中非高度重视语言的力量，推动中国与非洲各国语言互通，开辟多种层次语言文化交流渠道。中方着力加大汉语在非洲的推广力度，提升孔子学院办学水平，支持更多非洲国家将汉语教学纳入国民教育体系，同时健全中国高校外语学科体系，加快培养非通用语人才，不断提升中非语言交流互通能力。

4.3 进一步提升中非合作话语权和传播能力，防止和消除西方国家的干扰破坏

要改变并打破国际舆论"西强我弱"的局面，中国必须大力完善国际传播体系，提升国际传播能力。当今信息化时代，中国要着力打造具有国际影响力、易于被国外受众接受的全媒体和新媒体，进一步完善中国媒体在非洲的布局，同时推动中非新闻媒体、广播影视、出版机构等开展合作，做大做强"互联网＋人文交流"，充分利用互联网和虚拟平台开展中非人文交流与合作。与此同时，中国要加强同非洲国家的沟通与合作，共

同驳斥西方各种不实论调，防止和消除西方负面舆论对中非关系的干扰破坏。2018 年，习近平在中非合作论坛北京峰会上明确指出，任何人都不能破坏中非人民的大团结，任何人都不能阻挡中非人民振兴的步伐，任何人都不能以想象和臆测否定中非合作的显著成就，任何人都不能阻止和干扰国际社会支持非洲发展的积极行动（中国政府网，2018）。通过加强中非人文交流与合作，中非要牢牢把握中非合作话语权，讲好中国故事、非洲故事和中非合作故事，推动国际社会形成正确的中国观、非洲观和中非合作观。

　　综上，站在新时代的视域下，中非双方都应充分认识到人文交流与合作对于加深相互了解和彼此友谊、促进民心相通和文明互鉴、推动构建中非命运共同体乃至人类命运共同体的重要意义。尽管会面临各种困难和挑战，但是只要中非双方秉持共同的理念原则，坚持正确的目标方向，未来中非人文交流与合作就只会加强，不会减弱；只会扩大，不会缩小；只会升级，不会降级。

参考文献

伯高亚，2018."中国发展新现代与中非合作新机遇"国际研讨会上的发言[R]. 北京：中国社会科学院.

高莉莉，2019. 非洲孔子学院人才培养和可持续发展的思考 [J]. 天津职业技术师范大学学报，（1）：69-73.

古萍，2017. 中国与摩洛哥人文交流合作机制建设研究 [D]. 上海：上海外国语大学.

国务院新闻办公室，2021. 新时代中非合作 [M]. 北京：人民出版社.

胡登全，王丽平，2021. 非洲孔子学院研究述评（2006—2019 年）[J]. 中国非洲学刊，（1）：134-153.

姜洋，2013. 中非高等教育合作与交流探究 [J]. 重庆高教研究，（4）：109-112.

李安山，2014. 中国与非洲的文化相似性术——兼论中国应该向非洲学习什么 [J]. 西亚非洲，（1）：49-63.

李红秀，2015. 非洲孔子学院建设与汉语文化传播 [J]. 中华文化论坛，（1）：111-117.

刘官元，2019. 中非体育互动 60 年历史演进与现代意义 [J]. 武汉体育学院学报，（7）：19-24.

刘鸿武，林晨，2020. 人文交流推动中非合作行稳致远 [J]. 西亚非洲，（2）：22-32.

刘天南，蔡景峰，2018. 中非人文交流：机制、局限与对策 [C] // 中国非洲研究评论（2017）. 北京：社会科学文献出版社.

单思明，2018. 中国与埃及人文外交研究 [D]. 大连：大连外国语大学.

孙晓萌，2017. 南非新闻出版业现状与中南人文交流的拓展 [J]. 中国出版，（13）：65-68.

王战，等，2019. 人类命运共同体理论的构建与践行——以中法非人文交流为中心 [J]. 江汉论坛，（9）：62-67.

吴传华，郭佳，李玉洁，2018. 中非人文交流与合作 [M]. 北京：中国社会科学出版社.

习近平，2013. 共同谱写中非人民友谊新篇章——在刚果共和国议会的演讲 [N]. 人民日报，2013-03-30.

习近平，2014. 习近平谈治国理政 [M]. 北京：外文出版社.

习近平，2020. 习近平谈治国理政（第三卷）[M]. 北京：外文出版社.

新华网，2018. 习近平出席中非领导人与工商界代表高层对话会暨第六届中非企业家大会开幕式并发表主旨演讲 [EB/OL]. (2018-09-03) [2022-03-09]. http://www.xinhuanet.com/politics/leaders/2018-09/03/c_1123371924.htm.

邢丽菊，2019. 人文交流与人类命运共同体建设 [J]. 国际问题研究，（6）：11-24.

邢丽菊，2021. 中外人文交流概论 [M]. 北京：世界知识出版社.

徐丽华，2018. 非洲孔子学院：回视与前瞻 [M]. 上海：上海交通大学出版社.

徐丽华，包亮，2020. 非洲孔子学院探索与研究 [M]. 长春：吉林大学出版社.

徐薇，刘鸿武，2020. 中国—南非人文交流发展报告（2018—2019）[M]. 杭州：浙江大学出版社.

俞沂暄，2019. 人文交流与新时代中国对外关系发展——兼与文化外交的比较分析 [J]. 外交评论.（5）：34-53.

张宏明，2015. 非洲发展报告（2014～2015）：中国在非洲的软实力建设：成效、问题与出路 [M]. 北京：社会科学文献出版社.

张骥，丁媛媛，2019. 中国民间外交、地方外交与人文交流 70 年 [J]. 国际展望，（5）：54-72.

中国教育部网站，2019. 2018 年来华留学统计 [EB/OL]. (2019-04-12) [2022-3-20]. http://www.moe.gov.cn/jyb_xwfb/gzdt_gzdt/s5987/201904/t20190412_377692.html.

中国政府网，2018. 习近平在 2018 年中非合作论坛北京峰会开幕式上的主旨讲话（全文）[EB/OL]. (2018-09-03) [2022-03-15]. http://www.gov.cn/

xinwen/2018-09/03/content_5318979.htm.

中国政府网，2021. 习近平出席第三次"一带一路"建设座谈会并发表重要讲话 [EB/OL]. (2021-11-19)[2022-03-12]. http://www.gov.cn/xinwen/2021-11/19/content_5652067.htm.

朱伟东，2018. 文化交流助力中非合作行稳致远 [J]. 人民论坛，(32)：128-129.

庄礼伟，2017. 中国式"人文交流"能否有效实现"民心相通"[J]. 东南亚研究，（6）：67-84.

（编辑：王婷）

The Role of *Dyamu* and *Senankuya* Systems in the Manden Society[①]

Olga Yu Zavyalova
Department of African Studies, Saint Petersburg State University

Abstract: The *dyamu* (clans) and *senankuya* relationships (joking relationship) systems are important institutions and traditions common to all the Manden peoples in West Africa. It should be noted that these institutions had not lost their relevance today, and they even expanded their zone of influence. According to the surveys and interviews conducted among the Maninka students in Guinea in 2014, the identification by *dyamu* is more important for Maninka people than ethnicity and defines relationships in society at the present stage. Senankuya, in its turn, not only reduces social and interethnic tension, practically eliminating conflicts between *dyamu* themselves but also gradually penetrates other areas: these kinds of relations today have begun to be used even between the representatives of various confessions. The *dyamu* system as well as senankuya has long been in the field of interest of Africanists. The research aims to look at these relations from the point of view of the formation of the Manden society and the self-identification of both society as a whole and its individual representatives. How was this system formed and what is it aimed at? The representatives of the Manden culture themselves consider it to be a system of historical unification of members of different families and ethnic groups in the empire of Mali, a complex scheme of social fixed relationships, which is also a matter of pride for

① **Date of reception:** 2021-01-20

Author: Olga Yu Zavyalova, Associate Professor of Department of African Studies at Saint Petersburg State University; Research fields: Manding languages, African oral tradition, anthropology, ethnopsychology of the Asian and African peoples; Email: jontan@mail.ru.

all members of the society.

Keywords: Africa; Manden; *dyamu*; joking relationship; oral tradition

等级制度与戏谑关系在曼德社会中的作用

奥尔加·于·扎维雅洛娃

圣彼得堡国立大学非洲研究院

摘　要：等级制度与戏谑关系是西非曼德族群所共有的社会传统，这些机制至今仍发挥着重要作用。根据作者在 2014 年对几内亚马林凯族学生群体所做的调查和访谈结果，本文旨在论证对马林凯人来说，社会等级制度区分比族群区分更为重要，社会等级制度定义了现阶段不同群体间的社会关系。而戏谑关系不仅能够减少族群间的紧张关系，更能有效地缓解社会各阶级间的冲突，甚至能帮助达成族群之间的谅解。等级制度和戏谑关系长期以来一直是非洲学者感兴趣的领域。本研究旨在从曼德社会的形成、社会身份认同和自我身份认同的角度出发，来审视这种等级制度和戏谑关系是如何形成的以及形成的目的。曼德社会文化的继承者认为等级制度和戏谑关系是弥合马里帝国不同家庭、不同民族的重要机制，是维护曼德社会稳定的重要机制，也是曼德全体社会成员的骄傲。

关键词：非洲；曼登社会；等级制度；戏谑关系；口头传统

1　Introduction

The Manden peoples, mainly Mali and Guinea, inhabiting the West Africa, have a complex social system. One of its most significant parts is the so-called clan names system of *dyamu* or "*jamu*" in Bamana language. The *dyamu* system of the Manden peoples, about which many works have been written, is still not completely clear. The most complete list of *dyamu* can be considered a *dyamu* dictionary on the website of the Bamana corpus, based on the data obtained by V. Vydrin.

This study is based on data obtained from surveys and interviews conducted in Guinea and from analysis of the oral tradition as well as Internet sources, where such topics are discussed by bearers of the tradition themselves. During several expeditions in 1999 and in 2014, the relationship between *dyamu* in the Siguiri district (the Northern Guinea) was explored. It is the Manden region —

the heart of the Ancient Mali Empire. These questions were discussed from the colonial times, trying to describe and explain this phenomenon. This paper aims to describe the *dyamu* institution, taking into consideration of Manden peoples' conception of it, and tell how the Bamana and Maninka themselves explain the meaning and the origin of these institutions. That is why this paper is not intended to look through the numerous works about *dyamu* and *senankuya*.

Sometimes *dyamu* is called "caste", as all families are associated with a certain professional occupation, but this is not correct, since only *finɛ*[①], the only endogamous group, are suitable for the concept of "caste". It is also necessary to remember that some ethnic groups are also associated with certain professional activities. For example, Fulbe are originally cattle breeders and Bozo are fishermen. *Dyamu* is not only a clan system but also a kinship system, because when people really want to talk about their ancestors or their origin, they also operate with the concepts of "descendants of a certain person", and, as a rule, it does not intersect with the origin of *dyamu* itself. For example, Keita *dyamu* dominates in the Niagassola region, but they consider themselves the descendants of different Sunjata's sons (as they talked about 9 sons). *Dyamu* is the family name that entitles the belonging to the social group. Joking relationships are shared among the peoples of West Africa. *Dyamu* group is based on the idea of one ancestor as well as a common origin, common professional and marriage restrictions, and a certain system of interaction with other similar groups (*senankuya*)[②]. Today *dyamu* is more related to the kinship system.

The complete information about *dyamu* system, as well as about *senankuya*, belongs to griots (traditional narrators, guardians of epic stories and genealogies) and to representatives of the leaders' families, i.e., those who operate it. In

---

① *Finɛ, fina (funɛ)* consider themselves to be those who "say words that are pleasing to Allah". They are the griots category, who usually host events or help griots host events or meetings.

② In Bamana language *sànankuyá (senenkuyá, sìnankuyá)* — 'joking relationship, rite of ritual reviling'. Joking relationships are categorised as play by Bamana and Maninka peoples '*tlon*'.

Guinea, there are more than 30 major *dyamu*. Each *dyamu* has its own ancestor, who was the first to receive this name and *senanku* also — those *dyamu* with whom they are in so-called "joking relationship", or an animal totem. *Dyamu*, with whom the marriage is prohibited, and *dyamu*, with whom it is preferable.

The number of Maninka *dyamu* is less than the number of basic clans. For Keita the division into families by origin is the main one, as for the other *mansare* (the descendants of Sunjata, 4 ruling *dyamu*). In the past, everybody knew the ancestor or founder of his *dyamu*. Now the young people in the cities cannot name him. For 4 *mansare dyamu* Sunjata is the main ancestor. They are Keita, Konaté (the elders), Kulibali and Danwo (the younger ones). For Keita, Sunjata and Lawali Simbon (Simbon — the title of great hunter) are the ancestors; for Konate, Sunjata and Kabala Simbon; for Danwo, Sunjata and Kanin Simbon; for Kulibali, Sunjata, Kanin Nyogon Simbon and Biton Kulibali. According to the legends, they all (3 Simbons) descended from Bilali (Bilali Bunama was a companion of Mohammed (Niane, 1984), and Mamadu Kanu had three sons: Kanu Simbon, Kanu Nyogon Simbon, and Lawali Simbon (from Krikoroni).

According to Manden tradition, *dyamu* initially is a laudatory name. It should be noted that each *dyamu* has its own laudatory melody or slogan (*fasa*). Almost all *dyamu* have explanations of their name — the legend of its origin. The epic about Sunjata that is the source in which we can find some stories of the origin of the main *dyamu* and their *senankuya* histories[1].

The stories of griots tell us that the system of *dyamu*, in the form in which it is now, appeared during the founding of the Mali Empire as the subject of an agreement of representatives of the main clans who struggled together with the legendary founder of the empire Sunjata.

The griots explain the emergence of the *dyamu* institute as the following.

After the victory of Sunjata over Sumaoro and his Susu Empire, all the

---

[1] For example, see (Johnson, 2003; Niane, 1992; Cisse & Kamissoko, 2009; Kouyate, 2015).

ancestors of the main Manden clans met in Manden (the place of Kurukan Fuga) under the leadership of Sunjata. There were also Fa Koli, Sibi Kurula Kamandyan (ancestor of Camara/Kamara clan), Daman Diavara and others. "*Sunjata bɔra ka sɔrɔ jamu ɲini*" (Sunjata went out and started looking for inventing *dyamu* names) (Cisse & Kamissoko, 2009: 300).

According to oral tradition, the federation of Manden *dyamu* was established under the government of Keita in Kurukan Fuga and fixed in the Manden Charter. The laws and norms according to which people would live in the new empire were also established. *Senankuya* was also mentioned in the Charter, as well as other variants of "joking relationship".

2 The Charter of Kurukan Fuga

The Charter, adopted in Kurukan Fuga in 1236, the day after the victory of Sunjata Keita over Sumanguru Kante, is rather an agreement that determines the order and organisation of the society in the new Mali Empire. The concept of an agreement is the basis of relationship between the Manden people. On the one hand, the Charter has features of a constitution; on the other hand, it aims to regulate everyday life together and is partly something like an early declaration of human rights[1].

2.1 The history of the Charter

The Charter was fixed and recorded in 1998. Together with the *Manden Kalikan (The Hunters' Oath*, 1222), it is the main oral document that defines the relationship among the Manden peoples, concerning the interaction rules in the Manden society. One can find the bilingual Malinké-French text collected by Youssouf Tata Cissé, transcribed by Gérard Galtier.

The Charter, being a product of oral tradition, is not the historical document, but it rather sets the values and basic concepts of the Manden society.

---

[1] In 2009, the importance of the Charter of Kurukan Fuga was officially confirmed by UNESCO and it was added to the list of the Intangible Cultural Heritage of Humanity (UNESCO, 2009).

So, from the historical point of view, the level of its reliability is analogous to any epic story. But for Manden peoples not the date of its creation is important, but the fact of its existence. It plays a great role for the peoples of Mali themselves, and for all African peoples. In this case, its historical authenticity does not play a decisive role now. One way or another, this Charter appeared among these peoples, if not in 1236, then exactly in 1998. Its main statements confirm the *dyamu* system (the basic structure of society). They are important for the Manden self-identification, and African people's realization of their role in the modern world system.

Together with the *dyamu* system and the *senankuya* system, the Charter is the basis for the stability of the traditional structure of Manden society.

Some evidence of the existence of the Charter even before the 20th century is provided by the data that was obtained during the expedition to Guinea (Niagassola) in 1999. During this expedition and the second one in 2014 interviews with the most famous griots in the Siguiri region were conducted, as well as with the members of the majority of *dyamu* groups, and the Manden leaders' families of Keita from Niagassola, Balaninkoro, Balanindugu and Krikura. The residents showed me the sacred place and talked about it. It is the place of historical meeting similar in description to the Kurukan Fuga; it is also dated by residents by the date of the end of the war between Manden and the Susu Empire. Later the leaders of the Manden clans gathered there whenever they needed to solve their problems and this continued until the middle of the 20th century (as the elders from the Keita family in Krikura told me[1]).

And today we can find the place of gathering of 33 representatives of the main clans named *Kɛ-bɛn-so-kɔrɔ* "the meeting place of men under a bean tree (iseroelinia)", which is located between the villages of Krikura and Balaninkoro, Siguiri region in the Northern Guinea. There you can see 34 stones: 33 were for the elders of the main clans (for the descendants of Sunjata's sons), for

---

[1] *Kri Kura* (New Kri) is the new living place of those who have left *Kri kɔrɔ* (Old Kri) due to water problems (according to their history).

the representatives of all other *dyamu* and for three chiefs of the villages of Niagassola, Balaninkoro and Balandugu, and one stone was for Sunjata.

2.2 The Charter about dyamu

In the Charter we can find the social division of society into "warriors", "artisans" and "slaves". The griots and chiefs say that the division into *dyamu* has appeared as a result of this agreement.

In Manden society there are *dyamu*, referring to the *hɔrɔn* (free man or the noble). Now the word *hɔrɔn* is not used for it[①], but they are called only *tontigi* (master of quivers). Their main occupation is agriculture and war; while the professional castes of blacksmiths, griots (traditional story-tellers), *fina*, as well as leatherworkers are called *nyamakala*.

In 1236, "the day after the battle of Kirina, when Sunjata Keita defeated Sumaoro Kante, a Charter was adopted in Kurukan Fuga under the leadership of Kamadyan Camara, the ruler of Sibi. It was accepted by the representatives from 12 provinces of the new Empire. Discussion lasted for 12 days under the leadership of Samadi Bobo, the ruler of Bobo people" (Kouyate, 1999).

There it was announced the division of society into 16 clans of *ton tigiw*, or "quiver holders" and 4 clans *mansa da* or *mansare* (the rulers' families), 5 clans of *mori kanda* (marabouts), 4 professional castes of *nyamakala* (artisans). As for marabouts, they should have appeared later. It is known that 4 of their clans

---

① It is noteworthy that the attitude towards some words and concepts has changed: not only the word *hɔrɔn* "free" has been rejected, but the division into slaves *jɔnw* and *hɔrɔnw* has been denied. Despite the fact that slavery among the Manden has little to do with slavery in the conventional sense we know but it is a part of the traditional social structure. The Maninka refuse to use these words, focusing, rather, on the European attitude towards them. I witnessed an interesting behaviour of the head of the Tarawele family in Niagassola, who 15 years ago was very proud that his family belonged to slaves and only its members could be sacrificed to the patron-spirit of the village, before human sacrifices were replaced by the sacrifice of a bull or a cow. His father told in a conversation with me (and he himself confirmed it) that the patron-spirit of the Niagassola village said that only Tarawele could enter his house. So, the welfare of the village depended on the Tarawele family. In 2014, he stated that they have not been the slaves (according to the clan affiliation), and there was not any slavery for hundreds of years in Manden! So, we can see how the perception of the history changes when values change.

came to Manden from Wagadou.

In his epic story about Sunjata, the griot Fadigi Sisoko spoke about only 33 clans *tuntan mɔgɔ*: 16 *tuntan jɔn* (clans of warriors), 4 clans of "keepers of secrets" — *jabi fin jɔn*, 5 families of *Mamuru* (descendants), 5 clans of *mori* (one clan of patriarchs and 4 of those who came later) and 1 clan — *mɔgɔ fin mɔgɔ* (extra-caste) (Johnson, 2003: 112). In *Sunjata Fasa* (laudatory song for Sunjata), the griots told about a great meeting *Kalaben*, where Sunjata, his war lords and some leaders of clans discussed the creation of the Mali social system. As they said, there were "*Ton-ta-jɔn tan ni woro, jalifɛn cɛ seegi, mori kanda loolu ani mɔgɔ-fɛ-mɔgɔ konondo* (16 clans of noble, 8 clans of griots (artisans), 5 marabouts and 9 clans of other ethnic groups that took part in Mali creation)" (Smith, 2011: 31).

Griot Wa Kamissoko in his narration about the history of Mali noted that all 33 clans were warriors: "*Tuma min na n'a ye Nyani Mamaru lasigi yen Manden yan o lon, nwana min bɛ Manden yan, o ye siya bi saba ani saba le ye, o kelen kelen bɛ y'a ta mako nyɛ Manden*" (When Niani Mamuru settled in Manden, 33 clans of "knights, warriors" were in Manden, and they all served Manden) (Cisse & Kamissoko, 2000: 82). Siriman Kuyate, the leading griot of the Kuyate family from Niagassola, explained the text of the Charter in 1998 about the free men (*hɔrɔn*) of 29 clans as follows: (1) 16 *tontigi* families warriors are Traore, Condé, Camara (Kamara), Kourouma, Kamissoko, Magassouba, Diawara, Sako, Fofana, Koita, Dansouba, Diaby, Diallo, Diakité, Sidibé and Sangaré (Mangoné, 2006) [1]; (2) *mansare* (the rulers) are Koulibaly, Douno or Soumano, or Danhon or Somono, Konaté and Keita, but the leaders of the empire are Keita; (3) *mori* (marabouts) — Cissé, Bereté, Touré, Diané and Sylla, or Koma; (4) *jeli* (griots) — Kouyaté and Diabaté (today — Keita, Condé, Kanté, Kourouma, Koita, Touré, Diawara, etc.); (5)

---

[1] In different versions of the Charter, the list of warrior clans can vary, for example, the version of the Charter from the Guinean website, the version of the griot Karamoo Adama Diabate (Dioubate). This Charter or the Manden Constitution was transmitted orally by Balla Fasseke Kouyate.

fina or *finɛ* — only Camara; (6) *numu* (blacksmiths) — Kanté, Camara, Kourouma. At the same time, blacksmiths are divided into *numu fin* (those who work with iron, women of this clan are potters), *siaki* (those who work with precious metals making jewelry), *kule* (those who work with wood making wooden sculptures, masks); (7) *garanke* — leatherworkers, some of them — *sake* — specially made horse harness. They were mainly representatives of Sylla *dyamu*. All *nyamakala* could not be slaves. The people were afraid of them and had to give them livelihood and gifts (Niane, 2009; Kouyate, 2015).

As to dividing into the clans or castes, the Charter fixed the professional identity for certain *dyamu*; therefore, it happened after the victory of Sunjata. Three articles of the Charter are devoted to the *dyamu* division.

Article 1: The Great Mande Society is divided into sixteen clans of quiver carriers, five clans of marabouts, four groups of "*nyamakala*" and one group of slaves. Each of these groups has an activity and a specific role. (SK)[①]

The 4 royal families are Daon, Koulibaly, Keita and Konate.

The 16 quiver carriers are Traore, Kourouma, Diabate, Dembele, Cissoko, Kamissoko, Sinayoko, Fofana, Neita, Koita, Cherif, Ouattara, Conde, Dansoko, Camara and Ouedraogo.

The 5 families of marabouts are Diane, Berete, Toure, Cisse and Sylla.

The 4 mediators of Mandingo are:

(1) *Djeli* or griots;

(2) Thoroughbred *fina* or Camara (endogamy);

(3) *Noumou* or blacksmith;

(4) *Garanke* or leather worker.

The slave class are prisoners of war or bought slaves. (BF)[②]

Article 2: The "*nyamakala*" have a duty to tell leaders the truth, be their

---

① SK — the variant of Siriman Kuyate (Mangoné, 2006),

② BF — the variant of Balla Fasseke Kouyate (Diakite, 2015).

In the variant of Balla Fasseke Kouyate all *dyamu* are listed in detail, while Siriman Kuyate listed them separately in his "explanations" as was already written above.

advisers and defend with the verb the rules laid down, and the law and the order on the whole territory. (SK)

Article 2: The post of personal advisor to the king is granted to the *djeli*.(BF)

Article 3: The *morinkanda lolu* (five classes of Marabouts) are our masters and our teachers in Islam. Everyone owes them respect and consideration. (SK)

Article 3: The five clans of marabouts are our teachers and our educators in Islam. Everyone has to hold them in respect and consideration. (BF)

Article 13: Never offend the nyara (griots). (SK)

It should be added that although many scholars consider the Charter of Kurukan Fuga and *The Hunters' Oath* to be one and the same document, there is not a word in *The Hunters' Oath* about the social division of the society and about *dyamu*. *The Hunters' Oath* is an oral document of the Hunters' Union, and these two documents have something in common only in terms of declaration of a humane treatment among people and human rights.

3   The structure of the *dyamu* system

When one mentioned about *dyamu*, the freemen *hɔrɔn* (warriors or farmers) and the caste men *nyamakala* are always noted. The first are Manden families, as well as Fula and Soninke families; *mansare* are only the Manden, descendants of Sunjata; all marabouts are the Soninke.

As to the caste men *nyamakala,* only griots are the Manden. The blacksmiths are the Susu by the origin, as they originated from the ruler of the Susu empire Sumaoro Kante, while *fina* are from Soninke, only from the Camara family. And we can see that in both versions of the Charter the griots' role as personal advisor of the king, who have to defend with the verb the rules laid down, and the law and order on the whole territory are mentioned separately. So, that is why they must be from the Manden peoples.

It is interesting that during my research I always heard that some *dyamu* belonged to the Fula, while for others their nationality was not indicated. Moreover, in the conversations, the griot does not classify the Fula as free men, although the Fula, according to Siriman Kuyate's definition, belong to warriors. In the epic stories they are warriors, heroes, who serve the king, or enemies (they can steal cows from bamana). That is because only several Fula clans are the part of the Manden *dyamu* system.

So, the Manden peoples themselves turned out to be "free" (warriors and rulers), and only some of them are the griots, a caste which is most closely associated with the "free men", with *mansare*. All other families from different nations occupied other niches in the system and got a professional affiliation. The Soninke from the large Camara clan that owned the land of Manden were distributed among noblemen and caste men, and it was the Soninke who turned out to be the marabouts. The Fula herders, who joined first to the army of Sunjata, occupied their place among the warriors. It should be noted that the Bamana or Maninka most often use the word *siya* "people" when it comes to *dyamu*. Although marabouts occupied an exclusively professional niche, they are "noble" (but not warriors) and their status is much higher than that of the *nyamakala*. So we can construct the following table (see Table 1).

Table 1.   The correlation of *dyamu* and *ethnicity*

Social and Professional Affiliation		Ethnicity
free/nobles *hɔrɔn*	*mansare* (chiefs)	Manden (Maninka)
	tontigi (warriors)	Manden, Soninke, Fula
	mori (marabouts)	Soninke
caste men *nyamakala*	*jeli* (griots)	Manden (Maninka initially)
	numu (blacksmiths)	Susu
	garanke (leatherworkers)	(Often from the griot families)
	Fina	Soninke
Slaves *jɔn*	*mine jɔn* (who was captured in war) and *san jɔn* (who was bought)	Manden, Soninke, Fula (warriors , not *nyamakala*)
	woloso (who was born in the house)	

So *dyamu* is a social group. It is related to ethnicity and the origin, as well as to the history of the Mali Empire foundation. It has also become a kind of tool for the accession of new people to it. Representatives of other ethnic groups can enter this system by connecting their history with the history of the Manden, attributing to their ancestors' ties with Manden or entering the system through the so-called slavery (war slaves), when a slave in the third generation receives the *dyamu* of his patron. So, the Dogons turned out to be Keita's younger brothers, because according to their oral tradition their ancestors have come from the Manden just during the formation of the Mali Empire. Now the Dogons are the partners of Keita in joking relations (Куценков et al., 2020). The *senankuya* tradition is also connected with the *dyamu* system, and it introduces additional links between peoples or clans and ethnic groups.

4 Senankuya

In the Charter of Kurukan Fuga, the s*enankuya* institute is announced separately as it plays a great role in the West African society. It presumably appeared back in the era of the Ghana Empire, but officially (according to the oral tradition) it was fixed just in the Charter as the relationship of "joking kinship" between the corresponding *dyamu* and certain groups.

Article 7: "The *sanankunya* (joking relationship) and the *tanamaanyoonya* (blood pact) have been established among the Mandenkas[①]. Consequently, any contention that occurs among these groups should not degenerate the respect for one another being the rule. Between brothers-in-law and sisters-in-law, between grandparents and grandchildren, tolerance should be the principle" (Mangoné, 2006: 75).

Every member of the Manden society belongs to several groups. There are at least 4 types of joking relationship: *senankuya* (between *dyamu)*, *mamarenya* (between grandparents and grandchildren), *nimogoya* (between husband or wife

---

① *Mandenka*: the inhabitant of the Manden land.

and their younger relatives by marriage), *filanya* (between representatives of the same age class).

These types of joking relationships allow certain groups to avoid tensions in relationships between them and make communication to be more equal and open with the help of humour and play. This type of interaction includes teasing, verbal abuse, horseplay and so on. *Senankuya* is also a certain mechanism that allows members of other ethnic or professional groups into the system, to establish additional connections between all groups, which relieves tension in communication and makes the system more open. The whole ethnic groups are involved in the *senankuya* system, for example, Fula and Dogon peoples in Mali are the participants in the system of joking kinship along with castes. And in Mali one could hear the proposals to use their *senanku* (the partners in joking relationship) to resolve the modern conflict between them.

In general, the joking relationships are the same among all West African peoples. But there are also some nuances. For example, the Dogons (Mali) have at least two degrees of joking relationships (in the Tenkan language — *boinjangu*): relationship by blood or by brotherhood and neighborhood. The first type of *senankuya* Dogons have with Bozo, Maninka and some Kulibali (Bamana) families. This type of *senankuya* exists where several ethnic groups live side by side.[①] The second, "neighborly" variant of the Dogon joking relationships applies to the Fula, Tuareg and Arabs (Moors). It should be specially noted that among the Dogons, the institution of joking relationships continues to expand today. For example, Tuaregs and Arabs (Moors) were named Dogon's *senanku* for the first time only in the announcement of the II Dogon Culture Festival Ogobania (January 2016).[②] I suppose that this second "neighborly" variant of *senankuya* is common to all Manden peoples, though they do not distinguish it

---

① It can be assumed that this is a special relationship between any contacting groups that had or have the possibility of social conflict during integration into a single nation and their professional functions often lead to inevitable contradictions.

② The information was received by Kutsenkov Peter from Bokari Gindo (from Ende village, Mali) in January 2020.

separately. But Maninka also spoke about main *senanku* and some additional *senanku* in different regions.

There is a complex system of relationships in the Manden society. For example, the Union of Hunters is associated with the ruling system as all the leaders were also the hunters. The hunters themselves have connections with *soma* — "sorcerer, witch doctor", who help them with their work. Each group has its own secrets and fetishes. Each *dyamu* has its secrets concerning their main activity, as well as family fetishes. The leaders of the families in Niagassola and other villages of this region told me about these fetishes in 1999. Today due to the new rise of Islam in the society they don't like to talk about it. But I'm sure they don't abandon them. So, for the Kante family of blacksmiths, this is the secret of making iron. As to the ruling Keita family, their fetishes open them the secrets of power and social management. These fetishes are in the hands of the elders in the family and allow them to lead people correctly. Each *dyamu* also has its own patron spirits and a place of worship. In Niagassola, for example, there were patron spirits of the village itself, of the hunters, of the Keita family and the family of blacksmiths Kante. These are only those that I knew for sure and the legends about which were recorded.

Today a group has emerged that is of higher priority for the Manden people — a religious community — Islam, a group that unites the entire system. At the same time, other groups are losing their power and significance. Today, their system is simplified. In principle, the system of *dyamu* is changing its meaning today, approaching the surnames in the cities. But *senankuya* does not lose its significance, quite the contrary. Today, this kind of relations began to extend to the relationship between representatives of different faiths. A Muslim can joke about a Christian, marking that Christians drink a lot; a Christian can make a joke about the muezzin shouting too loudly, etc. The situation took place in a Dogon village and was told me by Kutsenkov in 2019. But none of them may offend the other. Everything happens as part of a joke, without any aggression.

5 The role of *dyamu* and *senankuya* in the Manden society

The *dyamu* system is the system of organisation of Mali Empire, so the main families of Soninke, Susu and Fula, interacting with the Manden peoples and residing on their territory, were included in it. The griot Fa-Digi Sisoko, for example, spoke about 12 clans of Soninke (*maraka*) and 16 Fula from Wagadou (Johnson, 2003).[①] One can assume that one of the functions of epic stories about Sunjata is an explanation of the history of the origin of Manden clans. As to *senankuya*, it reduces the confrontation between the ruling clans and others, as well as between some castes and ethnic groups. Therefore, in Manden, they say that since Keita is everywhere in Manden, they are *senanku* to everyone others.

Different regions of Mali and Guinea have different *dyamu* sets, which is quite natural. Accordingly, the griots store the information about the *dyamu* only of their region, and they often say that there are no such people here, and they do not know anything about them. Thus, the lists of joking relationship partners may also differ slightly. Sometimes griots say the main *senanku* (a partner in joking relationship) of *dyamu1* is *dyamu2*, but besides that, it is *dyamu3 and dyamu4*.

Griots say that all the Manden lands originally belonged to the Camara, therefore they are so numerous, and first they were not divided into professional castes. Now there are "free" Camara. Sometimes they are ranked among the rulers. Camara could be found among *nyamakala* of all castes, and Camara *fina* is the only fully endogamous group.

They were not conquered or uprooted from their lands. Manden and others only settled nearby and concluded the agreement with Camara as I was told by the people interviewed in Niagassola and Siguiri. The Guinean historian Tamsir Niani wrote that in Kurukan Fugan Sunjata had shared the lands, the blessed

---

① In Siguiri, it was said that not all Fula are participants of the *senankuya* relationship with Manden in Guinea, just several families. But all the Fula take part in joking relations with other ethnic groups.

Kita country had been retained for his people, but Camara remained the owner of the lands (Niane, 1960).

However, there are other interpretations of the history of Camara. Camara Lei told that Camara's leader had not agreed to bow to Sunjata and had been killed by the poisoned arrow of Fa Koli (Camara, 1953).

So, I suppose those Camara, who was the first to unite with Sunjata, became the warriors and those, who refused, became people of casts.

There are *dyamu* also, which are perceived as the same in different regions.

All these *dyamu* will have the same partners in joking relationships and prohibitions since they have the same ancestor. It indicates that the *dyamu* system has evolved over time, including more and more clans, as the empire of Mali itself expanded and the number of regions in the sphere of its influence increased also. Later the *dyamu* system turned out to be even more durable and stable than the Mali empire itself, and it continued the further expanding.

The *Senankunya* system, like the *dyamu* system, is very complex. There are some "original" *dyamu*, that, according to the legends, appeared, during the Susu-Manden war or even well before it.

Diarra are allies of Keita in bamana regions. sometimes they say that it's the same as Keita there. It leads to some variation in *Senankunya* ties as well.

So, just to summarise, the *dyamu* system as well as the division into the castes, was created to organise the relations between the Manden people and the Susu, Soninke and Fula families that joined them in the Mali empire. Although some *dyamu* names existed before. Respectively, it was Manden people who occupied the higher positions in the hierarchy according to their contribution to the victory and formation of the Mali Empire. The *dyamu* names are perceived as laudatory, and the main story of their origin or their etymology is recorded in the epic about Sunjata — the history of Manden peoples' victory. Often, the legends of some *senankuya* origins can also be found in the same place, as, for example, the history of the relationship between Diabate, Tarawele and Konate — the story about two brother-hunters and how they had brought the future mother of Sunjata to Manden.

The *senankuya* system was formed after the adoption of the Charter (as griots told), and aimed to reduce tension in the social interaction of various *dyamu*, as well as of other groups where inequality is implied.

When the interviews about the main characteristics of the members of different *dyamu* were conducted among the young Guinean people, first everyone named their professional qualities. So, even today *dyamu* is associated primarily with its professional activities. Neither stereotypes were revealed towards various *dyamu* groups, nor a disdainful attitude of "noble" *dyamu* to the "casted". At the same time, when we asked to name any well-known Maninka *dyamu* and to write three words characterising each of them, the absolute majority named Keita and Kuyate, the rest of the *dyamu* were little represented. So, for example, representatives of these two clans were characterised as follows: "Keita is a warrior. He is powerful, authoritative, a chieftain of the Manden, kind, amiable, honest/loyal, accepting decisions and allocator of income and expenses. Kuyate speaks a lot. He is energetic, amiable, a master of the word, educated, a historian who knows how to make a profit, a "storehouse" of speeches and histories, intelligent, peaceful, uniting people.[1]

Dyamu is not only the basis of the system of social organisation, but it is also the point of pride for all the Manden peoples, as well as their concept of *mɔgɔya* (humanity). These concepts distinguish them from other peoples, as they say.[2] As for their history, it is based on the epic about Sunjata and the Charter. They form every member of the Manden society. In this case, the degree of their real historicity is not a matter. The people believe them. As the Charter says, "A lie that has existed for 40 years can be considered as the truth."

During the expedition, we asked Maninka people to answer three times

---

① The information was obtained through surveys of Maninka students in Guinea in 2014.

② The concept *mɔgɔya* includes a notion of priority of society over an individual, interrelation of people, and their interdependency. According to *mɔgɔya*, people's relationships are based on unity, debt, understanding, intellect and reciprocity. *Mɔgɔ* is not a human being but a person as the part of society.

the question "Who are you?" (As if you need to say the most important information about yourself in one word). In 1999, most of the respondents said first: "I am the Guinean", and only after it they named their *dyamu*. In 2014, the overwhelming majority of respondents first of all mentioned their *dyamu*, and then they told about their professional activities, only after that all they said: "I am the Maninka" or "I am the Guinean".

Thus, it can be said with confidence that identification by *dyamu* is the most important in the Manden's self-identification system. In this case, however, it should be kept in mind that *dyamu* itself carries a significant amount of information about ethnic identification, since some *dyamu* belong to Maninka, others to Fula, etc. But it is obvious that nationality and ethnicity have still faded into the background compared to *dyamu*. It is also necessary to note a decrease in importance of such a concept as nationality among Guineans, which accordingly indicates a decrease in patriotism in the country in its turn. You can see that the people of Manden always identify themselves by local affiliation and, when speaking about themselves, always clearly define where they are from. This is also facilitated by the *dyamu* system, since *dyamu* are few and both the place and the ancestors are important for finding out one's exact origin, as well as for a person's self-identification.

The important norms and prohibitions associated with the *dyamu* system are essential for its existence. Prohibition of marriages with certain *dyamu* and establishing marital preferences ensure the preservation of the system in its original form and protect it from destruction, strengthening group cohesion as well as ethnic stability within the system. As it was the main goal to integrate various clans and peoples in the Malian Empire in one system, as well as to determine their place in accordance with the merits of their ancestors. In fact, today in Guinea the government tries to maintain interethnic ties both in families and in political organisations. It is necessary now in the multi-ethnic society, although it destroys the *dyamu* system. The regular addressing to the ancestors was necessary for concretisation of one's origin, and for connection with the history, which in its turn ensures the ties between generations and the preservation of traditions. Here it is necessary to remember one of the basic Manden rules — the respect for elders, which defines a real member of the society.

It is the *senankuya* system, which is precisely aimed at smoothing out the rigidity of the system, eliminating possible conflicts that could occur in relations between *dyamu*. Of course, *senankuya* is not the only mechanism aimed at reducing conflicts in the Manden society, but this tradition was based on the *dyamu* system.

One of the main functions of every culture is an adaptation. Each culture develops a mechanism for human adaptation not only to nature, but also to the society. Since every society has both internal and external conflicts, then, of course, it must also have mechanisms to resolve them. There are certain mechanisms in Manden society that allow you to maintain balance, mitigate internal and external social conflicts, and help members of the community to overcome psychological crises. These institutions not only smooth out interethnic and social contradictions, but also help a person to go calmly through all stages of psychological development, growing up, and to protect him from stress and disorientation. One of these mechanisms is *dyamu*; some others are the division into age classes, initiation tradition and joking relationships. Vydrin writes in this regard: "Ethnologists have repeatedly noted that the joking relationship in West Africa is a peculiar way to identify areas of potential and real conflicts between groups and to sublimate them, transforming them into a carnival form. It is not for nothing that it is actively (and, admittedly, effectively) exploited by the current government of Mali: "joking relationship" is viewed at the highest political level of the country as a serious means to prevent the emergence of interethnic tension" (Выдрин, 1998: 239).

Senankuya also equates interethnic relations with intergroup (inter-clan) ones. Fula's partners in joking relationships in Mali are all the blacksmiths. In Guinea Fula's *senanku* are the blacksmiths and the Tunkara clan. Since the Fula are shepherds, and one of the main consumers of the products of blacksmiths, disputes and conflicts are possible between these two groups, but they can solve the problems with the help of jokes. In Senegambia Fula's main partners are Serera. In Mali the Keita clan is the *senankuya* partners of Dogons. Dogons have their legend of the origin of this relationship.[1] Some other ethnic couples of *senankuya* can be named also: Dogon — Bozo, Maninka — Soninke, Looma — Maninka, etc.

So potential conflicts between these ethnic groups pass into the sphere of comic ritual and can be resolved.

6 Conclusion

Manden humor is one of the social regulators, through the various feelings that it can evoke. It affects members of society. Humor can cause a sense of shame, and guilty (for antisocial behaviour). For example, this is an effect of *Koteba* folk theater. Humor can make it easy to talk about the important things — this is how the *Koreduga* jesters do. As for the *senankuya*, within these relations humor and play allow people to relieve tension in communication between certain groups, allow them to express dissatisfaction with each other and even to express aggression in a humoristic way. In addition, play and joke make it easy to communicate even with strangers, to introduce strangers or representatives of other nations into the collective. As we can see there are many different variants of joking relationships. Some of them are dying off in the form in which it was

---

[1] "Once two brothers were traveling from the 'Mande Country'. On the way, the younger brother was completely exhausted from hunger and hardships and told the elder brother that he could not go further. Then the elder brother cut off a piece of meat from his leg, cooked it, and fed the younger one. After that, they went further and came to the place where Mopti is now. There the elder brother stayed (for fishing), while the younger went further to look for a place suitable for farming. He settled on the rocks of Bandiagara. A year later, the younger brother's son was born. According to an ancient tradition, he brought his firstborn son to the family of the elder brother to raise him. By that time, the first son was born in the elder brother's family also. Another year passed. The younger brother went to visit his son, but when he arrived, he found out that his son had died. The elder brother took the younger one to the grave of his son, and said that he buried his first child alive with his nephew" (Завьялова & Куценков, 2020: 153). The similar legend is about the origin of joking relationship of the Bozos and the Dogon (see ibid).

originally, such as *filanya* — between those, who were initiated at the same time (because the circumcision takes place in hospitals in infancy). But as Siriman Kuyate correctly noted, this kind of relationship will inevitably go over into the sphere of communication between people, who for a long time belonged to any closed group (classmates, colleagues, etc.), something similar exists in many other cultures (Kouyaté, 2003). So we can see how the traditional mechanisms can transform today.

Today *senankuya* does not need to change. This institution only expands and becomes more flexible, adapting to new realities; while *dyamu* system is transformed to a large extent, since some of its functions have already lost their significance today and do not correspond to the modern challenges facing multinational and multi-ethnic societies such as the societies of Mali or Guinea. Nevertheless, it can be argued that being a source of pride for the Manden peoples and a significant part of their tradition and history, *dyamu* will not lose its significance for them either.

Today in Mali, there is a strategy for the development of a "secondary" *senankuya*, an agreement on mutual friendship and joking kinship, supported at the government level. So, among the Dogons, for example, the Tuareg turned out to be "secondary" *senanku* and there is an attempt to declare the Fulbe as such, which will lead to a complete ban on attacks on each other. This could be observed at the Ogobagna festival in Bamako in 2022.

References

ВЫДРИН В Ф, 1998. "Fúlà tɛ́fóyi yé!" Образ малийских фульбе в баманских байках, анекдотах, размышлениях [C]. Язык. Африка. Фульбе. Сборник научных статей в честь Антонины Ивановны Коваль / ред. В. Ф. Выдрин и А. А. Кибрик. СПб.; М.: Европейский Дом.

ЗАВЬЯЛОВА О Ю, КУЦЕНКОВ П А, 2020. Смеховая культура народов Мали и Гвинеи (сенанкуя) [J]. Восток. Афро-азиатские общества: история и современность, (4): 150-160

КУЦЕНКОВ П А, ГИНДО Б, КАССАМБАРА М, ЗАВЬЯЛОВА О Ю, 2020.

Периодизация истории в устных исторических преданиях догонов и манден [J]. Вестник Санкт-Петербургского университета: Востоковедение и африканистика, 12 (1): 100-112.

CAMARA L, 1953. L'Enfant Noir [M]. Paris: Editions Plon.

CISSE Y, 2014. Manden donsolu Kalikan [EB/OL]. (2014-02-03) [2021-01-03]. https://fasokan.wordpress.com/2014/02/03/manden-donsolu-kalikan/.

CISSE Y, KAMISSOKO W, 2000. La grande geste du Mali [M]. Paris: Karthala. T. 1. Des origines à la fondation de l'Empire.

CISSE Y, KAMISSOKO W, 2009. La grande geste du Mali [M]. Paris: Karthala. T. 2. Soundjata la gloire du Mali.

DIAKITE D, 2015. La Charte du Mandingue [EB/OL]. (2015-08-09) [2020-11-01]. http://www.mandiana.com/publications/la-charte-du-mandingue.

JOHNSON J W, 2003. Son-Jara. The Mande Epic Performance by Jeli Fa-Digi Sisòkò [M]. Indiana: Indiana UP.

KOUYATE M, 2015. La variabilité dans quatre versions de l'épopée mandingue[D]. Bordeaux: Linguistics Université Michel de Montaigne — Bordeaux III.

KOUYATE S, 1999. La charte de Kurukanfuga [EB/OL]. (1999-09-30) [2020-11-12]. http://www.humiliationstudies.org/documents/KaboreLaCharteDeKurukafuga.pdf.

KOUYATE S, 2003. Le cousinage à plaisanterie: notre héritage commun [M]. Conakry: Ganndal.

MANGONÉ N, 2006. The Kurukan Fuga Charter: an example of an endogenous governance mechanism for conflict prevention [C] // Inter-generational Forum on Endogenous Governance in West Africa. Ouagadougou: Burkina Faso.

NIANE D T, 1960. Soundjata ou l'épopée mandingue [M]. Paris: Présence africaine.

NIANE D T, 1984. Mali and the second Mandingo expansion. Africa from the twelfth to the sixteenth century [M]. NIANE D T. International Scientific Committee for the Drafting of a General History of Africa. London: University of California Press.

NIANE D T, 1992. Sundiata: an epic of old Mali [M]. Harlow: Longman African Classics.

NIANE D T, 2009. La Charte de Kurukan Fuga aux sources d'une pensee politique en Afrique [R] Conakry: Republique de Guinee.

SMITH M C, 2011. The Mande kora: a West African system of thought. Collected writings, essays, and interviews from 35 years of ethnic music research [OL].

Tuebingen: Germany. https://www.yumpu.com/en/document/read/30392183/the-mande-kora-a-system-of-thought-university-of-maine-at-augusta.

UNESCO, 2009. Manden Charter, proclaimed in Kurukan Fuga [EB/OL]. [2020-12-18]. https://ich.unesco.org/en/RL/manden-charter-proclaimed-in-kurukan-fuga-00290?RL=00290.

VYDRIN V, MASLINSKY K, MERIC J J, 2019. Bamadaba/Jamu [EB/OL]. (2019-10-22) [2021-01-01]. https://github.com/maslinych/bamadaba/blob/master/jamuw.txt.

（编辑：李春光）

A Reflection on French Language Teaching and the Place of Evaluation in a Previously Disadvantaged Multicultural Setting: A Case Study of Rhodes University, South Africa[①]

Arthur Mukenge   Emmanuel Naancin Dami
School of Languages and Literatures, Rhodes University

Abstract: The teaching and learning of French in particular and foreign languages in general are, today, an integral part and parcel of many academic disciplines across the globe. Pursuant to this, several teaching models and learning manuals have been developed in an attempt to deliver a qualitative content and output to the various actors. However, these efforts cannot claim to have eradicated all the problems and difficulties encountered in the field of teaching and learning languages. The challenges vary according to the various geographical settings, culture, learning and teaching abilities and many other factors. Over the years, scholars and teachers of foreign languages have had to contend with a plethora of challenges in the teaching process. As such, there exists a body of research that has had to tackle several aspects of the concern raised. This paper targets information dissemination and experience sharing. French teaching as a foreign language forms the basis for this reflection. As such, adhering but not limited to conventional teaching

---

① **Date of reception:** 2021-01-10.

Authors: Arthur Mukenge, Associate Professor of French Language and Francophone Literatures at the School of Languages and Literatures of Rhodes University; Research fields: francophone African literature, French didactics and translation; Email: a.mukenge@ru.ac.za. Emmanuel Naancin Dami, Postdoctoral Fellow at the School of Languages and Literatures of Rhodes University; Research fields: African literature, and French didactics; Email: daminaancinemmanuelbelc@gmail.com.

patterns, it relates the path taken by two academics towards improving the teaching experience in practical terms. A special emphasis is laid on the importance of regular evaluation of the learning trajectory of the student and on the teachers' methods in a challenging environment. This article concludes that curriculum update, teacher-student extra-curricular fora, regular and sustained evaluation, teacher refresher training, student motivation and students' feedback are, *inter alia*, conditions in the success of a population that had previously been deprived of foreign language learning opportunities in South Africa.

Keywords: language teaching; language learning; evaluation; cultures; tutors/ teachers

对在具有历史性劣势的多元文化环境下法语教学与评估的反思：以南非罗德斯大学为例

亚瑟·穆肯盖　伊曼纽尔·那安钦·达米

罗德斯大学语言文学学院

摘　要： 外语教学和学习，包括法语教学与学习，是当今国际学术研究的一个组成部分。因此，研究者们提出了多种教学模式和学习指南，以期为实践者们提供参考。然而，这些努力并不能解决语言教学与学习中遇到的所有问题和困难。语言教学与学习的挑战随地理环境、文化、学习与教学能力等诸多因素的变化而变化。这些年来，外语教学相关学者和教师不得不面对教学过程中出现的诸多挑战。因此，针对不同挑战的相关研究也相继出现。本文旨在分享我们在外语教学，尤其是在法语教学中的反思和经验。在坚持常规教学模式的基础上，我们在教学实践中采取了一些改进措施。我们特别注重定期评估学生学习轨迹的重要性以及教师在南非这样一个充满挑战的环境中所采取的教学方法的重要性。通过实证研究，本文得出在这个很多人曾被剥夺了学习外语机会的南非，教学大纲的更新、师生课外活动论坛、定期与持续评估、教师进修培训、学生动机和学生反馈等因素是影响外语教学的重要因素。

关键词： 语言教学；语言学习；评估；文化；助教/教师

1　Introduction

In simple terms, "language education is the formal acquisition or learning

Arthur Mukenge   A Reflection on French Language Teaching and the Place of Evaluation
Emmanuel Naancin Dami   in a Previously Disadvantaged Multicultural Setting: A Case Study of
                        Rhodes University, South Africa

of communicative skills" (Enakome & Peter, 2015: 15). Therefore, to attain the lofty objectives of effective language teaching and productive learning, language manuals, for instance, the Common European Framework of Reference for Languages (2003) (CEFRL) clearly spells out four skills: writing, reading, speaking and listening. A reasonable acquisition of the said competencies is consequently the kernel of language teaching and learning activities. This, however, comes at a cost especially to the tutor who has to deal with myriads of challenges in the teaching process.

This study is a reflection on managing a language class in a multicultural and multiracial environment. French teaching in this setting is the subject of investigation. As such, Rhodes University, South Africa will be the case study. The study shall identify some of the challenges faced by tutors/teachers and the learners bordering on assessment and evaluation in such a multicultural setting and explain how such could be explored to the benefit of the learner. In addition, this paper is important since it details some steps and innovations taken by the teachers in an attempt to overcome the challenges and to assist the tutors to attain their objectives. If one of the goals the framers of the CEFRL had in mind was "[t]o encourage practitioners in the language field to reflect on their current practice, particularly in relation to learners' practical language learning needs, the setting of suitable objectives and the tracking of learner progress" (North, 2006: 2), then, by sharing our experience, we intend to challenge our readers all over the world to think out of the box and possibly push the boundaries of foreign language teaching to new limits when and if required. This would benefit other colleagues who could be facing similar issues in the field.

2 The Rhodes University working environment

In South Africa, like elsewhere in the world, the challenges of teaching French as a foreign language at the advanced and university levels abound. This is because the foreign language classroom setting is multicultural in nature. This is not different at Rhodes University. At this institution, a normal French class comprises different categories of learners ranging from "grands débutants, faux débutants" [1] and, more often than not, the descendants of the Huguenot tribes[2] conveniently considered native speakers when compared to the others. As such, the teacher is confronted with a scenario in which the true practice of French teaching is a curious blend of French as a native and foreign language because of the country's historical peculiarity.

The French Department is considered an asset of the School of Languages and Literatures at Rhodes University in South Africa. Rhodes University is a public research institution of higher learning located in the city centre of Grahamstown, Eastern Cape Province, South Africa. It is one of the four universities in the province. Established in 1904, Rhodes University is the province's oldest university. According to the Center for World University Rankings (2022), it ranks 10th of the 24 universities in the Country and 1313th in the world.

The university had an enrolment of over 8,000 multiracial and multicultural students in the 2020 academic year, of whom over half were residents in 51 residences on campus, with the rest (known as *Oppidans*) taking residence in digs (off-campus residences) or in their own homes.

On the other hand, the School of Languages and Literatures is an exciting and dynamic unit within the faculty of humanities. It currently offers courses in the following areas of language and literary studies: African language studies, Afrikaans and Netherlandic studies, Chinese studies, Classical studies, cultures and languages in Africa, French studies, German studies, modern fiction, and creative writing.

French as an academic discipline at Rhodes University and in most parts of the world is demanding in many ways since the tutor/teacher has to be an excellent speaker, writer and researcher in the field. Teaching the French language at Rhodes University equally presupposes a mastery of literature

① Absolute and false beginners.
② The contributions of the Huguenots in South Africa by Vilpen.

Arthur Mukenge   A Reflection on French Language Teaching and the Place of Evaluation
Emmanuel Naancin Dami   in a Previously Disadvantaged Multicultural Setting: A Case Study of
                         Rhodes University, South Africa

written in the language (French and Francophone). This is not out of place given the place of the language on the African continent and the world at large. French is an important tool of communication in the modern world. This romance language is one of the two most widely spoken European languages in Africa and is equally spoken on the five continents with an estimated 300 million speakers around the globe (Wood, 2019).

3 Background to the challenges of French language teaching and learning at Rhodes University

While sharing our personal teaching trajectory of the French language forms, the fulcrum of this article, considering a few facts and figures, might help in understanding the teaching dynamics in South Africa in general and at Rhodes University in particular. This has a direct nexus with the geographical and institutional context within which one teaches and students learn. Comparatively, South Africa has just emerged from one of the harshest and most dehumanising colonial pasts in Africa.

The World Population Review (2022) states that South Africa is home to five racial groups. Of the total South African population at the time, 79.4 percent declared themselves to be Sub-Saharan African while 9.2 percent were shown as whites, 8.8 percent colored and 2.6 percent Indian or Asian. There was a final category shown as unspecified/other but the results were negligible and as such were ultimately omitted. The country uses 11 official languages, including Zulu, Xhosa, Afrikaans, English, Sepedi, Setswana, Sesotho, Xitsonga, Swati, Tshivenda, and Ndebele.

If the above figures are anything to go by, the overall total number of Sub-Saharan South Africans in the country more than doubles the other races combined. However, the historical legacy of the apartheid system of government has left many Sub-Saharan South Africans with a huge gap in education. However, South Africa made significant changes in all spheres of its endeavours after the 1994 elections that brought Nelson Mandela, the first black man, to occupy the seat of power as president. This led to the abolition of the apartheid system of governance. Worthy of note is that the post-apartheid elites of South Africa embarked on the restructuration of the educational system to redress inequalities that hitherto, put a vast majority of its population at a huge disadvantage. For example, the apartheid governments restricted the blacks' education to what is today referred to as the "Bantu system of education". The reform is palpable at Rhodes University, an institution conceived as a "whites-only" centre of higher teaching and learning. Although huge leaps have been made in this regard, the university is still in the process of transforming to become more representative of the diverse South African demography. In the first year of the French course for instance, the number of black students has steadily increased over the years (since 2007). Therefore, one easily appreciates the great challenge in dealing with a student body that is very much conscious of its diversity.

Students at Rhodes have very different backgrounds. A significant percentage speaks more of the indigenous languages than English, which doubles as the language of instruction. This makes language teaching and learning arduous. It is needless to mention that the problem becomes hydra-headed for those who elect to learn French as another new language. They have problems understanding the English grammar and structure which share many similarities with Indo-European languages. Most of the students have no background knowledge of French. The varsity setting happens to be, more often than not, their first-ever encounter with the language. Therefore, teaching this course at that level gives us an opportunity to demonstrate innovativeness as teachers/lecturers.

Although French is spoken in most of the African countries, it was only a white privilege module in South Africa. Apartheid denied access to the majority of black students who desired to study the French language as a subject in various universities where French was taught.

This changed as part of the curriculum transformation upon our arrival at

Arthur Mukenge   A Reflection on French Language Teaching and the Place of Evaluation
Emmanuel Naancin Dami   in a Previously Disadvantaged Multicultural Setting: A Case Study of
                        Rhodes University, South Africa

Rhodes University in 2007. This happened at a critical time as the institution was going through some drastic measures of transformation. In the French Department, for instance, this was the very first time since its inception in 1904 that black lecturers were engaged to teach any "European language".

It was also the time when the institution was trying to boost the registration of socioeconomic and historically disadvantaged South African students. One must know that a good number of them come to Rhodes University with inadequate skills and a myopic cultural mind due to the tragic past. Most of this category of students is usually without any form of computer literacy. This is most appreciated when one considers the fact that these students are required to submit typed assignments and use electronic resources/devices for learning and practice. This is a big handicap in the learning process. Alan Kirkardly aptly captures it by asserting that "the Bantustan education promoted rote learning and stifled education" (Kirkardly, 1996: 21). It means that in general, white South Africans had more and better access to the French language than the vast majority of the population who, not only lacked basic literacy skills but also, were not culturally exposed and sensitive to other cultures. In this context, most post-apartheid curricula had to, at least take these issues into consideration. The post-apartheid government had the task of placing the historically disadvantaged South Africans on equal pedestals with those who had been privileged. As part of decolonising the curriculum, access to the French language is today more open to all and sundry. But this in itself created another challenge since most of the disadvantaged population never had the opportunity of learning French at basic or high schools. The university experience is almost always, their first encounter with the language as mentioned earlier. In this line, we applaud the emergence of the Outcome-Based Education (OBE), the South African Qualifications Authority (SAQA), and the Higher Education Quality Committee (HEQC), the National Qualifications Framework (NQF). All of them are saddled with the responsibility of enforcing quality and uniformity of standards across the board. These bodies describe the different levels and aspect-based outcomes at each level.

4 Situational paradigm shift and innovations

4.1 An introduction to the Preliminary French Programme

French Department at Rhodes University aims to foster a love for the French language, literature and culture; hence, a multi-media approach is used for teaching the language. The course offered, which starts at the beginners' level, enables students to understand the French and Francophone culture, speak, read, and write the language and study literature expressed in French. The practical components include business and tourism, knowledge of which has proven very valuable in a variety of careers.

In a bid to improve enrolment, the Department added a Preliminary French module geared towards equipping the absolute beginners with the necessary tools required for a deeper study of the language. French for beginners is a full-year's course consisting of 6 meetings of 50 minutes each per week. This lays the foundation upon which those who wish to take it as a major course could build. As such, the situation today is such that students at Rhodes can major up in French. The course is a 3-year major subject, that is to say, once students have satisfactorily completed French 1, they may proceed to French 2 and 3 respectively. Thereafter, if they so wish and have met all the requirements, they have the options of enrolling for French Honours, Masters and finally, the PhD.

The Preliminary French programme has turned out to be a positive experience for the department and for the students. With the post-apartheid reforms, everyone has equal access to learning provided that they meet the minimum requirements. As a result of this, the students have eventually realised that French is one of the languages that should be learned and used in the formal setting. Consequently, most African students from all over the humanities, take French as a subject — students who were previously disadvantaged by not getting a chance to learn English properly, *a priori*, and more often than not, developed a negative attitude vis-à-vis the French language. This has a significant impact on their determination to acquire the language and adversely influences their

Arthur Mukenge
Emmanuel Naancin Dami

A Reflection on French Language Teaching and the Place of Evaluation
in a Previously Disadvantaged Multicultural Setting: A Case Study of
Rhodes University, South Africa

attitude towards learning. However, after a while, we observed that they started developing a positive attitude and accepted French as one of the numerous African languages.

4.2　Innovations

Given the students' poor literacy background, we realised that deliberate and concerted efforts must be made to make the students work outside the regular class-contact periods. Although there are homework and assignments as would be discussed later, as lecturers, we go an extra mile by introducing the course on RUConnected, a Rhodes University electronic resource, to make students' learning easier and more interactive. This makes a huge difference because we notice that interaction begins at that point before the actual face-to-face contact. From the reactions or feedback we receive on this platform, we prepare and get more equipped for the next class interface. The students who have problems with some lessons in the class can connect to the online resource and continue learning at their own pace. In addition to this, we introduced extra lessons on Saturday mornings at no cost to the student. Although this is optional, we have made it a point of duty to identify the weakest students, point out their learning gaps to them and ask them to attend. This creates a strong mental attitude in the student as they feel carried along. It equally allows us to follow up on the week's objectives. At these extra classes, whatever was done or covered during the week is re-explained, retaught and the students are asked to redo their homework. This has proven to be quite effective as it enables slow learners to catch and make up for their deficiencies. This, to us, is a good step towards improving the students' understanding.

Another step taken to ensure we meet international standards in teaching and the evaluation of the French course is the introduction of the DELF[1]

---

[1] DELF (Diplôme d'Etude en Langue française) is a certification of French-language abilities for non-native speakers administered by the International Centre for French Studies by France's Ministry of Education in Paris.

preparatory classes and examinations in conjunction with the Alliance Française in Port Elizabeth. The organisation of DELF at Rhodes University came about as a result of many consultations that started in 2009 with the Alliance Française in Port Elizabeth, Pretoria and the French Embassy. After a series of meetings, all the collaborators came to an agreement to commence the DELF programme in the 2013 academic year. We went further afield to collect enough support material such as curriculum guidelines, textbooks, syllabuses and many more. These allow us to measure the students' progress at each stage of their learning and to conform to global practices. Rhodes thus, became the first DELF examination centre among the four universities in the Eastern Cape. Since then, students and members of the University community have, at their doorstep, the opportunity to obtain internationally recognised and acceptable certificates in French language proficiency.

After months of the DELF preparatory classes, the students are able to interact in a simple way: They speak about themselves and their immediate environment. In brief, the students are able to meet the objectives set out in the CEFRL. The department has recorded a significant number of enrollees and has attained a 98% success rate. Students who take the preliminary French course are able to pass the A2 and a few equally sit and pass the B1 examinations at the end of the academic session. This feat is not surprising as the Department of French has well-trained, accredited and certified DELF/DALF examiners by the Centre International d'Etudes Pédagogiques, Sèvres, France. In addition to this, the teachers have regularly attended courses facilitated by the Bureau Pour l'Enseignement de la Langue et de la Civilisation Française (BELC)[①] and organised by the Université d'été both within South Africa, France and elsewhere. Many students have found this programme very valuable, and have thus become very enthusiastic about it. This is evidenced by the fact that the 2013 French 1 students all sat for the examination even when it was made optional. As earlier mentioned, this qualification is internationally recognised;

① Office for the Teaching of French Language and Civilisation.

Arthur Mukenge   A Reflection on French Language Teaching and the Place of Evaluation
Emmanuel Naancin Dami   in a Previously Disadvantaged Multicultural Setting: A Case Study of
                        Rhodes University, South Africa

this is consistent with the international standard.

The French Department of the university is the first to be engaged on that route in South Africa. We hope that other universities will sooner or later, borrow a leaf from this.

Innovations and initiatives such as curriculum restructuring and reorganisation, for example, the replacement of some topics with new ones that on more modern teaching methods such as the *méthode actionelle*[1], have led to an improved pass rate over the years. We are also doing some formal consultations with students in connection with their learning. We have prioritised students' input in the learning and teaching process; we demand and get feedbacks which are taken into consideration when necessary.

But while trying to solve a problem in the French language teaching process, other challenges crop up. A case in point is the issue of assessing the students.

4.3   The challenge of assessing a multicultural, multiracial, multilevel class of French

If teaching has to be effective, there must be parameters with which the system should be able to measure and check its efficacy. "Assessment helps [us] to know whether students are mastering key concepts and skills, the quality of learning; whether [we are] being effective in [our] teaching process" (Race, 2002: 43). Therefore, assessment acts as a tool not only to impact students' learning but also to evaluate the efficacy of our teaching. Language teachers all over the world are expected to create a valid, reliable and credible assessment technic especially in a context like South Africa where the students have a lot of complexes and would easily be demoralised if there is any perception of inequality or what they may rightly or wrongly adjudge as discriminatory or preferential treatment. In French preliminary, the beginner level and point of entry for most students, assessment is regular and carried out on a weekly basis. Students' records are updated throughout the academic year and is put

---

① Active method.

at their disposal in an open and a very transparent way. Thus, there are weekly worksheets online (RUConnected/University website) and four tests (one test per term). The worksheets and tests comprise 20% of a student's final mark. The June examination includes both oral and written components and constitutes 20% of a student's final mark. The November examination, which tests the vocabulary, listening, oral and written skills, makes up 60% of the end-of-year result.

By the bye, on a personal note, we observe a considerable degree of students' apathy towards learning in general and to assessment in particular. It seems that acquiring knowledge is neither their first preoccupation nor a major priority. This is sometimes indicated by the marked but unclaimed worksheets, *Travaux Pratiques*①, test scripts and even essays, which stay in our offices on a weekly and yearly basis. We always think that this is not because the concerned students are not aware that their work has been marked and commented on, but that they are simply not interested in the feedback, especially when they suspect an underperformance. They do not want to know how they reacted, implemented and performed on the assessment tasks. This is counter-productive as it defeats the very objective for which the tests or examinations were conducted. Such assessments are geared towards identifying areas of weaknesses in the learning progress of the student. This is negative and should not be the case since students should be interested in feedback on their work to improve their performance in the assessment task. Our experience in other climes seems a little different.

For example, our personal experience as students, researchers and tutors in the vocational and technical education programmes in the Democratic Republic of Congo, Nigeria, France, Belgium, Canada and USA were more positive. A vast majority of the students showed greater commitment to learning and were enthusiastic about assessment. They always wanted to see their work in order to improve their performance based on the teachers' comments. On a face value, one could attribute this learning apathy and worrisome attitude among

① Work sheets.

Arthur Mukenge   A Reflection on French Language Teaching and the Place of Evaluation
Emmanuel Naancin Dami   in a Previously Disadvantaged Multicultural Setting: A Case Study of
                        Rhodes University, South Africa

some students at Rhodes University to many reasons among which could be the fact that they find that the course is tough due to their socio-cultural and poor educational background as had been mentioned earlier. Again, it could be said that many students, especially in the humanities elect to pick up French courses because they did not have other options open to them. Even those who did choose to do the language eventually regret and would normally prefer to withdraw midway into the course. However, once they were registered for the course, it was compulsory to finish the module at the end of the academic year as stipulated by the Rhodes study policy.

Consequently, we took a decision to reach out to the students. We realised that sensitisation could go a long way in raising awareness of the importance of all forms of assessments. To change this, we have made it a point of duty to make the purpose of the assessment clear and fully understood by all the students. This helps them to, not only appreciate the good, but also to come to terms with the way and manner that judgements and decisions are reached on their scripts. We are aware of the importance of feedback and the capital role it plays in improving students' performance. Thus, we agree with Lambert and Lines that "the student's involvement, in particular, student's self-assessment enhances student achievement and the more practical business of making it happen" (Lambert & Lines, 2000: 14). It is therefore pertinent for lecturers to understand that it is helpful and useful to have a good and perfect understanding of the multiple and various forms of assessment.

As lecturers, we play a big role in the assessment tasks. For instance, we have to carefully choose and consider assessment methods and techniques by designing and implementing valid and reliable assessment benchmarks. This has to be done painstakingly since "our assessment affects the rest of the life of a student and as such, there is need to pay particular attention to it" (Race, 2002: 4). This is also in line with Luckett and Sutherland's thought that "assessment helps institutions to evaluate the effectiveness of the learning environment, the quality of their graduates, as well as to monitor the quality of the education institution over time" (Luckett & Sutherland, 2000: 102). Therefore, it is much better for educational institutions to outline and indicate clearly the way in which the assessment is planned and implemented, what the modules' requirements are, how record books are kept, accessed and secured, the moderation and the training of staff in certain areas of assessment. In this regard, lecturers should have workshops/training, conferences, seminars that call for interactive discussions as is the case at Rhodes University. This component is vital in the sense that it does not only aid in teacher-upgrading but allows the institution to have clear-cut policy statements and a clear direction that ensures uniformity and conformity in its assessment criteria and guidelines.

Apropos, lecturers at Rhodes University have to be dynamic and innovative. There are no one-size-fits-all teaching or assessment methods as each case presents its challenges and should be treated on its own merit. Only the teacher who has physical contact with the learners appreciates this. As such, to tackle the issue, lecturers at Rhodes University are regularly trained, are provided with policy directions of the institution, and are expected to come up with personal but objective teaching and evaluation methods. All assessment methods are discussed with the head of the School. And to further achieve our set goals, we often manage to carry our tutors alone as they are part and parcel of the search for better criteria on methods, techniques and assessment strategies. We have really implemented many various forms of assessment and we lay emphasis on giving detailed comments on a students' worksheet.

Again, we have come up with a few ways to remedy this ill. Presently, we are planning to undertake trips to the University of Pretoria[①] and some other universities overseas in France specifically to exchange and share experiences with the view to finding solutions that can improve student conduct since the French Departments in these universities share similar challenges and demography as Rhodes.

---

① University of Pretoria has the highest number of students in the French Department in South Africa.

Arthur Mukenge   A Reflection on French Language Teaching and the Place of Evaluation
Emmanuel Naancin Dami   in a Previously Disadvantaged Multicultural Setting: A Case Study of
                         Rhodes University, South Africa

In terms of teaching methods, we consider our role as mentors who encourage students in ways that can henceforth help them and engage with the subject. So, we create an environment in which learning can take place and assessment becomes easier. We endeavour to serve as a learning compass to all the students, thereby helping out and attending to each individual's learning needs, regarding knowledge, techniques and encouragement. Furthermore, the kind of assessment given helps them to build sentences and develop writing skills. Through writing *Travaux Pratiques*[①], homework obligatorily done on a weekly basis, some of which has improved enormously in their French language grammar. We make the students realise that they are important and we (as lecturers) take their education seriously. Most of the time, we tell them that there will not be a class if you (students) are not there.

Nevertheless, our approach is also based on the principles supported by Ramsden (1992). In summary, all new methods, especially in terms of approach to learning, require interaction and students' participation, i.e., the learners play an active role in their learning process. As already mentioned, our teaching approach is a participatory one that requires attention on our part as well as a concerted concentration on the part of the learner. This method includes a real-life application of learning, such as the total involvement of students in reading, practising and conversation tasks. In the process, we are acting as a catalyst.

5 Conclusion

While there is a strong body of research on pedagogy and theories of teaching French as foreign language around the world, we have particularly noticed the dearth of same from colleagues in China. Very little work is available on individual experience in this field. However, studies, for example, "challenges native Chinese teachers face in teaching Chinese as a foreign language to non-native Chinese students in U.S. classrooms" by Xu (2012) are a

---

① Practical Activities.

proof that foreign language teachers around the world face problems that could potentially be tackled from sharing one's experience in the field.

As such, this article set out to share our personal and subjective experience in the teaching field in South Africa with academic colleagues and readers around the world. The goal is to challenge teachers to publish their experiences so as to enhance learning activities and teaching practices in different parts of the globe. To achieve this, we took the evaluation aspect of teaching. This component seems vital in that it measures, checks and balances not only the learner but the facilitator and guide.

Overall, the different levels of assessment: formative, summative and continuous are definitely crucial. Regarding student's assessment, we are happy to bear in mind the following: (1) What is required? What are students' expectations? What are the students' primary needs? (2) How can they perform against each of the set expectations? (3) How to close the gap between where one is now and where one will be in reaching improved achievement. (4) How to make room to close the gap, before meeting the next set of assessments.

We have also realised that, at the university level, in order to get the students to be fully committed to learning the French language, the tutor must make sure that the learners avoid passiveness. This can be achieved by luring the students to be fully involved in the educational process and to actively participate in all learning activities. Educators and lecturers must feel the need to justify what they decide to teach. In summary, students should be at the centre of the learning and teaching process.

References

Center for World University Rankings. 2022. Global 2000 list by the center for world university rankings. (2021) [2022-02-14]. https://cwur.org/2021-22.php.

ENAKOME P O, PETER G D. 2015. French language teaching in Nigeria: an issue of concern [J/OL]. Wilolud Journals, 8 (1): 17-19. (2015-06-18) [2022-01-10]. http://www.wiloludjournal.com.

Arthur Mukenge
Emmanuel Naancin Dami

A Reflection on French Language Teaching and the Place of Evaluation in a Previously Disadvantaged Multicultural Setting: A Case Study of Rhodes University, South Africa

KIRKARDLY A, 1996. Teaching in rural areas: The University of Venda [J]. African higher education, 24 (1): 17-23.

LAMBERT D, LINES D, 2000. Implementing effective classroom assessment: theory and practice [C] // LAMBERT D, LINES D. Understanding assessment: purposes, perceptions, practice. New York: Routledge.

LUCKETT K, SUTHERLAND L, 2000. Assessment practices that improve teaching and learning [C] // MAKONI S. Improving teaching and learning in higher education: a handbook for southern Africa. Johannesburg: Witwatersrand University Press.

North B, 2006. The common European framework of reference: development, theoretical and practical issues [EB/OL]. (2006/01/01) [2022/02/14]. https://www.researchgate.net/publication/251995323_The_common_European_framework_of_reference_development_theoretical_and_practical_issues.

RACE P, 2002. Why fix assessment? A discussion paper [J]. Staff and departmental development SDDU publication: 10-17.

RAMSDEN P, 1992. Learning to teach in higher education [M]. New York: Routledge.

WOOD E M, 2019. How many people speak French, and where is it spoken? [EB/OL]. (2019-09-17) [2022-02-16].https://www.babbel.com/en/magazine/how-many-people-speak-french-and-where-is-french-spoken.

World Population Review. 2022. South Africa population 2022 [EB/OL]. (2022-02-07) [2022-02-07]. https://worldpopulationreview.com/countries/south-africa-population.

XU H, 2012. Challenges native Chinese teachers face in teaching Chinese as a foreign language to non-native Chinese students in U.S. classrooms [EB/OL]. (2012-4-17) [2022-02-06]. https://digitalcommons.unl.edu/teachlearnstudent/20.

（编辑：马秀杰）

阿尔及利亚图书出版业的现状、困境和出路 ①

孟贤颖

外语教学与研究出版社

摘　要: 本文以阿尔及利亚图书出版业为研究对象,通过梳理该国出版行业现状,分析出版管理体制困境,展望出版行业的前景及出路。面对数字化发展机遇,阿尔及利亚在加速出版业发展的同时,通过坚持文化自信的价值追求,借助国际合作提升本国出版业的高质量发展,促进多元文化的发展与传播。

关键词: 阿尔及利亚;图书出版;出版体制;文化自信

The Current Situation, Predicament and Solution of the Book Publishing Industry in Algeria

Meng Xianying

Foreign language teaching and research press

Abstract: This paper takes the book publishing industry in Algeria as the research object, compares the current situation of the publishing industry in the country, analyzes the dilemma of the publishing management system, and looks forward to the future of the publishing industry in Algeria and the way out. In the face of the digital development opportunities, Algeria should accelerate the development of the publishing industry while adhering to its cultural self-confidence, enhancing the quality development of its publishing industry through international cooperation,

① 本文系国家语委"十三五"科研规划 2020 年度重点项目"非洲国家语言状况与语言政策研究"(项目编号:ZDI135-115)的阶段性研究成果。

收稿日期:2022-03-25

作者信息:孟贤颖,外语教学与研究出版社副编审,法语部主任,研究方向为法语专业图书出版,电子邮箱:mengxy@fltrp.com。

and promoting the development and dissemination of multiculturalism.

Keywords: Algeria; publishing industry; publishing management; cultural confidence

1　引言

非洲是人类古老文明的发祥地之一，早期非洲出版实践雏形可追溯至一万多年前岩画、铭文、莎草纸的创作及传播（万安伦、李仪、周杨，2019）。

殖民时期，随着印刷、出版技术在西方国家的快速发展，大量的欧洲商人、传教士、殖民者开始通过图书、报纸等印刷产品，巩固其在非洲国家的殖民统治及利益存在。19世纪初，随着法国对阿尔及利亚的入侵，殖民当局塑造了阿尔及利亚上流社会中单一法文报刊的格局，以此抑制本土语言、文化、思想的发展（刘欣路、许婷，2018）。20世纪50年代起，伴随着非洲民族解放运动的兴起，阿尔及利亚等国开始通过提升本国语言、文化和教育政策，促进图书出版行业的快速发展。目前，阿尔及利亚拥有400余家图书出版公司，图书出版发行行业进入快速发展阶段（宋毅，2021）。面对阿尔及利亚巨大的图书出版市场及其覆盖北非国家的辐射能力，部分学者认为应从多语种、差异化、数字化、本土化海外发行等角度拓展我国在阿尔及利亚及北非国家图书市场（宋毅，2021）。

本文在梳理阿尔及利亚图书出版业发展的历史和现状的基础上，认为面对阿尔及利亚广阔的出版市场前景，学界仍需注意到该国依旧脆弱的发行体系等问题。本文将在结合阿尔及利亚图书出版历史追溯及现实困境分析的基础上，思考数字化技术变革的背景下，阿尔及利亚图书出版行业的出路所在。

2　阿尔及利亚图书出版行业发展现状

自1962年独立至今，依托良好的社会人文背景和不断完善的图书出版机制，阿尔及利亚形成了较为完善的出版机构体系及相对畅通的出版发行渠道，具备了一定的出版发行能力。

2.1 良好的社会人文背景

自独立以来，阿尔及利亚积极摆脱殖民主义对本国语言、文化、思想的控制。出版业作为阿尔及利亚追求文化重建和精神自觉的重要窗口，发挥了不可替代的作用。

在语言方面，阿尔及利亚确定了阿拉伯语和塔马齐格特语的官方语言地位。目前该国的政府公文、宗教事务等书面文件已广泛使用阿拉伯语进行书写。在语言、文化、教育政策的规划下，该国的本土语言教材、反殖民题材等文学作品，在推动社会文化自信的基础上，也促进了该国出版业的发展（刘晖、于杰飞，2009）。目前，阿尔及利亚教育水平良好，义务教育入学比率较高。全国共有 111 所高等教育机构和近 200 万名大学生（Minisitère de l'enseignement supérieur et de la recherche scientifique, 2018），该国的成人识字率达 81.4%（UNESCO Institute for Statistics，2018）。这些客观因素都为图书行业的出版、发行、传播提供了重要的人文基础。

在公共阅读方面，阿尔及利亚重视全民阅读的推广工作，提高民众的阅读兴趣。根据 2018 年阿尔及尔国际书展上的调查，95.6% 的受访者表示热爱阅读，其中 30.3% 的人表示有在手机上阅读图书的习惯，55% 的读者认为图书价格偏高，57.7% 的人认为电子书将取代纸质图书。在阿尔及利亚读者的阅读语言方面，阿拉伯语排在第一位（68.8%），其次是法语（41.6%）和英语（12.7%）。调查数据还显示，35.5% 的阿尔及利亚人年平均阅读量为 1—5 本，每年阅读超过 20 本书的读者占 6.8%（Reporters,2018）。未来，阿尔及利亚的全民阅读普及率有望进一步提升。

此外，阿尔及利亚公共图书馆网络的建设与出版业相互呼应，从民众阅读习惯的培养、图书作用的发挥等多角度支撑起出版业的发展。2005年，阿尔及利亚开始兴建全国公共阅读图书馆网络。截至 2016 年，该网络包括位于首都阿尔及尔的国家图书馆和 14 个省级公共图书馆（Ministère de la Culture et des Arts, 2016a）。国家图书馆主要有两大职责：一是收集并处理全国出版物的信息，二是为正式出版物发放书号。阿尔及利亚实行出版物版本备案制度 ①。根据规定，所有正式出版物包括图书、期刊、报

---

① 见阿尔及利亚于 1996 年 7 月 2 日颁布的第 96-16 号行政法规和 1999 年 10 月 4 日颁布的第 99-226 号行政法规。

纸、文件、地图等均需在国家图书馆备案，以此保护作者的著作权并形成全国出版物总目录。省级图书馆则主要承担教育教学、文化中心、信息提供、文化传播等功能。例如，位于该国西部港口城市穆斯塔加奈姆的公共阅读图书馆，主要面向学生群体开放。该图书馆以著名历史学家贝勒哈米西（Belhamissi）的名字命名，经常通过举办阅读嘉年华和文学研讨会等活动推广全民阅读。

2.2　日臻完善的管理机构和出版网络

管理机构和执行机构的建立和完善是图书出版业发展的根本保障。阿尔及利亚图书出版的主管行政部门为该国文化和艺术部，其下设的国家图书中心主要负责图书产业的相关工作。这些工作包括从事出版经营活动的机构的审核和批准；对图书的印刷、出版和发行的管理；统计和收集出版发行和阅读情况的数据，开展与图书相关的社会、经济、文化调研；参加相关会议及展览；通过建设公共图书馆推广全民阅读等（Ministère de la Culture et des Arts, 2016b）。

在 1990 年以前，阿尔及利亚新闻出版主要由国家负责。1990 年，阿尔及利亚颁布了新的《新闻法》，放宽了对新闻出版的管控，独立的出版商、出版社开始逐渐形成。随着私有化改革的不断深化，2010 年起政府加大对图书产业的关注和支持。例如，在兴办图书沙龙、提供出版资助、举办图书文化节、减免进口纸张增值税等举措的实施下，阿尔及利亚的印刷媒体开始呈现出蓬勃发展的态势。

据阿尔及利亚文化和艺术部统计，阿尔及利亚目前共有 77 家较为活跃的出版社（Ministère de la Culture, 2019），包括私营出版社和国有出版社两类。私营出版社的业务相对广泛且灵活，部分出版社主要专注于某一领域的特色出版发行。例如，巴尔扎戈出版社关注当代非洲和阿拉伯世界主要文学作家，以出版文学研究和文学传记见长。该社曾于 2010 年获得克劳斯文化基金颁发的克劳斯文化和发展大奖。阿尔赫利亚出版社是关注人文社科领域的代表。该社曾在 2015 年"中阿典籍互译出版工程"项目中翻译出版中国当代作家刘震云的作品《手机》。绿色图书馆出版社和三个苹果出版社致力于少年儿童图书的出版。另有部分大型综合性出版社集团，例如，阿尔及利亚最著名的卡斯巴出版社出版内容覆盖文学、历史、传记、童书、教科书等多个领域。阿尔及利亚的国有出版社主要包括国家艺术和图画公司、国家出版发行社、大学出版局等多家出版机构，主要出版中小学教材、《古兰经》等宗教图书及科技文献等。在国家政策的支持和相关基础设施发展的推动下，阿尔及利亚出版物的数量逐年上升。2008年，阿尔及利亚图书出版量为 3,955 本，2010 年为 4,430 本，2011 年则上升至 5,401 本（Kherchi & Takouche, 2013）。出版物涉及教材、社科文献、文学作品等多个领域。

行业协会为凝聚不同出版集团作出了巨大贡献。自 2010 年，部分与出版行业相关的行业协会陆续成立，包括阿尔及利亚出版商协会、图书从业者协会、阿尔及利亚全国出版商组织、阿尔及利亚作家联盟等。在众多图书出版领域的协会中，阿尔及利亚出版商协会和全国出版商组织最为活跃。这两个非营利性组织分别成立于 2012 年和 2014 年，它们积极寻求政府层面对图书出版领域的资助和支持，努力团结全国出版行业力量，为推动阿尔及利亚图书产业的发展作出了巨大的贡献。阿尔及利亚出版商协会每年与文化艺术部共同组织盛大的阿尔及尔国际书展。全国出版商组织自2016 年发起国际书业博览会活动。该活动为图书出版领域的出版商、印刷商、纸张进口商、印刷设备进口商等打造交流和学习的平台，帮助业内人士了解最新技术和项目，提供同行之间的合作机会，推动图书产业的形成和发展，使其壮大成为国民经济的一部分。国际书业博览会持续举办并达成了一系列显著成果。例如，"国产图书标签"倡议的通过，使得印刷职业培训项目顺利达成；图书将会作为单独类别登记进商务部下一期出口商品计划中（Algérie 360°, 2018）；将降低纸张进口税率的呼吁上传至政府层面。2021 年，为刺激恢复受疫情打击的图书产业，阿尔及利亚全国出版商组织在文化艺术部的支持下，成功在首都阿尔及尔举办了第一届全国书展，吸引了 216 家出版社参展。

2.3 依旧薄弱的图书发行销售体系

目前，书店网络仍然是阿尔及利亚最主要的图书销售渠道。阿尔及利亚的大型出版社通常都有专门的图书代理，负责将图书分销给各家书店，而小型出版社的销售渠道相对有限。阿尔及利亚全国的书店数量没有确切的统计数字。该国商务部的统计并未将以图书销售为主的书店单独列出，而是与烟草商店、报亭、糖果店铺、纸制品销售店归为一类。相对于其国土面积和人口数量，阿尔及利亚的书店体系依旧相对薄弱，而且地区分布非常不均衡。大部分书店主要集中在北部城市。阿尔及利亚全国约有包括书店、超市、纸制品销售店铺、烟草店在内的 300—500 个图书产品销售网点，市场上 80% 的图书主要由其中的 50 家书店分销，10% 通过纸制品销售店进行销售，5% 通过超市卖出，线上销售仅占 3%（BIEF, 2021）。

图书线上销售在阿尔及利亚已经实现，但囿于网络支付尚未普及，支付结算系统不够便捷、运费昂贵、物流系统不够发达等原因，其使用规模十分有限。2018 年，阿尔及利亚第一家电子书店平台（https://aramebook.com/）正式上线，销售文学读物和阿拉伯语、塔马奇格特语、法语、英语等各类电子书。电子书店在售图书 300 余种，合作的出版社数量 22 家，其中还包含部分独立出版商。根据 2022 年阿尔及利亚网络使用统计情况，全国有 2,700 万网民，占全国人口的 60.6%，这一数量较 2021 年增长了 7.3%（Datareportal, 2022）。随着阿尔及利亚网络普及率的快速提升，线上销售和电子书店未来会有较大的发展前景。

阿尔及利亚最重要的书展——阿尔及尔国际书展，是阿拉伯国家规模最大的书展之一。在国内政局不稳、经济发展低迷的情况下，阿尔及尔书展仍然坚持举办，成为阿尔及利亚出版业的希望。2019 年，第 24 届阿尔及尔国际书展共有来自 36 个国家和地区的 1,030 家出版商参展（其中阿尔及利亚本土书商 298 个），展出 25 万种图书，吸引 110 万读者参与（Salon international du livre d'Alger, 2019），为阿尔及利亚图书市场带来了非常可观的销量。

2.4　多元广泛的国际合作建立

阿尔及利亚图书产业的快速发展，一方面得益于国内政策的推动，另一方面也离不开国际合作的助力。

阿尔及利亚在独立之初的数年中，仍保持着大量法语进口图书，这使得阿尔及利亚一度成为第四大法语图书进口国。但伴随着阿尔及利亚国家出版发行公司的成立以及第一本阿拉伯语图书的本地出版，阿尔及利亚逐步强化其与阿拉伯世界的联结。阿尔及利亚开始从叙利亚、黎巴嫩等阿拉伯国家引进图书，以阿歇特出版社为代表的法国出版商逐渐丧失了其对阿尔及利亚图书市场的垄断经营地位。

虽然法国仍然是阿尔及利亚重要的合作伙伴，但近些年来，阿尔及利亚从法国进口的图书金额在下降（见表1），其他马格里布国家（除摩洛哥外）也有类似趋势，市场正在逐渐摆脱对进口法国法语图书的依赖。

表1　2010—2020年法国向阿尔及利亚出口法语图书总额（单位：万欧元）

年份	数额
2010	1236.1
2013	1730.6
2015	1841.7
2017	731.4
2018	800.7
2019	773.8
2020	432

注：数据来源（La centrale de l'édition: Statistiques Export Livre, 2020）。

目前，随着本土出版业的发展，阿尔及利亚虽然仍从法国、比利时引进图书，尤其是少儿书籍，但这种引进出版更多是与法国有阿拉伯语出版业务的出版社进行平等合作出版。例如，阿尔及利亚绿色图书馆出版社和法国东方出版社合作出版少儿图书。这类合作出版的图书凭借其鲜艳的色彩和丰富的设计比阿尔及利亚本土图书更受读者青睐。本土出版社也在多样化的合作项目中积累出版经验，甚至也有机会探索本土阿拉伯语图书对法国的版权输出。

中国也是阿尔及利亚图书出版业的积极合作伙伴。20世纪60年代，阿尔及利亚独立之初，我国和阿尔及利亚就签署了第一个文化合作协定，旨在全面发展两国之间的文化关系，加强文化合作，其中包括涉及出版业互相尊重作者版权的明确条款。在随后数十年中，尤其是"一带一路"倡议提出以后，双方签署了多项文化合作框架协议，促成了图书出版领域一系列具体项目的实施。2014 年，中国作家代表团访问阿尔及利亚作家协会，双方签署《中阿版权交流合作谅解备忘录》，共同推动作品互译项目的出版。2015 年，中国诗人王久辛的诗集《狂雪》在阿尔及利亚胡马出版社出版，这是阿尔及利亚出版的第一部中国文学作品。随后，中国当代作家刘震云的作品《手机》在阿尔及利亚阿尔赫利亚出版社翻译出版。2018 年，作为主宾国，中国参加了第 23 届阿尔及尔国际书展，成功举办《中国对外开放 40 年》《因为爸爸》等主题图书联合版权签约仪式（中国出版集团公司，2018a）；中国图书进出口（集团）总公司与阿尔及利亚第三世界书店①、卡巴斯出版社签署合作备忘，在中国图书出口、互译出版等领域展开合作，并在第三世界书店开设"中国书架"（中国出版集团公司，2018b）。

3　阿尔及利亚图书出版行业面临的困难及前景分析

虽然阿尔及利亚出版业取得了较好的成绩，但是其面临的问题仍然复杂严峻。

首先，由于起步较晚，阿尔及利亚出版业相关法律法规尚不健全，导致盗版侵权现象频发。虽然出版物备案制度作为一项执行多年的出版制度相对比较完善，却并未得到诸多小出版商的遵守。在阿尔及利亚，盗版侵权现象比较多见，尤其是大学、中小学教材教辅的侵权盗版现象尤为严重。

其次，阿尔及利亚图书出版成本较高，给图书出版、销售等环节带来沉重负担。出版成本高的主要原因有两个。一是阿尔及利亚出版和印刷过程中需要的纸张、墨水和其他耗材完全依赖国外进口，导致图书印刷费用较高。二是政府对图书征收高昂的出版税，因此图书价格昂贵，尤其是部分引进版少儿图书大多由书商自己定价，价格很高。

---

① 第三世界书店成立于 1965 年，后由国有书店转为私营，是阿尔及利亚首都阿尔及尔最大的书店，在当地享誉盛名。

最后，阿尔及利亚的图书出版发行受到多重条件的束缚。例如，阿尔及利亚图书出版业的专业人才缺失严重，人力资源问题亟待解决；阿尔及利亚邮政系统不够发达，运费偏高且运力不足；图书馆数量不能满足当代读者的需求，部分设施设备欠佳；实体书店经营不景气。这些因素都是摆在阿尔及利亚图书出版业发展面前的现实问题。

不论是对于阿尔及利亚这样的北非较发达国家而言，还是对诸多欠发达的撒哈拉以南非洲国家，出版业的发展与民族文化的发展相辅相成，相互促进。非洲独特而多样的文化是人类文明宝库的重要组成部分，需要通过出版业的发展得到表达、输出和传播。文化自觉、文化自信是本土出版业发展的不竭动力，而本土出版业的发展反过来又会进一步推动民族文化自信的进程。非洲出版业的长足发展将有助于将更多非洲声音传向世界，有助于推动国际话语体系的变革，从而为本国发展营造有利的国际环境。为此，阿尔及利亚文化与艺术部专门设立了国家艺术和文学推广基金、阿里·马阿奇奖等资助项目，通过加大对本土文化艺术活动的鼓励和资助，对外积极寻求建立战略伙伴关系，促进带有文化自觉战略目标的图书出版。部分机构通过定期举办或参加国际性的研讨会、文化周等活动，将阿尔及利亚的本国文化艺术产品推向世界。

基于当下的全球出版语境和国际合作语境，阿尔及利亚除了继续加强国内出版业的法律法规建设、加强出版人才培养和完善出版发行网络以外，面对数字化出版的发展，阿尔及利亚还可通过借力国际合作来激发本国出版业的更多活力。

在数字出版方面，阿尔及利亚已经具备一定的网络基础设施和一定规模的潜在数字阅读人口。截至 2022 年 5 月，非洲已经拥有超过 6 亿的网民，约占人口总数的 43.1%，而阿尔及利亚有 3,784 万网民，占人口数量的 84%（Internet World Stats, 2022）。随着信息产业化的不断发展，网民数量不断攀升。阿尔及利亚数字阅读图书市场广大，越来越多的图书将走向线上。鉴于青少年读者往往倾向于在线阅读，面向青少年的数字阅读图书市场前景尤其光明。在后疫情时代，教育数字化的发展将进一步推动教材的数字化进程。相信阿尔及利亚数字出版将大踏步走进大发展时代，数字出版的范围和领域还会不断扩大。

阿尔及利亚出版商应乘互联网发展的东风，学习其他国家的先进经验，积极探索数字转型，努力打通从选题开发、内容撰写、编校出版到线上营销的一条龙模式，为传统出版赋能，为图书市场扩容。

在国际合作方面，阿尔及利亚可以继续发挥与阿拉伯世界以及法国等欧洲国家的良好合作关系，同时加大与中国出版业的合作，扩大阿尔及利亚出版业在世界的影响，提升阿尔及利亚的文化传播力。

中国与非洲的出版合作历史久远，基础坚固，近年来发展势头良好。"丝路书香出版工程""中外图书互译"等项目促进了中国和非洲优秀图书作品的互相传播，加深了中国和非洲各国对彼此文化的理解，更好地推动了非洲及世界各国的文明对话和交流互鉴。从上述阿尔及利亚图书出版业的发展状况来看，阿尔及利亚与中国图书出版合作主要可在以下几个方面发力。首先，阿尔及利亚拥有庞大的中小学生群体，本土少儿读物出版品种和数量难以满足巨大的需求，而欧洲进口的少儿图书价格昂贵，普通家庭难以负担。因此，阿尔及利亚出版社可以考虑与中国合作出版或翻译出版儿童文学、知识读本、绘画读本等类型图书，以填补市场空缺。其次，两国在"中阿典籍互译出版工程"框架下可继续扩充出版物品种，将更多的优秀作品呈现给双方读者，构建现代文化领域的"丝绸之路"，在文化交流中坚定文化自信。最后，阿尔及利亚需抓住数字出版的机遇。阿尔及利亚出版社可与中国出版企业合作，利用中国较为先进的数字出版和传播技术，合作搭建优质的阅读平台，提供阅读服务，从而培养读者的阅读习惯，逐步构建稳定增长的线上阅读市场。

4　结语

综上，阿尔及利亚自独立以来，文化教育事业取得了一定的发展，国民教育水平良好，全民阅读普及率高，公共图书馆网络建设初步成型，出版管理体制和机构不断完善，印刷媒体蓬勃发展。在文化艺术部的支持下，阿尔及利亚出版行业协会积极组织行业博览会，推动了了图书出版业的进步。

近年来，阿尔及利亚积极开展国际图书合作项目。除紧密联系阿拉伯国家外，阿尔及利亚出版社正在逐步转变与法国出版社的合作方式，通过政府互译项目与中国保持着积极的合作关系。阿尔及利亚图书出版建设框架已初步成型。未来，尝试打通线上线下的图书销售环节，拓宽图书销售渠道，进一步完善图书销售体系，应该是阿尔及利亚图书出版行业持续发展的主要发力点。

参考文献：

Algérie 360°, 2018. Industrie de livre: le 2e «bookprod» du 5 au 8 novembre prochain [N/OL]. Algérie 360° (2018-10-29) [2022-03-02]. https://www.algerie360.com/industrie-du-livre-le-2e-bookprod-du-5-au-8-novembre-prochain.

BIEF, 2021. Le marché du livre en français au Maghreb [R/OL]. (2021-04) [2022-03-06]. https://www.bief.org/fichiers/operation/4329/media/10602/FICHE%20MAGHREB%20-%20BIEF%20-%202021.pdf.

Datareportal, 2022. Digital 2022: Algeria [EB/OL]. (2022-02-15) [2022-02-26]. https://datareportal.com/reports/digital-2022-algeria?rq=algeria.

Internet World Stats, 2022. Internet usage and population statistics table for Africa [EB/OL]. (2022-05) [2022-06-05]. https://www.internetworldstats.com/africa.htm#dz.

KHERCHI M H, TAKOUCHE S, 2013. La situation du livre en Algérie: analyse statistique [J]. Revue des Sciences économiques de Gestion et de Commerce, 28 (1): 85-102.

La centrale de l'édition: Statistiques Export Livre, 2020. Exportations vers les pays francophones[R/OL]. (2020-12) [2022-03-09]. http://www.centrale-edition.fr/sites/default/files/la_centrale_de_ledition_-_statisitiques_2020.pdf.

Minisitère de l'Enseignement supérieur et de la Recherche scientifique, 2018. M. Hadjar participe à Paris aux travaux de la conférence internationale sur le processus de Bologne[EB/OL]. (2018-09-24) [2021-03-15]. https://www.mesrs.dz/fr_FR/accueil/-/journal_content/56/21525/52816.

Ministère de la Culture et des Arts, 2016a. Bibliothèque principale de lecture publique [EB/OL]. [2022-03-17]. https://www.m-culture.gov.dz/index.php/fr/lecture-publique/bibliotheque-principale-de-lecture-publique.

Ministère de la Culture et des Arts, 2016b. Centre nationale du livre [EB/OL]. [2022-03-09]. https://www.m-culture.gov.dz/index.php/fr/etablissements-sous-tutelle/centre-national-du-livre.

Ministère de la Culture, 2019. Les maisons d'éditions algériennes en activité [EB/

OL]. [2022-03-09]. https://web.archive.org/web/20190311135119/http://www.m-culture.gov.dz/mc2/fr/editeursalgeriens.php.

Reporters, 2018. Enquête sur les habitudes de lecture: Les Algériens lisent un à cinq livres l'année et de nuit [N/OL]. Reporters 2018-11-20 [2022-03-05]. https://www.reporters.dz/enquete-sur-les-habitudes-de-lecture-les-algeriens-lisent-un-a-cinq-livres-l-annee-et-de-nuit/.

Salon international du livre d'Alger, 2019. Le livre, un continent [EB/OL]. (2019-11) [2022-03-15]. https://sila.dz/2019/fr.

UNESCO Institute for Statistics, 2018. Algeria [EB/OL]. (2018) [2022-03-14]. http://uis.unesco.org/en/country/dz.

刘晖，于杰飞，2009. 阿拉伯语在阿尔及利亚的发展及现状调查 [J]. 阿拉伯世界研究，（4）：46-53.

刘欣路，许婷，2018. 阿尔及利亚新闻出版业发展管窥 [N]. 中国新闻出版广电报，2018-11-05 (004).

宋毅，2021. 北非出版市场的开拓路径与策略——以阿尔及利亚为中心的考察 [J]. 出版发行研究，(3)：27-32.

万安伦，李仪，周杨，2019. 论非洲对人类出版的历史性贡献 [J]. 出版参考，(2)：50-55.

中国出版集团公司，2018a.《中国对外开放 40 年》等主题图书联合版权签约活动在阿尔及利亚成功举办 [EB/OL]. (2018-11-06) [2022-03-15]. http://www.cnpubg.com/news/2018/1106/41107.shtml.

中国出版集团公司，2018b. 中国书架将走进阿尔及利亚 [EB/OL]. (2018-11-06) [2022-03-15]. http://www.cnpubg.com/news/2018/1106/41109.shtml.

（编辑：李春光）

《殖民主义与非洲社会变迁》书评 ^①

郭炯

湘潭大学法学院

摘 要： 当前，部分西方政府官员和媒体对中非合作的恶意指责呈现逐渐上升的
态势，其中最典型的就是"新殖民主义"论调。西方政客的"批评"和
西方媒体的炒作，试图歪曲中非合作的性质，损害中国形象，影响中非
友好关系的健康发展。鉴于西方故意混淆"新殖民主义"的概念和本质，
笔者认为有必要对西方在非洲的殖民史进行系统梳理。《殖民主义与非洲
社会变迁》一书从经济变革、城镇化、性别、家庭与人口、种族关系、大
众传媒、娱乐休闲与教育等方面对殖民统治时期非洲社会变迁进行了详细
的分析，将历史学理论思想和研究范式运用其中，具有立场客观、内容丰
富、观点新颖、资料翔实等特点，为非洲问题研究带来了诸多启示。

关键词： 殖民主义；非洲社会变迁；双重使命；"新殖民主义"

Book Review: *Colonialism and African Social Change*

Guo Jiong

School of Law, Xiangtan University

Abstract: Currently, some Western government officials and media are
increasingly making malicious accusations against China-Africa
cooperation, with the most typical one being the "neo-colonialism".
Western politicians' "criticism" and the Western media's hype attempt
to distort the nature of China-Africa cooperation, damage China's
image, and affect the healthy development of China-Africa friendly
relations. Given the intentional confusion of the concept and essence
of "neo-colonialism" by the West, it is necessary to systematically
sort out Western colonial history in Africa. The book *Colonialism and*

① 收稿日期：2022-2-10

作者信息：郭炯，湘潭大学法学院讲师，法学博士，研究方向为国际法、中非经贸法律，电
子邮箱：475477493@qq.com。

African Social Change provides a detailed analysis of the social changes in Africa during the colonial period from aspects such as economic reform, urbanisation, gender, family and population, race relations, mass media, entertainment and education, applying historical theory and research paradigms with objective positions, rich content, innovative perspectives, and ample data, which bring many insights to the study of African issues.

Keywords: colonialism; African social change; double mission; "neo-colonialism"

西方主流舆论将中非合作描绘成"负面的""罪恶的"，并且将中非合作加以标签化，捏造了诸如"新殖民论""资源掠夺论""破坏环境论""支持独裁和腐败论"，以及近年来的"债务陷阱论"等。当下，为了获得非洲国家的政治支持和能源供应，西方国家对所谓中国的"新殖民主义"指责更加激烈。

中国是否在非洲搞"新殖民主义"，非洲人最有资格评判，而不是西方人。讽刺的是，"新殖民主义"最早是非洲学者用来形容西方殖民者对非洲的行径。在对"新殖民主义"所作的诠释中，恩克鲁玛的观点最有代表性："那些在外部看来独立的主权国家，但是其实它的政治、经济、国防等都受制于原来的殖民统治国，它的一举一动都是在原宗主国的监控下进行的"（恩克鲁玛，1996: 1）。2006 年，英国时任外交大臣斯特劳（Straw）访问尼日利亚时，公然污蔑中国在非洲搞"新殖民主义"，蔑称"当前中国在非洲的所作所为与英国 150 年前如出一辙"，从而引发了西方对中非关系性质的恶意攻击（李安山，2020）。西方政客的"批评"和西方媒体的炒作，既给中非友好合作关系带来较大的负面影响，也损害中国形象，阻碍非洲的发展。因此，我们对非洲的殖民历史进行考察是十分必要的，这不仅具有重要的理论价值，而且具有积极的现实意义。李鹏涛所著的《殖民主义与非洲社会变迁》一书，从经济变革、城镇化、性别、家庭与人口、种族关系、大众传媒、娱乐休闲与教育等方面对英属非洲殖民地进行了详细的分析，贯穿了历史学理论思想和研究范式的运用，为非洲问题研究带来了诸多启示。

《殖民主义与非洲社会变迁》共分八章，分别是"殖民地国家与'传统的发明'""经济变革""城镇化""性别、家庭与人口""种族关系""大众传媒、娱乐休闲与教育""'第二次殖民占领'时期的非洲社会变迁与非殖民化"和"结语"。结语部分对全书内容做了总结和展望。全书呈现以下几个特点。

1 立场客观

全书贯穿运用马克思关于殖民主义"双重使命"的理论来解释殖民主义在非洲的"破坏性使命"和"建设性使命",真实、全面、客观地还原了非洲殖民史。例如,作者发现殖民主义的一个内在悖论,即殖民统治虽然需要引导和推动殖民地经济社会变革,重新组织当地生产,以满足宗主国本土需求,并为殖民地国家提供税收来源,但又必须将殖民地的经济社会变革限定在可控范围之内。在此基础上,作者引入了兰杰(Ranger)于1983年提出的"传统的发明"这一概念,围绕殖民当局所主导的社会建构过程中的三个产物,即族群、间接统治和习惯法进行了讨论,得出"不应夸大殖民者操纵非洲制度以建立霸权的能力;传统、族群和习惯法并非能够轻易制造或者操纵的,殖民统治依靠这些制度而得以维持,但与此同时,这也对殖民力量构成限制"(郑家馨,1997: 87-97)。这并非作者的首创,第一代非洲学者郑家馨先生率先将马克思关于"英国在印度要完成的双重使命"理论运用于非洲殖民问题研究。郑家馨先生指出,正是由于殖民主义有意识地全面忽视"工业化",甚至不准建立农产品加工工业,殖民时期非洲人根本没有受到任何接替欧洲人的训练,教育只是为了培养对殖民制度更有用的非洲人。在这种情况下,非洲如何为自己的"工业化社会"奠定必要的物质基础(郑家馨,1995: 50)?

2 内容丰富

该书立足19世纪90年代欧洲掀起瓜分非洲的狂潮,直至20世纪60年代大多数非洲国家获得独立这一时间段,描绘出殖民主义在非洲社会的渗透和干预日益加深的明显趋势。

第一章"殖民地国家与'传统的发明'"主要讨论了殖民主义在非洲

呈现出残暴性和剥削性，同时也暴露出了殖民霸权的脆弱性和有限性，即它无法有效控制殖民地的社会发展。这表现在经济变革、人口与传染病、生态环境、城镇化、性别与家庭、种族关系、宗教与教育、娱乐休闲与大众文化等诸多领域。

第二章"经济变革"讨论了交通变革、非洲劳动力的流动与控制、农业生产以及白人移民等影响殖民地经济发展的四个重要因素。作者认为，19 世纪以及整个殖民时期的非洲经济增长和进步是由非洲移民工人、可可农、花生收购者和公路运输者所推动的。作者发现，殖民统治虽然在客观上推动了以铁路和公路为代表的殖民地交通运输的发展，但是殖民地经济的发展往往是以满足殖民列强对于资源、市场等需要为前提的。为了满足财政自给自足等目的，殖民当局通过奴隶制、强制税收、推动非洲社会融入商品经济以及剥夺非洲人的谋生途径等方式获取劳动力，并强迫他们从事农业生产。这种畸形的经济发展甚至演变为依赖非洲农民生产的"西非方式"和白人移民控制的"南非模式"。

第三章"城镇化"重点讨论了殖民地国家城镇政策的变化以及城镇的社会和文化。作者发现，大多数殖民城镇，尤其是东非地区，更多的是政治的产物，其选址很少考虑经济因素。二战后，为了本土发展和偿还美国债务，英国和殖民地当局开始积极推动全方位的殖民地经济社会变革，加速了非洲城镇化的发展进程。在城镇环境中，虽然新的通用语言得以传播并被接受，但来自不同部落群体却无法获得新的身份认同。于是，一种全新的社会凝聚力形式——自愿协会出现了。例如，在桑给巴尔和苏丹，获释后的奴隶成为全新的工人阶级，在城镇中形成了全新的身份认同。

第四章"性别、家庭与人口"集中讨论了殖民时代非洲家庭变化的核心问题，即非洲妇女的地位，具体表现为非洲妇女的劳动权和迁徙权。作者发现，新兴城镇为非洲妇女提供了逃离男性控制的机会，很多妇女开始从事临时劳动。尽管殖民时代的新经济机会大多是面向男性的，但随着欧洲资本主义的渗透，城镇和贸易的发展创造出全新的机遇，非洲女性和男性同样从中获利。经济地位得以改善的妇女能够重新界定其与父亲、兄弟和丈夫之间的关系，从而削弱了男性对她们劳动力的控制。另外，从 20 世纪 20 年代开始，越来越多的妇女由于婚姻不和、与父母的争吵、寡居或无子等原因，离开农村来到城市，而殖民地国家出于对男性移民劳动力的需要，并未完全反对妇女的流动。然而，针对非洲社会业已经出现的性别间极为紧张的关系，殖民地国家开始通过法律措施限制妇女谋求独立发展的任何形式。非洲妇女往往能够适应这一新秩序，即通过宗教和政治活动回应她们所经历的社会和政治危机，并利用服饰和时尚装扮来表达全新的个人身份与文化认同。

第五章"种族关系"集中讨论了殖民地社会身份和地位的问题。通过对殖民地当局确立的种族界限进行深入描述，作者认为文化和种族间的混合在某些方面推进了帝国主义目标的实现，但在另一些情况下可能导致殖民秩序的破坏。为满足英国资产阶级的利益，殖民当局采取了重大措施来破坏停滞的自给自足的社会机体（艾周昌，1991）。作者发现，在英国殖民统治的种族政策推动下，殖民地社会形成了一种以肤色划分为依据的社会等级结构，包括欧洲白人、印度人、索马里人、黎巴嫩人和黑人。首先，建立在对非洲人压榨基础上的少数白人统治社会，构建了一种白人和男人至上的社会秩序。这点从殖民当局对待"黑祸（Black Peril，即黑人男性对白人女性的性侵犯）"和"白祸（White Peril，即白人男性对黑人女性的性侵犯）"的态度可以得到印证。其次，印度人在东非是最重要的"中间人"，即相对于非洲人而言享有部分特权，相对于欧洲人而言被剥夺了选举权。再次，索马里人在种族上是含混的，但由于其具备与阿拉伯人密切的文化和物质特征，尤其是在宗教信仰上趋同，因此在肯尼亚享有城镇居住权，并且缴纳非土著标准的人头税。最后，为躲避战乱而离开故土来到西非的黎巴嫩人，得益于家庭亲缘关系，加上生活节俭、头脑精明并具有个人牺牲精神，因而在西非地区的商业活动中扮演了重要的角色。但是，他们由于失去民族身份认同，也是非洲人仇视的对象。本地化的黎巴嫩人在西非国家独立后便选择了归化。

第六章"大众传媒、娱乐休闲与教育"主要关注殖民时期大众媒体、舞蹈、音乐、体育运动以及教育等方面的变化。作者发现，20世纪上半叶，电影在非洲的流行与殖民地社会经济变迁存在密切的关系。在这一时期，殖民者试图通过遴选、审查等方式，在工矿企业招工、非洲城镇化、宣传西方正面形象、树立西方电影偶像、防止犯罪、传播科学知识、推动非洲消费需求等方面巩固殖民统治。尽管殖民当局试图运用电影作为社会管理和控制的工具，但非洲人仍将其视为娱乐手段，折射出英国殖民文化霸权的有限性。另外，作为殖民者"文明使命"的核心，非洲的教育政策反映了殖民统治理念。但是，教会认为非洲人的教育应当"引导皈依者的信仰"，而殖民当局则认为教育是为了让非洲人能够成为廉价劳动力。即便如此，只有极少数非洲人有机会接受教育。到一战后，教育取代暴力成为殖民统治的重要手段。

3 观点新颖

作者梳理了非洲殖民地国家建立的过程，总结出欧洲殖民征服非洲过程的五大特点，包括工业文明的压倒优势、灵活多变的殖民策略、列强之间的合作妥协、广泛招募的非洲士兵、数十年的征服过程。作者注意到"殖民主义的日常表达要比想象的更为复杂"，认为殖民地国家按照自身意愿控制并塑造非洲社会的能力极为有限。

第七章"'第二次殖民占领'时期的非洲社会变迁与非殖民化"集中讨论了在非洲民族主义兴起和精英阶层形成的背景下，非洲城镇和农村民众反抗殖民主义的历史过程。作者认为，二战后，英国为了巩固大国地位并恢复经济，开始更深入地介入非洲社会，即"第二次殖民占领"，包括在政治上试图将间接统治制度转变为"地方政府"，在经济上推行"发展主义"。然而，政治上的变革导致了非洲社会精英阶层的出现，而殖民地农业发展计划也激起了农民对殖民统治的反抗。1945 年，泛非大会召开，未来的非洲民族主义领袖开始登上历史舞台。再加上"雅尔塔体系"的确立以及两极对立的世界新格局的形成，非洲民族解放运动蓬勃发展，原殖民地随后纷纷独立。

第八章"结语：殖民遗产与当代非洲国家"总结了殖民时期非洲社会的历史变迁，进一步论述了非洲人民在塑造殖民地社会进程中的能动作用。然而，所谓的"殖民地遗产"，包括被扭曲的政治体制和民族关系、畸形经济结构等，都对独立后的非洲国家产生了恶劣的影响（舒运国，2020）。作者直言，在殖民统治结束时，非洲国家的权力要比以往更为集中、更为强大，非洲民族国家的雏形到这时已经呼之欲出了。

4 资料翔实

非洲殖民历史的文献资料相对比较丰富。国内学者张星烺、向达和艾周昌还专门进行过中国载籍中非洲史资料的汇编工作，并取得了显著成绩。多种类型的资料可以比较，可以互证，也可以相互借助，更有助于非洲经济史乃至整个非洲史的研究（刘伟才，2018）。诚如作者在文中所言："丰富的殖民档案文献极大地推动了殖民时期非洲史研究，但非洲史研究者日益认识到这些殖民档案的局限性，并强调利用口头资料、司法记录、照片图像资料以及非洲文学作品等史料，试图更为全面地展现殖民时代的非洲社会变迁"（许永璋，2001: 51）。

《殖民主义与非洲社会变迁》的附录一中有详细的英属非洲殖民地大事年表（19 世纪至 20 世纪 60 年代），附录二中有英属 22 个非洲殖民地的历史概况。全书共计中文参考文献 114 篇（本），英文参考文献 289 篇（本）。该书中翔实的资料，无论是中文还是英文，均经过仔细地考证，避免盲从和模糊，具有真实性和科学性。

《殖民主义与非洲社会变迁》于 2019 年 5 月由社会科学文献出版社出版。该书观点明确、理论扎实、结构严谨、行文流畅，向读者较为完整地呈现出殖民时期非洲社会变迁的过程和画面，也为中国驳斥"新殖民主义"提供了理论支撑和历史依据，具有很高的学术价值和现实意义。

参考文献

艾周昌，1991. 殖民地时期加纳土地制度的变化 [J]. 西亚非洲，（5）：57-63+8+82.

恩克鲁玛，1996. 新殖民主义 [M]. 北京：世界知识出版社.

李安山，2020. 中非合作论坛二十周年：历程、成就与思考 [J]. 当代世界，（10）：17-23.

刘伟才，2018. 19 世纪英国人非洲行记中的经济史资料及其利用 [J]. 上海师范大学学报（哲学社会科学版），（4）：142-152.

舒运国，2020. 试析独立后非洲国家经济发展的主要矛盾 [J]. 西亚非洲，（2）：91-110.

许永璋，2001. 中国载籍中非洲史资料汇编问题漫谈 [J]. 西亚非洲，（5）：51-54+80.

郑家馨，1995.具体分析殖民主义在不同时期和不同地区的作用 [J]. 北大史学，
（3）：38-52.
郑家馨，1997.关于殖民主义"双重使命"的研究 [J]. 世界历史，（2）：87-97.

（编辑：张经纬）

《非洲语言文化研究》（中英文）征稿启事

　　《非洲语言文化研究》（中英文）由北京外国语大学非洲学院组编，外语教学与研究出版社出版，主要发表国内外学者关于非洲语言、文学、社会、文化以及中非文化比较和中非跨文化交际等研究领域的中文、英文优秀学术成果。重点关注的议题如下：非洲本土语言研究、语言教学与习得、国家语言政策与规划，非洲本土语言、英语、法语、阿拉伯语及葡语文学研究，非洲传统社会文化研究，中非文化比较研究以及中非跨文化交际。《非洲语言文化研究》设有非洲语言与文学、非洲社会与文化、中非文化比较与研究、专题研究、学术动态和书评等栏目，热诚欢迎国内外专家学者赐稿。

一、稿件内容要求

　　1. 来稿要求为原创性论文。论文内容要求充实，立意新颖，观点明确，论证严密，资料翔实，数据可靠，语言精练，注重学术性和理论性。

　　2. 来稿要求格式规范、要素齐全；各栏目的中文、英文文章篇幅一般为 8,000—12,000 字，书评篇幅为 4,000—6,000 字（文章和书评篇幅含中英文标题、摘要、关键词及参考文献）。

　　3. 书评栏目所评介图书限三年内出版的非洲语言、文学、社会、文化以及中非文化比较和中非跨文化交际类相关图书。

　　4. 来稿要求注意遵守学术规范。对直接引用的相关言论或观点，要标注出参考文献的具体页码，避免出现抄袭或内容上的重复；对间接引用的重要思想或观点，要注明文献来源，避免使用大量二手文献。

二、用稿格式体例说明

（一）来稿组成

　　1. 作者信息（单独页面）包括作者姓名、通信地址、联系电话、电子邮件和 100—200 字的作者简介。作者简介应包含作者的真实姓名、工作单位、学历、职称、职务、主要研究领域等信息。

2. 中文标题、摘要（200—300 字）、关键词（3—5 个，用分号隔开）。

3. 英文标题、摘要、关键词（用分号隔开）。

4. 正文、参考文献和附录。

5. 正文中文献引用均采用夹注。

6. 正文中的注释采用脚注，格式为①、②、③，以此类推。

（二）文件格式及板式

1. 来稿一律以 Microsoft Word 格式提供，单倍行距。标题用宋体小 3 号，一级标题用宋体 4 号，二级标题用宋体小 4 号，三级标题用宋体 5 号，正文用宋体 5 号。数字和英文一律用新罗马字体（Times New Roman）。

2. 标题层级序号限三级，全部左顶格写，编排格式为 1、1.1、1.1.1，数字后空一格再写标题文字。正文内例句等序号用带括号的阿拉伯数字序号，如（1）、（2）、（3）。

3. 文中图表各篇内部连续编号，图题位于插图下方，表题位于表格上方。图题格式为"图 1 图题"；表题格式为"表 1 表题"（序号和图题／表题之间加一个字空，序号后边不带标点）。中文稿件中的图题、表题以及图表中的文字一律采用中文。

（三）参考文献格式

文献引用要规范，文中与文末的参考文献要严格一致。作者在提交稿件前要对所有参考文献一一进行核实，避免出现信息错误或者缺失。英文及其他文献在前（按字母排序），中文文献在后（按拼音排序），具体格式参照以下范例执行。

1. 期刊论文

CARSTENS V, 2005. Agree and EPP in Bantu [J]. Natural language and linguistic theory, 23 (2): 219-279.

MAKONI S B, PENNYCOOK A, 2005. Disinventing and (re)constituting languages [J]. Critical inquiry in language studies, 2 (3): 137-156.

SUNSTEIN C R, 1996. Social norms and social roles [J/OL]. Columbia law review,

96: 903 [2012-01-26]. http://www.heinonline.org/HOL/Page?handle=hein. journals/clr96&id= 913&collecion=journals &index=journals/clr.

陆俭明，2018. 再谈语言信息结构理论 [J]. 外语教学与研究，（2）：163-172.

叶狂，潘海华，2012. 把字句的跨语言视角 [J]. 语言科学，（6）：604-620.

于潇，刘义，柴跃廷，等，2012. 互联网药品可信交易环境中主体资质审核备案模式 [J]. 清华大学学报（自然科学版），52（11）：1518-1523.

2. 论文集 / 汇编中的论文

CHOMSKY N, 2000. Minimalist inquiries: the framework [C] // MARTIN R, MICHAELS D, URIAGEREKA J. Step by step: essays on minimalist syntax in honor of Howard Lasnik. Cambridge, MA: The MIT Press: 89-156.

LEGÈRE K, ROSENDAL T, 2008. Linguistic landscapes and the African perspective [C] // PÜTZ M, MUNDT N. Expanding the linguistic landscape: linguistic diversity, multimodality and the use of space as a semiotic resource. Bristol: Multilingual Matters: 153-179.

刘丹青，1996. 东南方言的体貌标记 [C] // 张双庆 . 动词的体 . 香港：香港中文大学中国文化研究所吴多泰中国语文研究中心：9-33.

3. 专著

AYAFOR M, GREEN M, 2017. Cameroon pidgin English: a comprehensive grammar [M]. Amsterdam: Benjamins.

CHOMSKY N, 1995. The minimalist program [M]. Cambridge, MA: The MIT Press.

陆俭明，马真，1985. 现代汉语虚词散论 [M]. 北京：北京大学出版社 .

徐烈炯，2008. 中国语言学在十字路口 [M]. 上海：上海教育出版社 .

4. 译著

NEDJALKOV V P, 1983/1988. Typology of resultative constructions [C]. Trans, BERNARD C. Amsterdam: John Benjamins.

赵元任，1968/1980. 中国话的文法 [M]. 丁邦新，译 . 香港：香港中文大学出版社 .

5. 会议论文 / 报告

AELBRECHT L, 2008. Dutch modal complement ellipsis and English VPE [R]. Talk presented at CGSW 23, Edinburgh, June 12-13, 2008.

U.S. Department of Transportation Federal Highway Administration, 1990. Guidelines for handling excavated acid-producing material: PB91-1940001 [R]. Springfield: U.S. Department of Commerce National Information Service.

World Health Organization, 1970. Factors regulating the immune response: report of WHO Scientific Group [R]. Geneva: WHO.

宁春岩，2018-10-29/30. 形式语言学、语言获得、语言障碍及神经语言学间的通约问题 [R]. 北京语言大学语言学系成立仪式暨语言学前沿国际论坛论文. 北京：北京语言大学.

中华人民共和国国务院新闻办公室，2013. 国防白皮书：中国武装力量的多样化 [R/OL].（2013-04-16）[2021-07-10]. http://www.mod.gov.cn/affair/2013-04/16/content_4442839.htm.

6. 学位论文

HUANG C T J, 1982. Logical relations in Chinese and the theory of grammar [D]. Cambridge, MA: Massachusetts Institute of Technology.

张天伟，2012. 基于形式句法的现代汉语省略限制研究 [D]. 北京：中国传媒大学.

7. 电子资源

PAULSON S, 2019. "I am because we are": the African philosophy of Ubuntu [EB/OL]. (2019-06-22) [2021-08-11]. https://www.ttbook.org/interview/i-am-because-we-are-african-philosophy-ubuntu

UNESCO Institute for Lifelong Learning, 2010. Why and how Africa should invest in African languages and multilingual education: an evidence- and practice-based policy advocacy brief [EB/OL]. (2010-07) [2021-03-09]. https://uil.unesco.org/literacy/multilingual-research/why-and-how-africa-should-invest-african-languages-and-multilingual.

刘大龙，2011. 莫桑比克女孩辍学现象严重 [EB/OL]. (2011-12-01) [2018-12-25]. http://news.163.com/11/1201/08/7K660ICN00014JB5.html.

8. 报纸文章

Lusaka Times, 2018. Use of local languages in lower grades a success [N/OL]. Lusaka times, 2018-02-12 [2021-03-09]. https://www.lusakatimes.com/2018/02/12/use-local-languages-lower-grades-success/.

MACHANICK P, 2020. Covid logic beats "irrational" human logic [N]. Mail & Guardian, 2020-07-29.

田志凌，2005.《魔戒》的尴尬与文学翻译的危机 [N]. 南方都市报，2005-08-24.

张梦旭，李晓宏，2021. 推进非洲疫后重建，消除冲突根源 [N/OJ]. 人民网，2021-05-21 [2021-08-11]. http://world.people.com.cn/n1/2021/0521/c1002-32109168.html.

三、投稿方式及其他相关事宜

1. 投稿一律使用电子版稿件，请发送至 jalcs@bfsu.edu.cn。

2. 作者投稿时请自留底稿，所有来稿恕不退稿。

3. 审稿过程及审阅通知：来稿由两名同行专家匿名审阅；如意见有分歧，再由第三人审阅。编辑部在收到稿件3个月内把审阅结果通知投稿人。3个月后如未接到审阅结果，投稿人可自行处理。3个月内不可一稿两投，否则后果由投稿人自负。

4. 稿件内容文责自负，但编辑部有权对稿件进行必要的修改。

5. 稿件发表后，编辑部赠送作者当期样刊两本。

6. 编辑部联系电话：86-10-88816484。

Call for Papers

African Language and Culture Studies (Chinese-English) is compiled by the School of African Studies of Beijing Foreign Studies University, and published by Foreign Language Teaching and Research Press. It focuses on African languages, literature, societies, cultures, and cross-cultural comparison and communication between China and Africa, etc. It publishes outstanding academic papers on the related studies by Chinese and foreign scholars, with special focus on topics including studies of African indigenous languages, African language teaching and acquisition, language policies and planning in African countries, literature in African indigenous languages, English, French, Arabic and Portuguese, cultures of traditional African societies, comparative studies of Chinese and African cultures, and cross-cultural communication between China and Africa. It has the following columns: African languages and literature, African societies and cultures, comparative studies of Chinese and African culture, monographic study, academic trends, book review, etc. Experts and scholars at home and abroad are welcome to submit academic papers.

I. Submission requirements

1. The submitted papers should be original, academic and theory-based. Enriched content, novel viewpoints, rigorous logic, sufficient evidence, reliable data and concise language are expected from the submissions.

2. Submissions should comply with the style and formatting guidelines and have all necessary elements. Articles, including Chinese and English, for general columns should be between 8,000 and 12,000 words. Book reviews are expected to be between 4,000 and 6,000 words, inclusive of the title, abstract, keywords and references.

3. Books reviewed for the book review column should be academic publications on African languages, literature, societies, cultures, and cross-cultural comparison and communication between China and Africa published

within three years.

4. All submissions should comply with relevant academic standards. Sources of directly quoted argumentations and opinions should be cited with clear page numbers, for example, (Chomsky, 1995: 50). Plagiarism and repeated content should be avoided. Sources of key ideas or opinions that are indirectly quoted should also be cited, for example, (Chomsky, 1995). Excessive quotation of second-hand literature should be avoided.

II. Style guidelines

1. Structure

(1) Author details (on one single page) should include the author's full name, postal address, phone number, email address and biography (100-200 words). The biography should include the author's real name, affiliation, academic title, position and main academic interests.

(2) Chinese title, abstract (200-300 words) and keywords (3-5, separated by semicolons).

(3) English title, abstract and keywords (separated by semicolons).

(4) Main text, references and appendices.

(5) All citations should be parenthetical citations.

(6) All notes should be footnotes, using the format ① , ② , ③ .

2. Formatting guidelines

(1) Submit in Microsoft Word format with single line spacing. The font size of the main title should be 15pt. The first-level heading should be 14pt, the second-level heading 12pt, and the third-level heading and the main text 10.5pt. The English text and numbers should be typed in Times New Roman.

(2) The hierarchy of section headings should not exceed three levels, and all headings should stick to the left without spacing. The headings of different levels should be numbered as 1, 1.1, 1.1.1. There should be a space between the sequence number and the heading text. The numbering of example sentences in the main text

should be Arabic numerals in parentheses, for example, (1), (2) and (3).

(3) All figures and tables should be numbered consecutively throughout the text. Figure captions should be placed below the figures, while table captions must be placed above the tables, for example, Figure 1 Descriptive Caption, and Table 1 Descriptive Caption.

3. References guidelines

References should be compliant with relevant standards. Citations in the text and at the end of an article should be strictly consistent. The authors should verify every reference before submitting, so as to avoid erroneous or missing information. References in English and other languages should be placed before Chinese references. All references should be arranged in alphabetical order.

(1) Journal articles

CARSTENS V, 2005. Agree and EPP in Bantu [J]. Natural language and linguistic theory, 23 (2): 219-279.

MAKONI S B, PENNYCOOK A, 2005. Disinventing and (re)constituting languages [J]. Critical inquiry in language studies, 2 (3): 137-156.

SUNSTEIN C R, 1996. Social norms and social roles [J/OL]. Columbia law review, 96: 903 [2012-01-26]. http://www.heinonline.org/HOL/Page?handle=hein. journals/clr96&id= 913&collecion=journals &index=journals/clr.

陆俭明，2018. 再谈语言信息结构理论 [J]. 外语教学与研究，（2）：163-172.

叶狂，潘海华，2012. 把字句的跨语言视角 [J]. 语言科学，（6）：604-620.

于潇，刘义，柴跃廷，等，2012. 互联网药品可信交易环境中主体资质审核备案模式 [J]. 清华大学学报（自然科学版），52（11）：1518-1523.

(2) Theses in collections

CHOMSKY N, 2000. Minimalist inquiries: the framework [C] // MARTIN R, MICHAELS D, URIAGEREKA J. Step by step: essays on minimalist syntax in honor of Howard Lasnik. Cambridge, MA: The MIT Press: 89-156.

LEGÈRE K, ROSENDAL T, 2008. Linguistic landscapes and the African perspective [C] // PÜTZ M, MUNDT N. Expanding the linguistic landscape: linguistic diversity, multimodality and the use of space as a semiotic resource. Bristol: Multilingual Matters: 153-179.

刘丹青，1996. 东南方言的体貌标记 [C] // 张双庆. 动词的体. 香港：香港中文大学中国文化研究所吴多泰中国语文研究中心：9-33.

(3) Monographs

AYAFOR M, GREEN M, 2017. Cameroon pidgin English: a comprehensive grammar [M]. Amsterdam: Benjamins.

CHOMSKY N, 1995. The minimalist program [M]. Cambridge, MA: The MIT Press.

陆俭明，马真，1985. 现代汉语虚词散论 [M]. 北京：北京大学出版社.

徐烈炯，2008. 中国语言学在十字路口 [M]. 上海：上海教育出版社.

(4) Translation works

NEDJALKOV V P, 1983/1988. Typology of resultative constructions [C]. Trans, BERNARD C. Amsterdam: John Benjamins.

赵元任，1968/1980. 中国话的文法 [M]. 丁邦新，译. 香港：香港中文大学出版社.

(5) Conference proceedings/reports

AELBRECHT L, 2008. Dutch modal complement ellipsis and English VPE [R]. Talk presented at CGSW 23, Edinburgh, June 12-13, 2008.

U.S. Department of Transportation Federal Highway Administration, 1990. Guidelines for handling excavated acid-producing material: PB91-1940001 [R]. Springfield: U. S. Department of Commerce National Information Service.

World Health Organization, 1970. Factors regulating the immune response: report of WHO Scientific Group [R]. Geneva: WHO.

宁春岩，2018-10-29/30. 形式语言学、语言获得、语言障碍及神经语言学间的通约问题 [R]. 北京语言大学语言学系成立仪式暨语言学前沿国际论坛论文. 北京：北京语言大学.

中华人民共和国国务院新闻办公室，2013. 国防白皮书：中国武装力量的多样化 [R/OL]. （2013-04-16）[2021-07-10]. http://www.mod.gov.cn/affair/2013-04/16/content_4442839.htm.

(6) Degree dissertations/theses

HUANG C T J, 1982. Logical relations in Chinese and the theory of grammar [D]. Cambridge, MA: Massachusetts Institute of Technology.

张天伟，2012. 基于形式句法的现代汉语省略限制研究 [D]. 北京：中国传媒大学.

(7) Electronic resources

PAULSON S, 2019. "I am because we are": the African philosophy of Ubuntu [EB/

OL]. (2019-06-22) [2021-08-11]. https://www.ttbook.org/interview/i-am-because-we-are-african-philosophy-ubuntu.

UNESCO Institute for Lifelong Learning, 2010. Why and how Africa should invest in African languages and multilingual education: an evidence- and practice-based policy advocacy brief [EB/OL]. (2010-07) [2021-03-09]. https://uil.unesco.org/literacy/multilingual-research/why-and-how-africa-should-invest-african-languages-and-multilingual.

刘大龙，2011. 莫桑比克女孩辍学现象严重 [EB/OL]. (2011-12-01)[2018-12-25]. http://news.163.com/11/1201/08/7K660ICN00014JB5.html.

(8) Newspapers

Lusaka Times, 2018. Use of local languages in lower grades a success [N/OL]. Lusaka times, 2018-02-12 [2021-03-09]. https://www.lusakatimes.com/2018/02/12/use-local-languages-lower-grades-success/.

MACHANICK P, 2020. Covid logic beats "irrational" human logic [N]. Mail & Guardian, 2020-07-29.

田志凌，2005.《魔戒》的尴尬与文学翻译的危机 [N]. 南方都市报，2005-08-24.

张梦旭，李晓宏，2021. 推进非洲疫后重建，消除冲突根源 [N/OJ]. 人民网，2021-05-21 [2021-08-11]. http://world.people.com.cn/n1/2021/0521/c1002-32109168.html.

III. Submission and other issues

1. Only electronic submissions will be accepted. Contributions should be sent to jalcs@bfsu.edu.cn.

2. The original manuscript should be kept by the author since the journal will not return it.

3. Review process and response: Submitted papers will be first reviewed by two peer experts anonymously. If the two reviews differ widely, a third reviewer will be invited. The author will be informed of the final decision within three months after the journal receives the paper. If there is no response after three months, the author can submit the paper to other journals. The paper should not be submitted to other journals within three months, otherwise the author will be held accountable for the consequences.

4. The author takes sole responsibility for the submitted paper, but the editorial board reserves the right to make necessary modifications.

5. The journal will send two print copies to the author for free if the paper is accepted.

6. The phone number of the editorial office: 86-10-88816484.